Jahrbuch für Wirtschaftsgeschichte BEIHEFT 5

Im Auftrag der Herausgeber
des Jahrbuchs für Wirtschaftsgeschichte
herausgegeben von Reinhard Spree

Béla Tomka

Welfare in East and West

Hungarian Social Security in an International Comparison 1918–1990

Akademie Verlag

ISBN 3-05-003871-3

Das eingesetzte Papier ist alterungsbeständig nach DIN/ISO 9706.

Einbandgestaltung: Ingo Ostermaier, Berlin
Druck und Bindung: Druckhaus „Thomas Müntzer“, Bad Langensalza

Gedruckt in Deutschland

CONTENTS

ACKNOWLEDGEMENTS

The present study was prepared during the 2001-2002 academic year when I was a Fellow of the Alexander von Humboldt Foundation at the ZVGE (Zentrum für Vergleichende Geschichte Europas, Center for Comparative History of Europe), at Freie Universität and Humboldt Universität, Berlin, on leave from the University of Szeged. I am greatly indebted to the colleagues at the Center for their hospitality and help, particularly to Professor Hartmut Kaelble for the many occasions when he gave me the opportunity to discuss my project and shared his view on comparative social history, and also to Arnd Bauerkämper and Philipp Ther. My gratitude also goes to Susanne Nies and Regina Vogel in Berlin, Ilona Ostner, Sigrid Leitner and Stephan Lessenich in Göttingen for the talks we had on welfare and other topics. I am very grateful to the International Institute of Social History, Amsterdam, where I spent several weeks collecting materials and enjoying the inspiring atmosphere and the discussions with Lex Heerma van Voss, Jan Kok and Marcel van der Linden. Last, but not least I also wish to thank my Hungarian colleagues, Zsombor Bódy, Gábor Gyáni and István György Tóth for their valuable comments on the manuscript.

Berlin-Szeged, November 2002 Béla Tomka

LIST OF TABLES

ABBREVIATIONS

ÁMH	Állami Munkásbiztosítási Hivatal, State Office of Workers' Insurance
Ft	Forint
ILO	International Labour Office
K	Korona
MABI	Magánalkalmazottak Biztosító Intézete, Institute of Insurance for Private Employees
OECD	Organization for Economic Cooperation and Development
OMBP	Országos Munkásbetegsegélyző és Balesetbiztosító Pénztár, National Fund for the Health and Accident Insurance of Workers
OTBA	Országos Tisztviselői Betegsegélyezési Alap, National Clerk's Health Insurance Fund
OTI	Országos Társadalombiztosító Intézet, National Social Security Institute
P	Pengő
SZETA	Szegényeket Támogató Alap, Fund Aiding the Poor
SZOT	Szakszervezetek Országos Tanácsa, National Council of Trade Unions
SZTK	Szakszervezeti Társadalombiztosítási Központ, Social Security Centre of Trade Unions

INTRODUCTION

The objective of this study is to describe Hungarian welfare development in the 20th century in a European context with a main focus on analysing the convergent and divergent features. There are several reasons that account for this research interest. On the one hand, it is increasingly acknowledged that reaching a full understanding of social developments in any particular country is only possible if its experience is set in the context of wider changes. This fact is reflected in the continuously growing body of comparative historical literature. In the past decades comparative history has become a major field, characterised by ever higher degrees of refinement in methodology, sophistication of the institutional background, and, consequently, effectiveness in research. In spite of this, no systematic comparative study of 20th century Hungarian welfare development has been carried out yet, although a comparison may lead to the identification of the unique features of 20th century Hungarian welfare development and those that followed general European trends. Furthermore, the study of a "late-comer" country, subsequently ruled by a communist regime may yield lessons for international research as well, by opening new perspectives in the study of supranational tendencies in 20th century welfare development. Our research interest is not only revealing similarities and differences but also the dynamics of the Hungarian welfare development. One of the most important questions we would like to answer is, whether the whole 20th century can be viewed as one period, in which Hungary clearly differed from Western European societies; or there has been a specific dynamic in the relationship of Hungary and Western Europe, with periods of growing social similarities and/or dissimilarities.

Beside the general interest in the long-term comparative study of Hungarian welfare, a more specific interest in the problem of European social integration will constitute the basis of the present investigation. Current discussions of European integration focus in particular on economy and politics, but much less on the social side of the integration process. Another important feature of the ongoing debates is that issues revolving around European integration have been dealt with little reference to historical processes. The interest in social integration also leads us to the problem of convergence in welfare development. The analysis of this issue will show the extent to which the route Hungary took in the past decades regarding social and, more specifically, welfare development conforms to Western European trends and constitutes an integration process in social areas.

Consequently, in this book we primarily seek to explore the relationship between Hungarian and Western European welfare state development by answering the following questions: Have 20th century changes in Hungarian welfare state converged to or diverged from Western European trends? In which periods and in which areas of welfare development can convergence and divergence be observed?

The introductory chapter is structured as follows: We first deal with some important features of comparative research carried out on welfare state and social convergence in Europe and in Hungary. Then we describe the research design, the major sources of data, as well as the limits of the present investigation, and consider other methodological problems posed by comparative research.

Comparative approaches to welfare

The long traditions of the comparative study of the welfare state makes it one of the most advanced fields of comparative history and historical sociology.[1] Comparative studies have significantly contributed to the analysis of the characteristics of the welfare state as well as to drawing a picture of the determinants of the formation and development of welfare systems. It is the abundance of such research that makes it impossible to give even an outline of a literature review here. Instead, related literature will be cited where appropriate in the discussion that follows.[2] It can be stated here, though, that international research is concentrated in several respects, favouring specific aspects of welfare and neglecting others. First of all, there is chronological and geographic concentration as the main subject of studies is the post-Second World War era and the comparison of Western European states or that of Western European and overseas Anglo-Saxon countries. Research on the first half of the 20th century is rather more scarce

1 Citing only a few important works in the comparative history of welfare, Peter Flora and Arnold J. Heidenheimer eds., The Development of Welfare States in Europe and America. New Brunswick and London 1981; Peter Flora ed., Growth to Limits. Vol. 1-4. Berlin 1986-1987; Jens Alber, Vom Armenhaus zum Wohlfahrtsstaat. Analysen zur Entwicklung der Sozialversicherung in Westeuropa. Frankfurt/M. New York 1987; Gerhard A. Ritter, Der Sozialstaat. München 1989; Hugh Heclo, Modern Social Politics in Britain and Sweden. From Relief to Income Maintenance. New Haven and London 1974; Peter Baldwin, The Politics of Social Solidarity and the Bourgeois Basis of the European Welfare State, 1875-1975. Cambridge 1990.

2 For literature reviews, see e.g. Alber, Vom Armenhaus zum Wohlfahrtsstaat; Manfred G. Schmidt, Sozialpolitik. Opladen 1988; Catherine Jones, Patterns of Social Policy: An Introduction to Comparative Analysis. London 1985; Joan Higgins, States of Welfare: Comparative Analysis of Social Policy. Oxford 1981; Christopher Pierson, Beyond the Welfare State? The New Political Economy of Welfare. Cambridge 1991, 6-140; Gosta Esping-Andersen, Welfare States and the Economy, in: Neil J. Smelser ed., Handbook of Economic Sociology. Priceton/NJ 1994, 711-732; for comparisons, see Allan Cochran and John Clarke, Comparing Welfare Sates: Britain in International Context. London 1993, 1-18, 239-269; James Midgley, Social Welfare in Global Context. London 1997, 89-110; Jochen Clasen ed., Comparative Social Policy: Concepts, Theories and Methods. Oxford 1999.

and countries outside the regions mentioned are rarely discussed even regarding the post-1945 era.

There is a striking thematic and methodological concentration in surveys, too. Especially the early welfare research focused on the comparison of the relative size of *welfare expenditures* in different countries.[3] A latent hypothesis of these endeavours was that the level of the expenditures (or, rather, their level relative to the gross national product or other indicators of economic output) is a good proxy for the development of the welfare state. The level of expenditures does indeed deliver important and comprehensive information on a welfare system, and thus it is definitely worthy of analysis. In addition, the inclusion of data on welfare costs helps to operationalise long term comparisons of a high number of welfare systems. However, as argued by several authors,[4] differences in such expenditures as a whole do not necessarily reflect either the structure of individual welfare systems, or their other important characteristics, or demand for welfare services, or the effects of the system on welfare. In other words, what is important is not simply how much is spent on welfare but how it is spent,[5] because it is possible, for example, that there is a growth in welfare spending as expressed in the ratio of GNP, but this may only be the result of an economic recession, a decrease in economic output or it may be due to growing assistance brought about by increasing unemployment.

Although the analysis of welfare expenditures constitutes an important area of research even today, the criticism that ranking welfare states based on the levels of such expenditures has provoked, led to the investigation of other areas, such as the ratio of welfare recipients, the significance of specific welfare institutions, the degree of redistribution, etc. Furthermore, many have argued that individual characteristics of the welfare state cannot be analysed separately. They proposed the consideration of complex welfare regimes the components of which are interrelated. Among alternative approaches, *typologies* for the classification of welfare systems based on both quantitative and qualitative criteria elicited especially large response. Though dual and four-way classifications are also known, triarchic typologies are the most widely used.[6] One of the classic and most cited typologies of welfare states was created by Richard M. Tit-

---

3 For a recent work on the first third of the century, see Peter H. Lindert, The Rise of Social Spending, 1880-1930, in: Explorations in Economic History, 31 (1994), 1-37.

4 Gosta Esping-Andersen, The Three Worlds of Welfare Capitalism. Cambridge 1990, 19; in the Hungarian literature, see Iván Csaba and István György Tóth eds., A jóléti állam politikai gazdaságtana. Budapest 1999, 16-18.

5 Michael Hill, Social Policy: A Comparative Analysis. London 1996, 42.

6 For the two-way residual-institutional division, see Harold L. Wilensky and Charles Lebeaux, Industrial Society and Social Welfare. New York 1965; for a four-way division, including a radical-type in addition to those discussed later, see Francis G. Castles and Deborah Mitchell, Worlds of Welfare and Families of Nations, in: Francis G. Castles ed., Families of Nations. Patterns of Public Policy in Western Democracies. Aldershot 1993, 93-128.

muss who distinguished between three types of welfare states: in the "residual" welfare model (United States) state welfare institutions operate only as a last resort when the private market or the family is not able to fulfill welfare needs; in the "industrial achievement-performance" type (continental Western Europe) state welfare provisions are intended to help the proper functioning of the economy; in the "institutional redistributive" states universal benefits are distributed by the state on the basis of need (Sweden, United Kingdom).[7] A similar categorisation though with different placement of some countries was proposed by Norman Furniss and Timothy Tilton, assigning welfare systems into one of three groups, the "positive state" (United States), the "social security state" (United Kingdom) and the "social welfare state" (Sweden).[8]

These works clearly laid down the foundations for Gosta Esping-Andersen who carried out the most influential analyses of welfare regimes of the past fifteen years and distinguished three welfare state regimes, the liberal, the conservative or corporatist and the social democratic welfare state. The regimes differ according to the role of major institutions in producing and allocating social security (the state, the market and the family); the degree of decommodification (i. e. the degree to which social services are available as a matter of right, and one can maintain a socially acceptable standard of living without relying on the market); and the dominant mode and locus of solidarity and the kind of stratification system promoted by social policy. The liberal welfare state favours the logic of the market in welfare, social rights and welfare transfers are modest and social benefits are based on the means-test principle. The liberal regime characterises Ireland and the United Kingdom from among the countries in the scope of the present study. The conservative/corporatist welfare regime has a strong commitment to state provisions as a result of which private insurance is minimal. It also has an emphasis on social policy measures that preserve status differences and protect the family. This regime can be identified in France, Finland, Germany, Italy, Switzerland, Austria, Belgium and the Netherlands. The social democratic type can be found in Denmark, Norway and Sweden, characterised by strong state intervention, universal social rights, commitment to full employment and a high degree of de-commodification, i. e. it reduces greatly the market dependence of wage-earners.[9]

Gosta Esping-Andersen's work received wide critical acclaim and became a modern classic, or, at least, is on the way to achieve that status, determining the agenda for much of the current scholarly discourse on the welfare state. Many of the researchers dealing with welfare systems do not fully accept the proposed framework; however,

---

7 Richard M. Titmuss, Social Policy. London 1974; an earlier, less explicit formulation, Essays on 'The Welfare State'. London 1958, 34-55.

8 Norman Furniss and Timothy Tilton, The Case for the Welfare State. From Social Security to Social Equality. Bloomington and London 1979, 15-20.

9 Gosta Esping-Andersen, The Three Worlds of Welfare Capitalism. 21-22, 37; Gosta Esping-Andersen, Social Foundations of Postindustrial Economies. Oxford 1999, 74-86.

even most of the critics define their own position vis-a-vis the Esping-Andersenian approach.

A number of factors have contributed to the popularity of Esping-Andersen's welfare regime paradigm. With its straightforward but still plausible and empirically founded typology it has offered a much needed compass for the vast research literature on welfare. It has also addressed the tension between "grand theorizing" of welfare state development based on large-scale regression analyses of social and economic indicators on the one hand, and "micro" studies dealing with only one or some cases and specific welfare areas on the other.[10] The welfare regime paradigm quite successfully incorporated the two approaches, and at the same time attempted at a methodological compromise of different and usually exclusive comparative research traditions, such as a more qualitative, institutionally-oriented and a variable-oriented quantitative research strategy. In addition, it emphasized the multi-dimensional character of welfare effort (instead of ranking states along one or some combined indicators) and the interaction between social policy, economic and political institutions.[11] As a result, much of the literature is willing to accept the idea that the development of welfare states is not "linearly distributed, but clustered by regime-types".[12]

Despite its obvious achievements, criticisms emerging are quite diverse, too. One major line of critique is that Esping-Andersen misspecificated several countries, such as the Mediterranean ones, Australia or New Zeeland. It was suggested that the Mediterranean countries form a "Southern" or "Latin Rim" model of social policy with their lack of an articulated social minimum and right to welfare, along with strong familialism.[13] In a similar way, Castles and Mitchell suggested that Australia and New Zeeland had a more inclusive approach to social policy than the other countries belonging to the liberal form, therefore they represent a model of their own.[14] Another related problem is "Swedocentrism", the bias for the social democratic model, implicitly assuming its superiority over other welfare regimes, though presumably not supported by its achievements in the 1980s and 1990s.[15] Esping-Andersen, however, insisted that the Mediter-

10 Jochen Clasen, Introduction, in: Clasen ed., Comparative Social Policy. 6.

11 Deborah Mabbett and Helen Bolderson, Theories and Methods in Comparative Social Policy, in: Jochen Clasen ed., Comparative Social Policy: Concepts, Theories and Methods. Oxford 1999, 34-56.

12 Esping-Andersen, The Three Worlds of Welfare Capitalism. 26.

13 Stephan Leibfried, Towards a European Welfare State? On Integrating Poverty Regimes into the European Community, in: Zsuzsa Ferge and Jon Eivind Kolberg eds., Social Policy in a Changing Europe. Frankfurt/M. and Boulder/Co. 1992, 245-279.

14 Castles and Mitchell, Worlds of Welfare and Families of Nations, in: Castles, Families of Nations: Patterns of Public Policy in Western Democracies. 93-128.

15 Manfred Schmidt, Wohlfahrtsstaatliche Regime: Politische Grundlagen und politisch-ökonomisches Leistungsvermögen, in: Lessenich and Ostner (Hrsg.), Welten des Wohlfahrtskapitalismus. 179-200; Kees van Kersbergen, Social Capitalism: A Study of Christian Democracy and the Welfare State. London 1995, 23-26.

ranean and Antipodean countries form subgroups of the continental/conservative and liberal model, respectively, and he opted for fewer rather than more regime types.[16]

According to another line of criticism, the regime approach concentrates on income maintenance and labour market constellations, neglecting other major welfare schemes, and, more generally, major components of human needs (e.g. quality of work). National patterns found in health, social services, housing, education and social assistance do not necessarily fit the ones in social security and the labour market.[17]

In the attempts to refine the theory of the regime approach, it has also been argued that the concentration on class analysis led to the neglect of other dimensions of stratification, such as status, ethnicity, and, in particular, gender. The latter one is the point where Esping-Andersen seems to be the most receptive to criticism, as a sign of which he systematically discussed the family's place in the provision of welfare in a later book and recognized the household economy as the foundation of post-industrial welfare states.[18]

The intensive but somewhat inconclusive debate over variables and contradictory empirical results clearly shows that introducing more variables and more precise statistical techniques alone cannot address properly the unresolved research problems. Fundamental methodological issues might be at the roots of diverging opinions and the determinants of welfare state changes are too complex to be understood fully by the restrained perspectives of any approach.

Several of the criticisms that are most important from our point of view refer to theoretical and methodological shortcomings of the typology. Although some critics doubt that typologies as such have explanatory value and might contribute to fruitful theorizing about welfare states,[19] most of the participants of the debate seem to accept that typologies can be useful in comparative research from several respects: they can promote greater analytical depth, contribute to a greater understanding of causal relationships, and provide a tool for hypothesis formulation and testing.[20]

However, the regime approach, and typologies in general, seem to lack historical sensibility in several sense. One the one hand, it is not explicit and clear what historical relevance it has, and what kind of historical validity it claims.[21] On the other hand, the model cannot handle properly changes in welfare systems and shifts between them, al-

16 Esping-Andersen, Social Foundations. 88-94.

17 Ian Gough, Welfare Regimes: On Adapting the Framework to Developing Countries. University of Bath, Institute for International Policy Analysis. Working Paper. 2000, 5.

18 Esping-Andersen, Social Foundations.

19 Peter Baldwin, Can We Define a European Welfare State Model?, in: B. Greve ed., Comparative Welfare Systems: the Scandinavian Model in a Period of Change. London 1996, 29-44.

20 Esping-Andersen, Social Foundations. 73.

21 Jens Borchert, Ausgetretene Pfade? Zur Statik und Dynamik wohlfahrtsstaatlicher Regime, in: Stephan Lessenich and Ilona Ostner (Hrsg.), Welten des Wohlfahrtskapitalismus. Der Sozialstaat in vergleichender Perspektive. Frankfurt/M. and New York 1998, 137-176.

though welfare states underwent a powerful transformation process in the 20th century and are still in a state of dynamic change. Systematic data for the typology outlined above span only one or two decades, almost exclusively from the second half of the 20th century, that is, Esping-Andersen's model reflects only the situation of the 1970s and 1980s. Therefore, it is possible that welfare had three worlds in 1980 or in certain other periods, but two or four in another. If the major variables introduced by Esping-Andersen (rules for entitlements, the degree of income replacement, the degree of universalisms etc.) were applied in the investigation of welfare systems, almost all Western European countries would qualify as conservative or liberal in the first third of the century, since there would show hardly any difference between the individual systems. The welfare system termed social democratic emerged much later in Scandinavia.

Esping-Andersen does admit typologies are static by definition and insensible to changes and dynamics.[22] Even more, his typology is not simply static, but it is based on a strong continuity thesis. He argues that regime shifts happen rarely since nation states cannot escape their historical legacies. Existing institutional arrangements decisively determine national welfare developments, the way states respond to internal or outside challenges and pressures. In this way the regime theory can cope with some social change, however, it is not well equipped to understand profound transformation of welfare systems, such as the United Kingdom's move from a social democratic model to a more liberal type of welfare state in the decades after circa 1970.[23] Expressing arguments based either on path dependency or institutional inertia, the model seems to be somewhat deterministic and calls for an opening up to incorporate not only path dependency but path changes as well.[24] As a way out it has been suggested that a specific typology for every major phase of welfare development should be developed.[25] The proposed new typology based on the determination of "critical junctures" in the development of welfare states, is, however, admittedly only a speculation without any empirical foundation, and in this way it cannot yet be regarded as a real alternative. In addition, it is somewhat tautological: typologies are needed to accommodate and explain changes in welfare development, however, they are produced as a result of the analysis of changes.

Arguably, the typology outlined above, and typologies in general, are not easy to adjust to assist historical comparisons. Furthermore, the aspects included in the existing typologies disregard the distinct features of communist welfare regimes and thus they cannot be used in a comparison like the one designed here.

As mentioned above, the problem of convergence versus divergence between 20th century Hungary and Western European societies is an important aspect of the present

22 Esping-Andersen, Social Foundations. 87.
23 Gough, Welfare Regimes. 7.
24 Schmidt, Wohlfahrtsstaatliche Regime. 181.
25 Borchert, Ausgetretene Pfade? 152-171.

work. The existence and extent of convergence between industrial societies has been a subject of debate and controversy in social sciences for generations. One can encounter the idea of decreasing differences among societies over time in several works of nineteenth-century century social thinkers. In the 1950s and especially in the 1960s, social scientists have continued the convergence debate very intensively. The emerging convergence theory suggested that industrial nations were becoming more and more similar despite different cultural and historical legacies and various political and economic systems. At that time convergence theory was closely connected to modernisation theories on the one hand, and to the assumption of growing similarities between the capitalist and communist countries in industrial organisation, social structure, etc. on the other hand.[26]

More recently, controversies over convergence have been especially fierce among economists, dealing with the problem both theoretically and with regard to regional development.[27] The significance of cohesion objectives in the European Union, and indeed the effect of the Cohesion Fund itself on the harmonious development of the European Union, has resulted in numerous studies seeking to find out whether economic disparities between member states, regions and social groups have diminished over time. Economic convergence also appears to be a hot topic for both the European Union and the member candidates, since it obviously reduces the dispersion of countries on the scale of economic development. The narrower the distribution, the lower the cost of future European Union enlargement, because it lessens the burdens of transfers from the European Union to the new members, such as structural, cohesion and agricultural supports.[28]

Although the issue of economic convergence clearly received the highest attention in research, considerable empirical research on the convergence thesis has been carried out by sociologists, historians, demographers, and other social scientists as well. Sociologists have been particularly active in such areas as stratification systems, industrial sociology and welfare systems, producing conflicting evidences with respect to convergence in all these areas.[29] In the last decade a renewed interest can be seen in conver-

---

26 Citing only a few classic publications, see Clark Kerr et al., Industrialism and Industrial Man. Cambridge/Mass. 1960; Pitirim A. Sorokin, Mutual Convergence of the United States and the U.S.S.R. to the Mixed Sociocultural Type, in: International Journal of Comparative Sociology, 1 (1960), 143-176; J. Tinbergen, Do Communist and Free Economies Show a Converging Pattern?, in: Soviet Studies, 12 (1961), 333-341.

27 We only refer to a widely cited theoretical work on economic convergence here, Robert J. Barro and Xavier Sala-i-Martin, Economic Growth. New York 1995, 26-39, 382-413.

28 Wladimir Andreff, Nominal and real convergence, in: Jozef M. van Brabant ed., Remaking Europe. The European Union and the Transition Economies. Lanham 1999, 111-138.

29 John B. Williamson and Jeanne J. Flemming, Convergence Theory and the Social Welfare Sector: A Cross-National Analysis, in: International Journal of Comparative Sociology, 18 (1977), 3-4, 242-253; Robert Erikson and John H. Goldthorpe and Lucienne Portocarero, Intergenerational Class Mobility and the Convergence Thesis: England, France, and Sweden,

gence among sociologists, when several of them (e.g. G. Therborn, C. Crouch) took up the problem of European social convergence quite explicitly.[30] In the historical research of the past few decades, it was the German social historian, Hartmut Kaelble, who carried out the most systematic research on social convergence. He showed that the developments of Western European societies have converged in significant areas of social life during the 20th century.[31] Kaelble analyses Western European social integration through examining different areas of social history, such as welfare development. He has mostly dealt with Western Europe, however, some Central and Eastern European countries have also been included in his latest works.[32]

As indicated above, no systematic comparative study has been carried out on 20th century Hungarian welfare development. With a few exceptions, only the comparison of post-1960 welfare attracted attention and, within this, mostly the changes in expenditures.[33] Regarding the solution of methodological problems involved in comparisons in

---

in: British Journal of Sociology, 34 (1983), 303-343; Pekka Kosonen, European Welfare State Models, in: International Journal of Sociology, 4 (1995), 81-110.

30 Göran Therborn, Europan Modernity and Beyond. The Trajectory of European Societies, 1945-2000. London 1995, 352-353; Colin Crouch, Social Change in Western Europe. Oxford 1999, 404-409; Simon Langlois et al., Convergence or Divergence? Comparing Recent Social Trends in Industrial Societies. Frankfurt/M. and London 1994.

31 Hartmut Kaelble, Auf dem Weg zu einer europäischen Gesellschaft. München 1987; Hartmut Kaelble, A Social History of Western Europe, 1880-1980. Dublin 1990; most recently, Hartmut Kaelble, Europäische Vielfalt und der Weg zu einer europäischen Gesellschaft, in: Stefan Hradil and Stefan Immerfall (Hrsg.), Die westeuropäischen Gesellschaften im Vergleich. Opladen 1997, 27-68.

32 As examples, see Harmut Kaelble, Der Wandel der Erwerbstruktur im 19. und 20. Jahrhundert, in: Struktur und Dimension. Festschrift für K. H. Kaufhold. Stuttgart 1997, 73-93; Hartmut Kaelble, Europäische Besonderheiten des Massenkonsums, 1950-1990, in: Hannes Siegrist, Hartmut Kaelble, Jürgen Kocka (Hrsg.), Europäische Konsumgeschichte. Frankfurt/M. 1997, 169-203; H. Kaelble also deals with employment structures, social mobility, social inequality, the quality of urban life, family, labour relations, and in his recent studies he includes the patterns of mass consumption. Kaelble, Europäische Vielfalt. 40-42.

33 Regarding exceptions, see e.g. Susan Zimmermann and Gerhard Melinz, A szegényügy "szerves" fejlődése vagy radikális reform? Kommunális közjótékonyság Budapesten és Bécsben (1873-1914), in: Aetas, 8 (1994) 3, 37-70; Susan Zimmermann, Prächtige Armut. Fürsorge, Kinderschutz und Sozialreform in Budapest. Das "sozialpolitische Laboratorium" der Donaumonarchie im Vergleich zu Wien, 1873-1914. Sigmaringen 1997; Susan Zimmermann, Geschützte und ungeschützte Arbeitsverhältnisse von der Hochindustrialisierung bis zur Weltwirtschaftskrise. Österreich und Ungarn im Vergleich, in: Andrea Komlossy and Christof Parnreiter and Irene Stacher and Susan Zimmermann (Hrsg.), Ungeregelt und unterbezahlt. Der informelle Sektor in der Weltwirtschaft. Frankfurt/M. and Wien 1997, 87-115; Dorottya Szikra, Modernizáció és társadalombiztosítás a 20. század elején, in: Mária Augusztinovics ed., Körkép reform után. Budapest 2000, 11-27; recently in the international literature, see Lynne Haney, Familial Welfare: Building the Hungarian Welfare Society, 1948-1968, in: Social Politics, 7 (2000) 1, 101-122; contemporary comparison for the pre-1945 period, Kovrig Béla, A munka védelme a dunai államokban. Kolozsvár 1944.

this area, significant attempts have been made only with respect to the 1980s.[34] In addition, several comparative works treated Hungary only marginally, as a part of the Eastern Block, and mostly concerning the period after 1960.[35] Only two of the comparisons can be mentioned here as examples. Among the analyses, it was Bob Deacon's that devoted perhaps the most extensive discussion to the Hungarian welfare system. At the same time, his work covers only the 1960s and 1970s and the comparison in essence involves only other communist countries. His aspects of analysis are too normative, addressing goals rather than real experience, and seems to overrate welfare achievements.[36] The latest and perhaps most notable attempt to include Eastern European welfare systems, mostly disregarded elsewhere, in comparison with Western European ones, was published by Göran Therborn. He uses three variables in the analysis, the relative size of welfare spending, the role of the state and the patterns of welfare entitlements. Still, these aspects are used for a systematic comparison only regarding the 1970s and 1980s. Therborn's variables are definitely worthy of consideration, although should be supplemented and the place he assigned to Hungary is based on improper observations in some respects.[37] If studies not applying a comparative approach are taken into account, the literature on the Hungarian welfare system naturally proves to be more extensive. Still, as regards the first half of the century, only a few historical studies are available[38] and the historical perspective has obviously been secondary in economic and sociological research on welfare. Because of the late establishment of this field in Hun-

---

34 Endre Gács, Szociális kiadásaink nemzetközi összehasonlításban, in: Statisztikai Szemle, 63 (1985) 12, 1226-1236; Csaba and Tóth eds., A jóléti állam politikai gazdaságtana; for Hungary and Finland, see Rudolf Andorka, The Use of Time Series in International Comparison, in: Else Oyen ed., Comparative Methodology. London 1990, 103-223; Zsuzsa Ferge, A szociálpolitika hazai fejlődése, in: Zsuzsa Ferge and Györgyi Várnai, Szociálpolitika ma és holnap. Budapest 1987, 41-48; Zsuzsa Ferge, Social Policy Regimes and Social Structure, in: Zsuzsa Ferge and J. E. Kolberg eds., Social Policy in a Changing Europe. Frankfurt/M. and Boulder/Co. 1992, 201-222.

35 See, e.g., Francis G. Castles, Whatever Happened to the Communist Welfare State?, in: Studies in Comparative Communism, XIX (1986) 3-4, 213-226.

36 Bob Deacon, Social policy and socialism. London 1983, 81-89, 154-161, 199-207.

37 Therborn, European Modernity and Beyond. 96.

38 Gábor Gyáni, Könyörületesség, fegyelmezés, avagy a szociális gondoskodás genealógiája, in: Történelmi Szemle, XLI (1999) 1-2, 57-84; Gábor Gyáni, A szociálpolitika múltja Magyarországon. Budapest 1994; Gábor Gyáni, A szociálpolitika első lépései hazánkban: Darányi törvényei, in: Darányi Ignác emlékkonferencia. Budapest 2000, 94-110; Péter Hámori, A magyarországi agrár-szociálpolitika kezdetei, in: Századok, 137 (2003) 1, 3-42; István Csöppüs, Komáromi norma – egy szociálpolitikai kísérlet, in: Századok, 126 (1992) 2, 259-283; Zsuzsa Ferge, Fejezetek a magyarországi szegénypolitika történetéből. Budapest 1986; for two recent syntheses, see György Kövér and Gábor Gyáni, Magyarország társadalomtörténete a reformkortól a második világháborúig. Budapest 1998; Tibor Valuch, Magyarország társadalomtörténete a XX. század második felében. Budapest 2001, 344-350.

gary, sociology concentrates on the period from the 1960s on, with a special significance of Zsuzsa Ferge's studies.[39]

Research design and the scope of research

In the following we shall compare the Hungarian and Western European development of welfare systems in the 20th century, relying on findings from previous research on the welfare state but attempting to avoid its biases. As previous research does not offer appropriate frameworks for a study covering a long period, the first task was the selection and development of the variables and methods of the study. In this, our objectives were:

a) to reflect, as much as possible, the main aspects identified in research on (Western) European welfare states, also considering the diversity of these states beyond welfare expenditures or any other single dimension;
b) to make historical research possible, as well as the assessment of the dynamics of changes in some form. For the latter, quantitative analysis is an important, though not exclusive, method. Our aim was to compile data series on welfare development so that long term analysis becomes possible; and, finally,
c) not to be biased for any welfare system, i. e. to develop a framework for the examination of all welfare systems, appropriate for identifying the characteristics of 20th century Western European as well as Hungarian welfare systems, including the post-1945, communist era.

Considering the above, the major variables of the comparison are:

1. welfare expenditures (the relative size of welfare expenditures based on different methods of calculations, and expressed as percentage of the economic output);
2. relative importance of welfare institutions (the timing of the introduction of programs; the sequence of introduction; the process of expansion and differentiation regarding the programs; the changes in the structure of expenditures);
3. the characteristics of welfare rights (what percentage of the population receives benefits based on what principles; the level of benefits); and
4. organisational forms of welfare programs, the degree and characteristics of state involvement; the control exercised by those eligible for benefits over welfare institutions and vice versa, and the control of welfare institutions over those receiving benefits.

---

39 Probably the most noteworthy work regarding the social policy in the second half of the century is Zsuzsa Ferge, A Society in the Making: Hungarian Social and Societal Policy, 1945-1975. New York 1979.

Obviously, there are other possible aspects for analysis, e.g. the degree of redistribution through welfare institutions, the role of state and public organisations in different areas of welfare, issues of legal regulation, the decentralisation vs. centralisation of administration, the role of gender in welfare, etc.[40] Nevertheless, the aspects selected cover most of the important elements discussed in the literature, including Esping-Andersen's major variables, Jens Alber's aspects of analysis for social insurance, Göran Therborn's variables mentioned above, as well as Romke J. van der Veen's economic-social rights-administrative/organisational dimensions.[41]

At this point it seems necessary to clarify a few conceptual issues regarding the welfare state. The term welfare state is rather blurred in everyday use, but also in academic discussions; or, to put it differently, it is a concept used in several meanings.[42] It does have a comprehensive interpretation in political economy, according to which the analysis of the welfare state should involve the examination of almost the whole economic role of the state, including policies regarding employment, wages/incomes and the problems of macro-economic control, because all these are relevant in the distribution of welfare. However, there exist narrower meanings of the term, which are used more commonly than the former. These spring from the understanding of the welfare state as guaranteeing a set level of well-being for its citizens through income transfers and the system of welfare services.[43]

This latter interpretation is still wide enough, however, to give rise to different definitions of the welfare state. The OECD classification of *social expenditures* includes health care, various pensions, unemployment benefits as well as expenditures on education and other social services, maternity benefits, disability assistance and guaranteeing minimal wages.[44] In contrast, the International Labour Office (ILO) distinguishes be-

---

40 For possible aspects, see Ritter, Der Sozialstaat. 102.

41 Esping-Andersen, The Three Worlds of Welfare Capitalism. 70-71; Alber, Vom Armenhaus zum Wohlfahrtsstaat. 42; Therborn, European Modernity and Beyond. 96; Romke J. van der Veen, Social Solidarity: The Development of the Welfare State in the Netherlands and the United States, in: Hans Bak and Frits van Holthoon and Hans Krabbendan eds., Social and Secure? Politics and Culture of the Welfare State. Amsterdam 1996, 60-61.

42 For the origin and interpretation of the welfare state, social state, social security state and similar notions, see Ritter, Der Sozialstaat. 4-29; Peter Flora and Arnold J. Heidenheimer, The Historical Core and Changing Boundaries of the Welfare State, in: Peter Flora and Arnold J. Heidenheimer eds., The Development of Welfare State in Europe and America. New Brunswick and London 1981, 17-34; Bent Greve, The Historical Dictionary of the Welfare State. Lanham/Md. and London 1998, 129-132.

43 Esping-Andersen, The Three Worlds of Welfare Capitalism. 1-2; Ritter, Der Sozialstaat. 7-10.

44 Paul Johnson, Welfare States, in: Max-Stephan Schulze ed., Western Europe: Economic and Social Change Since 1945. London and New York 1999, 123; recently the OECD has not been considering educational expenditures, but their calculations include, in addition to the above, the costs of active measures regarding the labour market and housing supports. OECD, Social Expenditure Statistics of OECD Member Countries. Labour Market and So-

tween (1) *social insurance expenditures* (occupational injuries insurance, as well as health, pension and unemployment insurance), which are provided in return for the contribution of the insured, and (2) programs of social assistance where this individual contribution is missing (public health, means-tested assistance, benefits for public servants, benefits for war victims and family benefits). Still, the ILO does assess expenditures in all 9 areas as *social security expenditures*.[45] Similarly to the OECD but disregarding education, the European Union classifies under *social protection expenditures* spendings related to illness, invalidity/disability, work-related injuries and illnesses, old age, survivors, maternity, family, unemployment, placement, vocational guidance and resettlement, housing, and there is also a miscellaneous category.[46]

Furthermore, some argue that, rather than assessing welfare efforts (somewhat ironically also called the *accounting approach*), a *functionalist approach* must be applied. This implies a focus on welfare outcomes (such as the mitigation of poverty and inequality, educational opportunities or the quality of employment). That is, welfare states should be described not from the viewpoint of measures taken but from that of actual output or results.[47] In fact, what is considered important here is not the study of the welfare state but that of welfare society, in which the activities of non-governmental institutions are also included, because welfare objectives cannot only be realised through state programs. Some argue that the whole "welfare mix" should be studied, i. e. all the institutions contributing to welfare, but at least the households, the market and the state.[48] This idea has been gaining ground from the 1980s with the perspective of privatising welfare institutions, although the welfare mix is naturally an old phenomenon and has obviously survived even the greatest expansion of state welfare activities.[49]

This functionalist approach is undoubtedly plausible, since it can lead to the formation of complex and authentic interpretations of welfare systems. At the same time, the inclusion of a wide range of welfare activities, and especially private activities and expenditures rather expands the notion of the welfare state/regime. To give an example, unemployment can be relieved through benefits, but through the creation of new jobs as well. However, if public expenditures on new jobs are included, a consistency requires the inclusion of similar private expenditures in the spirit of the functionalist school. An-

---

cial Policy Occasional Papers. No. 17. Paris 1996, 3-7.

45 ILO, The Cost of Social Security. Geneva 1949 ff. (different volumes)

46 Commission of the European Communities, Social Protection in Europe, 1993. Luxembourg 1994, 44.

47 Johnson, Welfare States. 123-127; Walter Korpi, The Democratic Class Struggle. London 1983, 183-193.

48 Adalbert Evers, Shifts in the Welfare Mix – Introducing a New Approach for the Study of Transformations in Welfare and Social Policy, in: A. Evers and H. Wintersberger eds., Shifts in the Welfare Mix. Frankfurt/M. 1990, 7-30.

49 Christoph Conrad, Mixed Incomes for the Elderly Poor in Germany, 1880-1930, in: Michael B. Katz and Christoph Sachsse eds., The Mixed Economy of Social Welfare. Baden-Baden 1996, 340-367.

other example may be the care for old age through private savings, which also belong to welfare expenditures in the above line of argument. However, besides pension funds, bank savings may in part also serve this purpose. Similarly, if the definition includes private expenditures on health insurance, it must comprehend other expenditures realising the conservation of health, too, such as sports and holidays. These examples clearly show that the consistent application of the functionalist approach would make the assessment of welfare expenditures almost impossible, at least in historical research.

Thus the difficulties of interpretation of different welfare activities as well as practical reasons, namely, the accessibility of comparable data justify the choice of a much narrower definition. At the same time, we do not find it justifiable to include only state welfare expenditures, as Peter Lindert has done, and exclude e.g. most of the Bismarckian pension and other security systems from the analysis.[50] The state can contribute to the operation of the welfare system not only through its expenditures, but also through legislation. Therefore, searching for the middle ground, we have settled on the study of state and state regulated welfare activities.

It must be noted here that notions of the welfare state, welfare policies, welfare society are mostly used in relation to market economies based on private property with a democratic political system and not so much in the discussions of communist countries.[51] As regards terminological issues, we apply a pragmatic approach, accepting the use of other notions as well, such as the welfare system.[52] At the same time, both the idea of collective responsibility for citizens' welfare and the corresponding institutions did exist in communist countries. The state was obviously not the only actor here either, taking responsibility for the citizens, but it was part of the welfare mix, however, having prime importance. Thus in contrast with others but not in the least singularly, we do not find it justified to avoid the use of the above terms.[53]

Our most important thematic limitation is comparing the development of welfare states primarily, though not exclusively, through the development of *social security*, and first of all its major component, the social insurance systems.[54] This choice is sup-

---

50 Peter Lindert, The Rise of Social Spending, 1880-1930, in: Explorations in Economic History, 31 (1994), 1-37.

51 Richard Hauser, Soziale Sicherung in westeuropäischen Staaten, in: Stefan Hradil and Stefan Immerfall (Hrsg.), Die westeuropäischen Gesellschaften im Vergleich. Opladen 1997, 521.

52 The suggestion to use of this notion regarding communist countries emerged, in: Endre Sik and Ivan Svetlik, Similarities and Differences, in: A. Evers and H. Winterberger eds., Shifts in the Welfare Mix. Frankfurt/M. 1990, 274.

53 Zsuzsa Ferge, The Changing Hungarian Social Policy, in: Else Oyen ed., Comparing Welfare States and their Futures. Aldershot 1986, 152; for the use of the notion in a Hungarian context, Lynne Haney, Familial Welfare: Building the Hungarian Welfare Society, 1948-1968. 101-122.

54 We use the term social security to refer to social insurance and its assimilated schemes (family allowance, maternity benefits). Although we try to employ the terms in their exact meanings, because of the relatively minor significance of the latter programmes in most countries

ported by the significance of social security programs. Although social security has been associated with other welfare institutions (e.g. aid programs or housing policy) right from the beginnings, it was a basic institutional breakthrough in the process of the formation of the welfare state.[55] These social security programs differed significantly from the welfare institutions of previous decades and centuries, which were characterised by a low level of benefits, incalculable and often arbitrary provisions and the stigmatisation of those receiving them.[56] In contrast, though the new social security programs were not generous initially, the possibility of dynamic growth was already inherent, because the objective of social security was not simply to help the needy in emergency, but it was primarily intended to prevent such situations. In addition, one of the main characteristics of the new programs was that they were regulated by state legislation and compulsory membership was prescribed for certain groups. The new systems obliged potential beneficiaries to contribute. However, they redistributed not only the contributions of the insured persons but resources were supplemented by the state and/or employers. The contributions paid created individual legal claims, not to be downgraded by any consideration, e.g. adequate means or other similar conditions. Furthermore, the new social security was a functionally more differentiated system than earlier poor relief. Its programs covered specific standard risks (e.g. occupational injuries, illness, the loss of ability to work in old age, disability, the death of relative or unemployment, and their coverage extended to more than narrow, individual occupational groups. Another characteristic is that social security concentrated on male wage earners and not on women and children, as did poor relief earlier.[57] The significance of social security is exemplified by its gradually becoming the most important welfare institution everywhere in Europe in the second half of the 20th century, regarding both its expenditures and its effects on welfare. – Furthermore, the wide time-span and the high number of countries included in our study requires a constraint on issues examined in order to keep the analysis feasible. Technical considerations also played a part, because this area of welfare services offers more reliable comparative data on a wider scale than any other.

This limitation can undoubtedly reduce the validity of findings significantly, since other welfare programs also target the elimination or prevention of social inequalities, though through means different from those of social security. At the same time, stylistics is not the only reason for using the term "welfare state" while mostly discussing

---

and periods, social security is virtually interchangeable with the term social insurance.

55 Abram de Swaan, Der sorgende Staat. Wohlfahrt, Gesundheit und Bildung in Europa und den USA der Neuzeit. Frankfurt/M. 1993, 170-186.

56 Gerold Ambrosius and William Hubbard, A Social and Economic History of Europe. 116.

57 Alber, Vom Armenhaus zum Wohlfahrtsstaat. 27; Flora and Heidenheimer, The Historical Core and Changing Boundaries of the Welfare State. 27; Arnold J. Heidenheimer and Hugh Heclo and Carolyn Teich Adams, Comparative Public Policy. The Politics of Social Choice in America, Europe, and Japan. New York 1990, 229.

social security. Despite the constraints, we find that the importance of the areas examined means that they are good indicators of the main tendencies in the development of the welfare state. Thus our approach might be appropriate for the intended comparisons and could serve as a starting point for further, more comprehensive comparisons. The exploration of the field, however, poses challenges in methodological respects as well.

Methodology, sources, data analysis and statistical problems

There are a variety of different designs in comparative research with considerable methodological consequences.[58] It is possible to single out two or a small number of societies to compare over a defined period of time, such as some years or decades. However, it is also a widespread practice to compare a large number of countries, over a period of several decades. Needless to say, each research design has weaknesses and strengths. With the first approach, preferred by many historians, one can take into consideration the context and the factors which are difficult to quantify. However, with this approach it is obviously not possible to address all kinds of relevant questions – some of the answers need a comparison of a larger number of cases, over a long period of time. Researchers applying the second approach are likely to be sensitive to quantitative factors and to look for general trends. With this research design, widely used by sociologist and other social scientists, researchers can also test the validity of concepts/theories, and weigh the importance of different factors more precisely. On the other hand, the use of a quantitative research strategy does not allow to be really sensitive to the context and the exact meaning of the numbers.

The questions we would like to answer about social convergences in 20th century Europe obviously need the analysis of a large number of societies over a long period of time. Therefore, we have applied a quantitative approach quite extensively but not exclusively. Such research, by its very nature, demands greater compromises in methods than research more limited in its scope. Thus the present comparison is constrained beyond the thematic limitations indicated above. In addition, distinguishing convergent

58 For the methodology of comparisons, see e.g. Larry J. Griffin, Comparative-historical analysis, in: Edgar F. Borgetta and Marie L. Borgetta eds., Encyclopaedia of Sociology. Vol. 1. New York 1992, 263-271; Else Oyen ed., Comparative Methodology. London 1990; for the comparison of welfare systems, see Thomas Janoski and Alexander M. Hicks eds., The Comparative Political Economy of the Welfare State. Cambridge 1994; Harold Wilensky et al., Comparative Social Policy: Theories, Methods, Findings, in: Meinolf Dierkes and Hans N. Weiler and Ariane Berthoin Antal eds., Comparative Policy Research. Learning from Experience. Aldershot 1987, 381-457; Harold L. Wilensky et al., Comparative Social Policy: Theories, Methods, Findings. Berkeley 1985, 5-47.

and divergent features between Hungary and Western Europe as our main research interest resulted in the neglect of other approaches. Furthermore, important practical difficulties arose, as indicated above, from the unevenness and gaps in the available literature regarding Hungary which is reflected in the present work. Probably the most obvious of such problems is chronological. Namely, the discussion of the pre-Second World War period is of a smaller scale than would be reasonable because of the lack of sources.

An important methodological problem present in many comparative studies is that of what is compared to what, i.e. what are regarded to be the *units of comparison*. Hungary as the unit of comparison is given in this case. The comparison with other Central and Eastern European countries would obviously be a legitimate exercise, because these countries have shared several distinct social features with Hungary throughout the 20th century. However, the similarity of developmental paths does not allow a "contrasting type" or "individualising" comparison, which is also a useful research strategy.[59] This version of comparison is only possible if there are clear-cut differences between the units of comparison, which makes a case for the comparison of Hungary to units with highly distinct structures, such as Western Europe. In addition, a comparison of Hungary with other Eastern European societies would obviously need another focus, different from convergence. As we noted earlier, convergence between the European Union and prospective EU members, such as Hungary, appears to be a hot topic. In contrast, the convergence between the Central and Eastern European countries has not attracted significant interest so far.

It is not evident either which countries are regarded as Western European ones. When selecting the Western European countries into the sample, an effort was made to include ones that produced similar socio-economic and political development in the 20th century. Thus among the countries analysed, beside Norway and Switzerland, the present EU member states are included with the exception of Spain, Greece, Portugal and Luxembourg. The inclusion of the latter was hindered by very practical reasons, the unavailability of sources. Nevertheless, no attempt has been made to claim that other countries could not have been considered for inclusion in the sample.

Comparative studies published in the past decades have amply documented that the social and welfare development of Western Europe was not unified, therefore it is not without problems if one treats this region as a unit of comparison.[60] This methodologi-

---

59 On classification of historical comparisons, see Hartmut Kaelble, Der historische Vergleich. Frankfurt/M. 1999, 25-36; A. A. Van den Braembussche, Historical Explanation and Comparative Method: Towards a Theory of the History of Society, in: History and Theory, 28 (1989), 1-24; Theda Skocpol and Margaret Somers, The uses of comparative history, in: Comparative Studies in Society and History, 22 (1980), 174-197; Charles Tilly, Big structures, large processes, huge comparisons. New York 1984, 82 ff.

60 Flora and Heidenheimer, The Historical Core and Changing Boundaries of the Welfare State. 17-34; Peter A. Köhler and H. F. Zacher (Hrsg.), Ein Jahrhundert Sozialversicherung in der

cal difficulty may be balanced out in the interpretation by a differentiated treatment of developmental processes within Western Europe. Also, obvious differences between individual societies cannot obscure the fact that 20th century modern industrial states, and especially their Western European forms, do show certain similarities in their treatment of welfare problems. H. Kaelble considers it as an indicator of similarities that one of the three types in the most influential typology, also cited in the present work, was able to comprise the whole of continental Western Europe.[61] Besides the correct presentation of differences within the region, these similarities may form the basis for comparing Hungary to Western Europe in the above sense. In addition, the statistical methods applied do not simply assess convergent and divergent processes within Western Europe. They enable us to compare Hungary and Western Europe even when the differences in the latter are significant and even when, as will be shown, divergence can be detected between the development of individual Western European societies. It is quite obvious, however, that the comparison we are embarking on will be an asymmetrical one with all its methodological consequences; first of all, the development of the societies that make up Western Europe cannot be analysed with such a depth as the Hungarian trends.[62]

The present study covers the period between 1918 and 1990, sometimes called the "short 20th century" by historians. The end of World War I and the fall of European communist regimes were significant historical turning points for Europe and the whole world and there are plausible arguments to support that intra-European wars and tensions give an inner unity for this period. However, these major political changes do not necessarily demarcate major social changes as well. Especially the starting point seems to be somewhat arbitrary in this sense, so we go back further to pre-World War I times when necessary.

There are several international *data sets* containing welfare data.[63] However, none of them covers the whole period under investigation, and all of the areas and 14 countries we intend to incorporate into the study. Using different types of sources, we compiled own our data set which contains several indicators of welfare change. This set of indicators also has its limitations. For some periods (interwar years), and some areas (welfare expenditures) we were unable to obtain appropriate data and the quality of some of

Bundesrepublik Deutschland, Frankreich, Grossbritannien, Österreich und der Schweiz. Berlin 1981; Hugh Heclo, Modern Social Politics in Britain and Sweden. New Haven and London 1974; Alber, Vom Armenhaus zum Wohlfahrtsstaat; Peter Flora ed., Growth to Limits. The Western European Welfare States Since World War II. Vol. 1-4. Berlin 1986-1988.

61 Hartmut Kaelble, Wie kam es zum Europäischen Sozialmodell?, in: Jahrbuch für Europa- und Nordamerika-Studien, 4 (2000), 45.

62 On asymmetrical comparisons, see Jürgen Kocka, Asymmetrical Historical Comparison: The Case of the German Sonderweg, in: History and Theory, 38 (1999), 40-50.

63 ILO, The Cost of Social Security. Geneva 1949 ff. (different volumes); OECD, Social Expenditure, 1960-1990. Paris 1985; Peter Flora ed., State, Economy, and Society in Western Europe, 1815-1975. Vol. I. Frankfurt/M. 1983; Flora ed., Growth to Limits. Vol. 1-4.

the existing data might be unequal. However, we believe these limitations do not seriously restrict the intended comparison. (Tables 1-18)

Based on our data set, the development of Hungarian welfare will be examined in comparison to Western Europe through statistical procedures as well. The appropriate Hungarian data can obviously be compared to the Western European means to reveal the degree of convergence or divergence. This method is widely used in comparative research, and, indeed, it is suitable to pointing out some important trends. Still, this method in itself seems not to be fully satisfactory: the interpretation of the Western European means is not without its problems, as it fails to take into consideration the variations in the indicators of the different countries.[64]

Common alternatives for measuring convergence are the standard deviation or variance and the coefficient of variation. We also calculate the convergence of Western European countries by using the coefficient of variation because it is adjusted for shifts in the mean (i. e. a 10 point spread is likely to have a different interpretation around a mean of 50, than around a mean of 20). The greater the decrease in the coefficient of variation over a specified period of time, the greater the convergence, and the greater the increase in the coefficient of variation, the greater the divergence.

However, in contrast to the studies cited above, which measure convergence among countries, in the present analysis convergence is assessed between one specific country, Hungary, and a group of countries, Western Europe. For this purpose the coefficient of variation seems to be not suitable. In order to overcome this difficulty, we measure convergence of Hungary and Western European societies using the standardised Hungarian data. This indicator takes into account both the changes in the Hungarian data and the Western European standard deviations and means, and therefore provides more comprehensive information. Standardisation is the transformation of the values of a distribution, so that it has a mean of 0 and a standard deviation of 1. We can produce the standardised Hungarian data through subtracting the respective Western European means from the Hungarian data and then dividing it by the Western European standard deviations. The difference of this number from zero shows the degree of diversion from the Western European data. The greater the decrease in the standardised data over a specified period of time, the greater the convergence and vice versa.[65] These indices are not only suitable for properly indicating convergent or divergent tendencies, but they

---

64 On forms of convergence, see Alex Inkeles, Convergence and Divergence in Industrial Societies, in: Mustafa O. Attir et al. ed., Directions of Change. Boulder/Co. 1981, 13.

65 As a result, the standardised data take into account both major forms of convergence described in the literature: the absolute convergence (beta convergence), which occurs when the observed values come closer to each other; and the convergence in deviation (sigma convergence), which occurs when the dispersion of the observed values decreases over time. Barro and Sala-i-Martin, Economic Growth. 26-39, 382-413; Xavier Sala-i-Martin, The Classical Approach to Convergence Analysis, in: Economic Journal, 106 (1996), 1019-1036.

also make it possible to measure the convergence of Hungarian development even when Western European societies diverge in an area of welfare development.

It is also possible to offer a measure of the mean convergence/divergence per year. True, this statistics implicitly assumes that any one-year period is equivalent to another, although, in reality, there is at least some variation in the rate of convergence from one year to another. The mean convergence per year also neglects the so-called crossover pattern of trends. The interpretation of average annual change is relatively easy, when a simple convergence or convergence from different directions occurs with a movement towards a common point from the same or the opposite direction, respectively. However, converging trends may meet, not fuse but cross each other and then start to diverge.[66] This crossover pattern can be observed in some cases in our investigation, when the standardised Hungarian data approach the zero level, then cross it and start to diverge. In this case average annual changes of the standardised data cannot be interpreted as a measure of the dynamics of convergence or divergence and were left out from the computations (Appendix).

The structure of the study

The foci of our research discussed above basically define the structure of the present work. Chapter 1 describes changes in welfare expenditures in the course of the 20th century by applying different definitions. Chapter 2 reveals the development of welfare institutions, including variables such as the timing and sequence of the introduction of programs, the process of differentiation, and the changes in the structure of individual welfare programs. Chapter 3 examines the development in eligibility for welfare benefits, primarily through the changes in those under social insurance and social security, the eligibility and the relative level of benefits. Chapter 4 focuses on the organizational forms of programs, the role of the state and control mechanisms related to the welfare systems. Although the focus of our work is the examination of convergences and divergences between Hungary and Western Europe, a question central in the literature, primary determinants of welfare development, shall also be discussed in Chapter 5. Finally, Chapter 6 summarises the results.

In the individual chapters, using different criteria, we will first present the 20th century welfare development of Western European societies highlighting convergent and divergent tendencies inside that region. Following this, we will show the Hungarian welfare trends by relying on the same analysis criteria to the extent possible and dealing with the pre-Second World War and Communist eras separately. At the end of this part

66 Inkeles, Convergence and Divergence. 14-27.

we will point out the convergent and divergent trends of Hungarian and Western European welfare development.

1 CHANGES IN WELFARE EXPENDITURES

One of the most remarkable aspects of the history of the welfare state in the 20th century is the scale and the universality of the growth in welfare expenditures in all the industrialized countries.[67] The levels of the expenditures is symptomatic of the welfare efforts, although, as pointed out earlier, their analysis must be supplemented by other aspects, such as the structure of social rights and other characteristics of the welfare institutions.

There are considerable differences between various definitions of the welfare state and welfare services, resulting in discrepancies in welfare expenditure calculations and thus making comparisons a difficult exercise. While some definitions include expenditures of the whole welfare system, others are restricted to central governmental expenditures; some calculations take educational expenditures into account while others do not. Such differences are natural in that the individual calculations serve different purposes. However, even the intention to use the same definition will not guarantee comparable figures, because data providers in various countries and periods may interpret certain concepts differently. Moreover, there are periods for which little or no data are available. There are especially scarce data collected along the same criteria from the first half of the 20th century, hence data must be approached with special caution regarding this period. In order to make expenditures comparable it is expedient to define them as a proportion of economic output, such as the GDP. However, comparative analysis is further hindered by the fact that the methods for calculating the GDP also vary, furthermore, figures are often scarce, as is the case with Hungary. Therefore, the best way is to analyse the various types of expenditures in parallel and indicate the main methodologycal features of the calculations.

In the following, the changes in expenditures in Western Europe and Hungary will be examined in four different areas. First, the major *social insurance programs* (accident, pension, sickness and unemployment) and public expenditure on health will be explored (Tables 1 and 2). In the first decades of the 20th century these data are complemented by indices of *government social spending* (health care, pensions, housing and unemployment) (Table 3). The ILO data collection of *social security expenditures* provides information about the period following the Second World War based on a broader definition including family, maternity, invalidity, war victims and survivors benefits, as well as special transfers to civil servants besides the four main social insurance programs and

67 Studies based on the analysis of expenditures, Frederic Pryor, Public Expenditures in Communist and Capitalist Nations. Homewood 1968; Jürgen Kohl, Staatsausgaben in Westeuropa. Analysen zur langfristigen Entwicklung der öffentlichen Finanzen. Frankfurt/M. 1985.

public health expenditures (Tables 4 and 5).[68] Finally, the OECD data collection on *social expenditures* has an even wider scope, embracing education and housing-related public expenditures as well as investments in the welfare sector in addition to the programs surveyed by the ILO (Table 6). The ILO and OECD publications and other sources used generally do not include any data on Hungary until 1990, or they publish data which we find unreliable. Therefore new calculations have been made for Hungary, achieving comparability by adopting the established international methods, an effort not smoothly and effectively accomplished in some cases for reasons discussed below.

The research literature usually regards Germany as a vanguard on the turn of the century with regard to *social insurance expenditures* and social expenditures in general. In 1900 about 1% of the gross domestic product was spent on these services, while 2.6% of the GDP was spent on social insurance and poor relief before World War I (Table 1).[69] However, a relatively large body of comparable data regarding West European social insurance expenditures is available only from as late as 1930.[70] At this point it was still Germany where the most resources, 5.2% of the GDP was allocated for these purposes.[71] Great Britain was second on the list with 4.6%, closely followed by Austria with 4.4%. Ireland and Denmark came in the middle of the list (2.8 and 2.6%), while other Scandinavian countries spent a markedly lower percentage of their domestic product, 0.7% (Finland) and 1.1% (Sweden), on social insurance (Table 1).

When inquiry is restricted to *government social spending*, i.e. when social security services financed by employers and employees are excluded while other types of social expenditures (e.g. assistance) are included, a completely different picture emerges. According to Peter Lindert's calculations, in 1900 the governmental welfare expenditures in Denmark amounted to 1.41% of the GNP, followed by 1.24% in Norway, but indices of the United Kingdom and Sweden also exceeded the 0.59% found in Germany, the

68 ILO, The cost of social security. Eleventh international inquiry, 1978-1980. Geneva 1985, 1-2.

69 Peter Flora, Solution or source of crises?, in: W. J. Mommsen ed., The Emergence of the Welfare State in Britain and Germany, 1850-1950. London 1981, 359.

70 For social insurance and social security expenditures in Western Europe see, Flora ed., State, Economy and Society in Western Europe. Vol. I. 456; ILO, The cost of social security. Fourteenth international inquiry, 1987-1989. Geneva 1996, 108-165 and other volumes of the series; Flora, Solution or source of crises? 359; Statistisches Bundesamt, Bevölkerung und Wirtschaft, 1872-1972. Stuttgart 1972, 219-260; Wolfram Fischer (Hrsg.), Handbuch der europäischen Wirtschafts- und Sozialgeschichte. Bd. 6. Stuttgart 1987, 217; Alber, Vom Armenhaus zum Wohlfahrtsstaat. 60.

71 Our own computation based on the following work, Statistisches Bundesamt, Bevölkerung und Wirtschaft, 1872-1972. 219-224, 260; According to the data of Jens Alber 1930 social insurance expenditures accounted for 7.8% of GDP in Germany. Alber, Vom Armenhaus zum Wohlfahrtsstaat. 60.

country leading in terms of social security expenditures.[72] For the next few decades all the countries examined are characterised by dynamic growth, Germany showing the highest rate, so much so that by 1930 it became the leader also in terms of government social spending, which reached almost 5%. Ireland was close behind, while the United Kingdom and Scandinavian countries were in the middle of the list (Table 3). It must be pointed out here, though, that Lindert does not include either pensions paid for public employees or any other social benefits among government social spending, but considers them to be part of the earnings. As mentioned in the Introduction, this method is justifiable to a certain extent, however, the inclusion of benefits for public employees would significantly alter the amount of expenditures in a number of countries, Hungary being one among them.

Returning to social security expenditures, from 1950 onwards complete data sets are available regarding the four main programs in the examined West European countries, which are of better quality and consistency than the former ones. Figures from the middle of the century exceeded those two decades earlier everywhere, though statistics from this period onwards will include public expenditures on health as well.[73] The only exception was Germany, badly hit by the war and unable to reach the relatively high level of expenditures of the first half of the century. Growth in the fifties was also steady, although its rate was lower than in the preceding two decades. It was the 1960s and the first half of the 1970s that saw the most dramatic increase. In the latter period, for example, in a number of the countries (Italy, Ireland, Switzerland and West Germany) the ratio of social insurance and public health expenditures to the GDP rose by 50% over only a few years. Although up to the middle of the 1970s growth was universal, the dynamics of expenditures and their levels were uneven across countries. In 1975 Sweden, having the highest rate of growth alongside with the Netherlands and Italy in the previous decades, spent twice as much on social security and public health than the United Kingdom. The most striking change took place in the relative position of the United Kingdom: in 1950 it was at the top of the list closely behind Germany, but, its expenditures stagnating, by the mid-1970s it was the country in Western Europe that spent the least on social security compared to its GDP.

The middle of the 1970s can be regarded as a watershed in a sense. From this time on there is an almost general decline in the growth rate of expenditures in most countries.

---

72 Peter Lindert, The Rise of Social Spending. 10. Lindert excludes the pensions of public employees; also from Lindert, see Peter Lindert, What Limits Social Spending?, in: Explorations in Economic History, 33 (1996), 1-34.

73 Between 1950 and 1977 public health expenditures includes free hospitalization, medical care, and sanitation. From 1978 onwards a narrower definition applies. In countries with state health care system (United Kingdom, Italy, Denmark, Finland, Ireland, Norway, Sweden) the costs of the systems are included in the public health expenditures until 1977 and in social insurance expenditures from 1978 onwards. ILO, The cost of social security. Eleventh international inquiry, 1978-1980. Geneva 1985, 2-3, 78.

Moreover, in the second half of the 1980s the ratio of social insurance expenditures already stagnated or even decreased in a number of the countries. The most dramatic fall took place in Ireland, Finland (which saw the fastest growth at the beginning of the 1980s) and in the United Kingdom. The Western European average at the end of the 80s is lagging behind the average of five years earlier and only slightly exceeds the level of 10 years before (Appendix). This occurred in tandem with a further differentiation between the countries of Western Europe. At the end of the period examined, the Netherlands, having the second highest ratio (20.9%) was lagging well behind the 28.6% of Sweden, while the countries spending the least on social insurance relative to their GDP were the United Kingdom (9.9%) and Switzerland (11.4%) (Table 1).

Beyond the methodological problems already mentioned, the comparability of the figures in Table 1 is limited somewhat for the reason that the special schemes for public employees are not included. This affects countries to different degrees, depending on whether they had a program of this kind and, if such programs existed, how developed these were. Consequently, the data of the countries where these programs had a major role (e.g. Germany and Austria) appear to be lower than they actually were, due to the fact that a proportion of their citizens received benefits through these programs and not through the normal social insurance schemes.

The ILO data collection on *social security expenditures* provides better figures for comparison than social insurance expenditures in the narrow sense.[74] The wider definition of ILO includes not only the four main social insurance services and public health service, but also family, maternity and social insurance expenditures to public servants and also expenditures on certain types of assistance (for example, non-contributory pensions) as well as benefits to war victims. By adopting this definition, most of the comparative methodological pitfalls can undoubtedly be eliminated, although some inconsistencies in statistics still remain, because the ILO survey underestimates expenditures by some percentage points for certain countries against other data sets using a similar approach.[75] However, for the decades succeeding the Second World War, social secu-

---

74 Cf. ILO, The cost of social security. Eleventh international inquiry, 1978-1980. Geneva 1985, 57-58; ILO, The cost of social security. Fourteenth international inquiry, 1987-1989. Geneva 1996, 74-75; ILO, World Labour Report 2000. Income Security and Social Protection in a Changing World. Geneva 2000, 313; Flora ed., State, Economy, and Society in Western Europe. Vol. I. 456.

75 The difference in 1983 is 4.8 percentage points in the case of Germany, and 3.7 that of Great Britain as compared to EC-statistics. The Nordic Statistics shows a deviation of 3.4 percentage points for Finland in 1984 and some 7-8 percentage points for Norway at the end of the 1980s. Nordic Social-Statistical Committee, Social Security in the Nordic Countries. Scope, expenditure and financing, 1990; Pekka Kosonen, European Integration: A Welfare State Perspective. Helsinki 1994, 52. It is not possible to discuss here the problem of different taxations of welfare benefits either, which can also affect the relative level of net social expenditures considerably. Data are only available in this case for some countries and for some years in the last two decades. In the Netherlands such taxes accounted for 5.1% of the GDP

rity expenditures by the ILO definition show a pattern of growth similar to social insurance expenditures in the narrow sense, with slower rise at the beginning and end of the period and rapid increase in the 60s and 70s. The path taken by individual countries was also similar to what could be seen in the case of social insurance. West Germany had the highest rate of expenditures in 1950, and France, Belgium and Austria alike spent large amounts on these purposes. At this time Scandinavian countries, the Netherlands and Switzerland were among the countries spending the least. The highest rate of growth is characteristic of exactly this latter group of countries, with the exception of Switzerland, where the rate of growth was steadily low from the middle of the 50s until the end of the examined period. Countries that had been traditionally big spenders (West Germany, Belgium and Austria) were surpassed by the Netherlands at the end of the 60s and a decade later it was Sweden heading the list. Regarding the period between 1950 and 1990, Sweden had the highest rate of growth, with the Netherlands and Denmark close behind. France also witnessed a high rate of growth in this period, while the United Kingdom had the lowest percentage of rise in social security spending and the West German rate of growth was also moderate. By the end of the 80s Sweden's expenditure rate of 35.9% was the highest, leaving the almost identical rates of the Netherlands (28.5%) and Denmark (28.4%) well behind (Table 3).

Social security plays a special role among social welfare programs for the above mentioned reasons, and its development is also in the focus of the present study. It has to be noted, though, that this category, even with public health expenditures and family and maternity benefits included, covers only a part of all welfare expenditures. Social assistance in the broader sense, education and housing expenditures as well as investments in the welfare sector not included in the statistics above can all be included among *social expenditures*. Therefore, it seems expedient to give a brief account of the OECD data collection based on such broad definition for the last decades.[76] These data

---

in 1990 and for 5.9% in 1993. Also in 1993 they made up 5.3% of the GDP in Sweden, 3.9% in Denmark, and only 2.6% in Germany and 0.2% in the United Kingdom. The differences in taxation decreased the gap between the United Kingdom and the Netherlands in the level of social expenditures. OECD, Net Public Social Expenditure. OECD Working Papers. Vol. V. Occasional Papers, No. 19. Paris 1997, 14; for similar methodological problems, see Willem Adema, Uncovering Real Social Spending. The OECD Observer, No. 211, April/May 1998, 20-23.

76 At the same time the OECD data exclude special benefits for public employees, such as pensions, probably based on the usual consideration that these benefits constitute a part of the income. Fraternité Rt., Jelentés a társadalombiztosítás reformjáról. Budapest 1991, 57; for OECD-data, see Peter Flora ed., Growth to Limits. The Western European Welfare States Since World War II. Vol. 4. Berlin and New York 1987, 325-815; OECD, Social Expenditure, 1960-1990. Paris 1985, 80; OECD, Social Expenditure Statistics of OECD Members Countries. Labour Market and Social Policy Occasional Papers. No. 17. Paris 1996, 19; UNESCO, Statistical Yearbook. 1993. Paris 1993, 416-418; OECD, National Accounts. Main Aggregates, 1960-1997. Vol. I. Paris 1999.

are not complete either for the first half of the 20th century, but for the second half they can be practically regarded as complete (Table 6).

Employing this broad definition, the ratio of expenditures to the GDP will significantly increase, in some cases it will double or even triple compared to social insurance expenditures. This was the case already in the beginning of the century. In 1913 Germany spent 6.1% of its GDP on welfare purposes in the wider sense, such as social insurance, education, public health, which was the highest ratio in Western Europe. In the early 20th century Switzerland, the United Kingdom and Ireland also had a high expenditure ratio.[77] In the interwar period the ratio of social expenditures showed a steady growth and exceeded 5% in all the countries with the exception of Finland and Italy. Growth after the Second World War shows little divergence from that of social insurance and social security, all reaching their peaks at about the same time, and the countries with the highest and lowest expenditure ratios roughly coincide, too. In the years following the Second World War welfare legislation intensified, which affected welfare expenditures as well. Great Britain is a very obvious example here and so is Finland, a country with a modest welfare state between the two world wars, where the annual growth of social expenditures amounted to 22.2% between 1945 and 1950. In Ireland social policy gained momentum as well.[78] The 1950s, on the other hand, can be considered a period of relative stagnation, because the relative level of resources spent on welfare increased only slightly. From approximately 1960 a new era began, spanning to the middle of the 1970s, which is characterised by the highest rate of growth in Western European social expenditures for the whole period examined. Denmark and Norway had the most dynamic rise in this period with more than 8% per annum in real value, while the United Kingdom and Austria had the lowest rate (less than 4%).[79] The average rate of growth approximately halved between the mid 70s and the mid 80s (Table 6). The relative ratio of social expenditures to the GDP reached their peak at the beginning or middle of the 1980s in most of the countries. In 1980 the Netherlands and Sweden headed the list with around 40%, while Switzerland and the United Kingdom spent the least on these purposes; the Western European average was at about 30%. Expenditures in the 1980s increased further but the steady growth characterising the previous decades in all the countries was superseded by a more complex pattern. While the rate of expenditure growth remained high in Finland and Norway in this decade as well, in other countries it stagnated or even decreased slightly (e.g. in the United Kingdom, Ireland, the Netherlands and Belgium) (Table 6).

Various indicators examined show that in terms of the relative level of welfare expenditures there were remarkable differences between West European countries in the first

---

77 Christopher Pierson, Beyond the Welfare State? Cambridge 1991, 111.

78 Pierson, Beyond the Welfare State? 136.

79 OECD, The Future of Social Protection. Paris 1988, 11.

half of the 20th century, but these significantly decreased by the 1950s, and the tendency of convergence continued steadily in the next two decades. Subsequently, the coefficient of variation from the middle of the 1970s onwards displayed different patterns for the various types of expenditures. With social insurance expenditures narrowly defined, the trend reversed and variation increased until the end of the examined period.[80] Though this indicated a significant divergence, differences between Western European countries were slightly smaller in 1990 than in 1950, and were far smaller than the differences between the two world wars. On the other hand, social security expenditures by the ILO definition, which detected smaller differences between individual countries from the start, show only a slight increase of the coefficient of variation at the end of the period examined. In the case of social expenditures based on the broad OECD definition, in contrast with the two indices discussed before, the trend of levelling out continued, and in 1990 the coefficient of variation indicating the differences between individual countries was only one-fourth of the coefficient found four decades earlier (Appendix).

* * *

Only a small body of data is available regarding *Hungary*'s welfare expenditures in the first half of the century. However, available sources clearly suggest that in 1930 the 1.6% ratio of *social insurance expenditures* relative to economic output is lagging well behind the 2.5% average of the examined Western European countries, accompanied by high variance (we have no data on Italy, France and Belgium from this period), but surpasses the countries at the end of the list such as Finland, Norway, Sweden and Switzerland (Tables 1 and 2).[81]

Relying on Peter Lindert's data collection cited above and supplemented, in terms of the state's role an even wider gap can be found, provided that social benefits to public employees are not involved in the calculations. In this case government social spending in Hungary in 1930 amounted to 0.64% of the GNP, exceeding the corresponding data of Belgium and Italy only (Table 3).[82]

---

80 Alber, Vom Armenhaus zum Wohlfahrtsstaat. 161; Schmidt, Sozialpolitik. 137.

81 For the Hungarian social security data, see ILO, International Survey of Social Services. Studies and Reports, Series M., No. 11. Geneva 1933, 361-390; Magyar Statisztikai Évkönyv. 1940. Budapest 1941, 59; Statisztikai Évkönyv. 1970. Budapest 1971, 419; Népesség- és társadalomstatisztikai zsebkönyv. 1985. Budapest 1986, 208; Magyar Statisztikai Évkönyv. 1980. Budapest 1981, 387; A magyar állam zárszámadása az 1930-31. évről. Budapest 1932, 60-153; A Világbank szociálpolitikai jelentése Magyarországról, in: Szociálpolitikai Értesítő, 1992, 2. szám, 54.

82 Lindert, The Rise of Social Spending. 10. Our own calculations for Hungary based on the sources and methods used by Lindert with a considerable higher result than the 0.1% published by Lindert. The correction was necessary because Lindert's compilation is inconsistent regarding the social expenditures of communes and the state as an employer.

Although not affecting the 1930 figures, the 1927 pension insurance reform, to be discussed below, can be regarded as an important move, a sort of breakthrough in the social security of the Hungarian population employed outside agriculture and the public sector. In his contemporary analysis Béla Kovrig already argued convincingly that this reform set pensions at a level that compares favourably with the international standard, though it applied only to new pensioners and contributors. His statements were supported by the contemporary ILO surveys as well (Table 16).[83] Therefore, with the gradual maturation of eligibilities the significant increase of welfare expenditures was to be expected, although due to the waiting periods the reform's impact on social security expenditures can hardly be detected sooner than from the end of the 30s. Expenditures stagnated during the years of depression only to pick up again after it was over: their ratio to economic output amounted to 2.3% in 1935 and 2.7% in 1940. We have comparable data from Germany for this decade, where social insurance expenditures relative to gross domestic product decreased for roughly the same period (1930-1938). Consequently, the gap between the Hungarian and German expenditure levels narrowed in the 30s (Table 1).[84]

A much larger body of data is accessible on Hungarian welfare efforts from the period following the Second World War. Nevertheless, difficulties do arise when comparing these data with those from Western Europe. One type of difficulty is revealed by the fact that in Western Europe welfare expenditures are calculated in proportion to either the GDP or the GNP, while in Hungary it had been the practice for decades to publish data only relative to the Net Material Product. As a result of the communist approach to economics, this latter figure only covered material production and so called material services, therefore welfare expenditures expressed in its percentages are not suitable for direct comparison with Western European figures. Surprisingly, historical calculations so far, including ILO publications and other major works, used these figures with no corrections for comparative purposes.[85] Still, there exist retrospective GDP calculations for Hungary. Despite some shortcomings they are great help in calculating Hungarian indices which are directly comparable with Western European figures. In several cases our own estimations supply missing data.[86]

83 Béla Kovrig, Magyar társadalompolitika. 1920-1945. I. rész. New York 1954, 125-129; Kovrig, A munka védelme a dunai államokban. 275-294; ILO, International Survey of Social Services. Studies and Reports, Series M., 361-390.

84 For German data, see Statistisches Bundesamt, Bevölkerung und Wirtschaft, 1872-1972. Stuttgart 1972, 219-224, 260.

85 Cf. ILO, The cost of social security. Eleventh international inquiry, 1978-1980. Geneva 1985, 112; Zsuzsa Ferge, A szociálpolitika hazai fejlődése, in: Zsuzsa Ferge and Györgyi Várnai eds., Szociálpolitika ma és holnap. Budapest 1987, 53.

86 Our analysis is based on data published by Alexander Eckstein and the partly retrospective GDP-data of the Hungarian Central Statistical Office (KSH); NNP 1930-1940: Alexander Eckstein, National Income and Capital Formation in Hungary, 1900-1950, in: Simon Kuznets ed., Income and Wealth. Series V. London 1955, 219; 1950 GDP is our own estima-

In 1950 social insurance and public health expenditures in Hungary equalled 3.2% of the estimated GDP (Table 2).[87] This percentage cannot be directly compared with pre-war Hungarian data because of the inclusion of public health expenditures (prevention of epidemics, etc.), and that of the pension and other welfare benefits of state and public employees. It is not possible to separate the latter from the benefits of other social groups, therefore corrections have been made to pre-war figures for comparative purposes.

If the pensions of state employees (public servants, teachers, railway officers, state factory employees) and those of their relatives and survivors, financed by sources other than social security, are taken into account, rather higher social expenditure percentages emerge for the pre-war period.[88] In 1930 224.7 million Pengős were allocated for these purposes from the state budget.[89] Adding this amount, significantly exceeding contemporary social insurance expenditures, the total expenditures amount to 326.7 million Pengős and account for 5.2% of the NNP.[90] This percentage further increased in the years of the recession due to the shrinking national product. In 1932, for example, the total sum allocated for pensions, including the benefits of state employees, health insurance and occupational injuries insurance expenditures amounted to 380.27 million Pengős. This means that 7.7% of the 4.9 billion Pengős NNP was allocated for these purposes.[91] Therefore, if the calculations of the 1930s are made according to the definitions of the post-1950 period, figures will indicate that the percentage of social insurance expenditures in the 1930s in Hungary was considerably higher than in the fist decades of the communist era. This ratio to the GDP of expenditures allocated for pensions, health-

tion based on the following publication United Nations, Statistical Yearbook. 1961. New York 1961, 486. The NMP of 1950 was 46.5 billion Forints of which we estimated a GDP value of 20 per cent higher; other sources of GDP-data include Statisztikai Évkönyv. 1970. Budapest 1971, 74-75; Magyar Statisztikai Évkönyv. 1980. Budapest 1981, 89; Magyarország nemzeti számlái. Főbb mutatók. 1991. Budapest 1993, 4.

87 The same expenditures made up 3.8% of the NMP in 1950.

88 For social benefits of public employees offered outside the social security programs, see Gusztáv Ladik, Jóléti intézményeink. Budapest 1940, 342-349.

89 A magyar állam zárszámadása az 1930-31. évről. Budapest 1932, 60-153, 306-310.

90 The data refer to contributions paid by insured persons and employers and state contributions. Dénes Bikkal, Társadalombiztosítás Magyarországon, in: Közgazdasági Szemle, LVIII (1934) 6-8, 389; for the pensions of public employees, see István Hollós, A közszolgálati alkalmazottak nyugdíjkérdése és a megoldási lehetőségek. Budapest 1940, 3-55. Bikkal, Társadalombiztosítás Magyarországon. 389; Eckstein, National Income and Capital Formation in Hungary, 1900-1950. 165. The NNP-indicator applied by Eckstein differs from GNP to the extent that it also contains the depreciation of capital stock. As a result, Eckstein's NNP data only slightly differ from the GNP and GDP in the 1930s.

91 Excluding public health expenditures. Bikkal, Társadalombiztosítás Magyarországon. 389; Eckstein, National Income and Capital Formation in Hungary, 1900-1950. 165; László Béry and Andor Kun, Magyarország évkönyve. 1934. Budapest s. a., 65.

care, other welfare services and public health services was not reached again in Hungary until the beginning of the 1970s.[92]

The growth of social security expenditures in the 1950s turns out to be especially low in the light of the significant increase in the number of those eligible, which was due to the maturing of the eligibilities of the 1928 pension reform on the one hand, and the extension of coverage after the Second World War on the other. The level of benefits and the regulation of eligibility will be discussed in more detail below.

The level of social security expenditures in the 1950s and 60s was also relatively low in comparison with Western European figures, equalling approximately two-thirds of the Western European average. In the 1970s the gap between Hungary and Western Europe seems to have become narrower, although it has to be noted that this can be partly attributed to the fact that from 1978 onwards Western European figures do not include public health expenditures, while Hungarian ones still do. Taking this difference also into account diminishes Hungary's rate of convergence. The 1980s saw a slight fall in the rate of growth in Hungary, but there was a sharp increase at the end of the decade. For example, between 1989 and 1990, in just one year, the ratio of expenditures to the GDP rose from 14.5% to 15.8%. This is, however, already closely related to the so called transformation crisis, which resulted in a fall in economic output on the one hand, and, with the actual emergence of unemployment an increase in the demand for social allowances on the other. This growth, in parallel with the slump in the growth rate of social expenditures in Western Europe (and even the stagnation of, or fall in, expenditures in some cases), resulted in the first significant convergence under the communist regime between Hungary and Western Europe in this area in the 80s. However, social insurance expenditures in Hungary could not reach the West European average even at the end of the 1980s (Table 1, Appendix).

As pointed out above in another context, there are two major differences in the methodology of post-Second World War social insurance calculations in Hungary and Western Europe. On the one hand, the special social insurance benefits of public employees by the state and, on the other hand, war victims benefits are not included in West European figures, which limit the validity of the comparison. These difficulties can be mostly overcome by the ILO social security calculations based on a broader definition of expenditures (social insurance, maternity and family benefits, disabled/war widow assistance, public health expenditures).[93] These expenditures rose dynamically in Hun-

92 Our computation is also based on the NNP in this case, which excludes the appreciation of the capital stock. This difference, however, only slightly affects the results.

93 ILO, The cost of social security. Eleventh international inquiry, 1978-1980. Geneva 1985 and the other volumes of the series; Magyarország adataira, Statisztikai Évkönyv. 1970. Budapest 1971, 419; Magyar Statisztikai Évkönyv. 1980. Budapest 1981, 387; Népesség- és társadalomstatisztikai zsebkönyv. 1985. Budapest 1986, 208; A Világbank szociálpolitikai jelentése Magyarországról, in: Szociálpolitikai Értesítő, 1992, 2. szám, 54. (Original English edition: International Bank for Reconstruction and Development, Hungary: Reform of social

gary as well after the Second World War, especially in the 1970s and 1980s, and their ratio to the GDP was five times as high in 1990 than in 1950 (Table 5). The manifold increase, however, was to a large extent due to the low basis – 3.8% in 1950. Despite its steady growth, the ratio of social security expenditures became as high as 20% only by the end of the period examined, amounting to four-fifths of the West European average. As mentioned before, however, this was partly due to the recession of the Hungarian economy, as the GDP, and especially its officially registered portion started to shrink, resulting in the relative rise in the level of expenditures (Table 4). Nevertheless, following the divergence of the 1950s, in the discussed periods of fast growth, clear-cut convergence can be observed between Hungary and Western Europe in this area (Appendix).[94]

If trends of social expenditures are measured by the broader method of calculation used by the OECD, slightly different dynamics emerge both in terms of the changes in the Hungarian level and the differences between Hungarian and Western European levels.[95] In 1960 11.3% of the GDP was spent on welfare purposes, which rose to 13.9%, 19.6% and 27.8% in 1970, 1980 and 1990, respectively.[96] That is, the moderate rate of growth in the 60s was followed by a relatively sharp rise. The first half of the 1980s saw the reoccurrence of a slow down, almost equalling stagnation. At the end of the decade acceleration can be seen, which is obviously the result of the recession in Hungary: for example, from 1989 to 1990, in the course of one year, the ratio of expenditures rose from 25.4% to 27.8% (Table 6).[97]

In summary, in the period between 1960 and 1990 the relative level of social expenditures in Hungary was lagging far behind the Western European average. In 1960 it amounted to 70% of the Western European average, which was followed by a sharp then a moderate increase in the difference until in 1980 it was considerably higher than two decades before. The fast growth in the second half of the 1980s was enough only to reach four-fifths of the West European average. Moreover, the gradual decrease in the

---

policy and expenditures. Washington DC 1992, 121.)

94 For other communist countries with considerably different growth patterns, see Castles, Whatever Happened to the Communist Welfare State? 213-226.

95 OECD, Social Expenditure, 1960-1990. Paris 1985; OECD, Social Expenditure Statistics of OECD Members Countries. Labour Market and Social Policy Occasional Papers. No. 17. Paris 1996, 19; UNESCO, Statistical Yearbook. 1993. Paris 1993, 416-418; OECD, National Accounts. Main Aggregates, 1960-1997. Vol. I. Paris 1999. Unlike Western European data, the Hungarian data exclude social benefits for public employees.

96 For the Hungarian data, see Gács, Szociális kiadásaink nemzetközi összehasonlításban. 1228; Magyarország nemzeti számlái. Főbb mutatók. 1991. Budapest 1993, 85; Beruházási Évkönyv. 1980. Budapest 1981, 18; Népgazdasági mérlegek, 1949-1987. Budapest 1989, 66; A lakosság jövedelme és fogyasztása, 1960-1980. Budapest 1984, 21; A Világbank szociálpolitikai jelentése Magyarországról. 54.

97 For welfare expenditures in the era of transformation crisis, see István György Tóth, A jóléti rendszer az átmenet időszakában, in: Közgazdasági Szemle, XLI (1994) 3, 313-340.

variance in Western Europe also contributed to the divergence observed in the examined period between Hungary and Western Europe except for the last few years (Table 6, Appendix).

There is another problem, even greater than the ones discussed above when compareing post-Second World War Hungarian and Western European welfare expenditures.[98] It is a dilemma whether the subsidies to consumer prices, typical of communist countries and absorbing huge resources, should be included in social expenditures or not. In one, undoubtedly plausible argument, the ILO and OECD statistics often used in the comparative analysis of welfare systems reflect the principles underlying the welfare systems of Western countries and ignore the unique structure of social rights in communist countries.[99] In these countries state subsidies to the prices of basic consumer goods and services were a major tool of welfare policy. The explicit goal of these measures, i.e. the improvement and nivellation of the purchasing power of incomes, was not unlike the objectives to be realised by other means of welfare policy. However, we believe that including price subsidies in welfare expenditures would also present considerable difficulties in the comparison, exactly because the principles underlying these subsidies differed so significantly from the principles behind welfare benefits discussed above. If the definition of welfare benefits was extended to include subsidies as well, it would be not welfare systems but entire social-economic systems that we were to compare. This, even disregarding the difficulties involved, is not our ambition. These subsidies served not only welfare purposes but had a more complex function, e.g. the support of inefficient firms and economic branches. Moreover, evidence from research shows that they had a moderate impact on social policy, primarily because affluent segments of the society had much better access to them than the average. Furthermore, in certain areas, such as health care or consumption of basic foods, they resulted in the large-scale waste of resources.[100]

Price subsidies in communist Hungary definitely increased the expenditures of the national budget, although never grew so much out of proportion as in the GDR in the 80s, where the funds allocated for subsidies surpassed social security expenditures.[101] The growth pattern of price subsidies was considerably different from the benefits of social policy. The growth, excluding housing benefits, was highest in the 50s, the 70s and in the first half of the 80s, and after reaching its peak in 1986-1987 it fell sharply.[102]

---

98 For methodological problems of international comparisons of Hungarian welfare expenditures in the 1980s, see Tóth, A jóléti rendszer az átmenet időszakában. 314-315.

99 Therborn, European Modernity and Beyond. 95.

100 Rudolf Andorka and István György Tóth, A szociális kiadások és a szociálpolitika Magyarországon, in: Rudolf Andorka and Tamás Kolosi and György Vukovich ed., Társadalmi riport. 1992. Budapest 1992, 442.

101 Therborn, European Modernity and Beyond. 95.

102 A Világbank szociálpolitikai jelentése Magyarországról. 54; Rudolf Andorka and Anna Kondratas and István György Tóth, A jóléti rendszer átalakulása Magyarországon: felépítése,

Including price subsidies in Hungarian welfare expenditures, we find their ratio to the GDP equal to or slightly exceeding the level of the West European average in 1960, and, after a decline, reaching it again and remaining steady at this level until the end of the 1980s.[103]

In conclusion, first it has to be noted that due to the lack of appropriate data both in the case of Hungary and Western Europe, considerable methodological difficulties arise in the comparison of welfare expenditures, especially in the first half of the century. This in itself makes reliance exclusively on expenditure data methodologically unacceptable in welfare comparisons.

However, if definitions of international organisations (ILO, OECD) extensively used in international comparative studies are employed, it can be clearly seen that Hungary was lagging well behind Western European societies in terms of welfare expenditure ratios, and in the second half of the century the actual gap is much wider than it has been estimated before.[104]

Due to the lack of long-term data sets it is hard to make any definitive statements about the first half of the century regarding the convergence/divergence of Western European and Hungarian welfare expenditures. Considering trends in Germany, intensifying Hungarian welfare legislature in the late 1920s and in the 1930s as well as the welfare programs launched in this period provide sufficient grounds only to formulate the hypothesis that social insurance and social security expenditures in Hungary converged to those of Western Europe in the 1930s.

Although 1945 or other political turning points cannot be regarded as divides in terms of welfare expenditures, the most striking feature of the communist regime establishing itself is the moderate welfare efforts both compared to efforts in Hungary in the interwar period and in international comparison. In terms of social insurance expenditures, social security expenditures and social expenditures relative to the GDP, Hungary diverged from Western Europe until the end of the 1970s. Moreover, in 1980 Hungary was still more behind the West than it had been in 1930.

If there is a turning point in the relationships of corresponding Hungarian and Western European welfare expenditures, it must be the 1970s and the 1980s. In terms of social insurance and social security expenditures, a narrowing of the gap can be observed from the 1970s, a process accelerating at the end of the 1980s. The latter was due to, first, the recession in Hungary which was reflected in the stagnation of the GDP, and secondly, to the relative stagnation of Western European expenditures. This dynamics does not hold for total social expenditures, as these show divergence between Hungary

---

kezdeti reformjai és javaslatok. A Magyar-Nemzetközi Kék Szalag Bizottság 3. sz. Gazdaságpolitikai tanulmánya. Budapest 1994, 17.

103 For price subsidies, see Mária Barát ed., A magyar gazdaság vargabetűje. Budapest 1994, 447; A Világbank szociálpolitikai jelentése Magyarországról. 54.

104 See Ferge, A szociálpolitika hazai fejlődése. 41-48.

and Western Europe in the 1970s and 1980s, with the exception of the last few years of the observed period, mainly due to an increasing uniformity of the countries of Western Europe.

The dynamics described above with respect to Hungarian trends reinforce the arguments that communist regimes increased welfare expenditures primarily in periods of crises for purposes of legitimisation, but welfare policy was not an inherent priority for them. This thesis is also supported by the practice of other communist countries, where, with the exception of the GDR and Czechoslovakia, the rate of growth in welfare expenditures was even lower than in Hungary.

2 MAJOR STRUCTURAL CHARACTERISTICS OF WELFARE

The changes in welfare expenditures yield important information but are not sufficient in themselves to characterise welfare states. A more accurate picture can be drawn by analysing the mechanisms and institutions for relieving poverty in 20th century Western Europe and Hungary and by examining how their relative importance changed over time. In this chapter the most important structural characteristics of social security will be examined. The questions posed include: 1. what major social security programs existed and when they were introduced; and 2. how these developed after their establishment, how they differentiated and what structural changes occurred to them. Further details of institutional characteristics will be discussed in later chapters.

Although collective welfare provision had already existed for more than a hundred years in Western Europe by the 19th century, the real breakthrough in the development of welfare institutions was represented by the establishment and development of social security. For smaller social groups such as sailors or miners, experiments with social security systems had been ongoing since the mid-19th century, but the birth of modern social security is generally considered to be the German legislature of the 1880s. In Germany, compulsory state health insurance for industrial workers was introduced in 1883. Then the same decade saw the introduction of similar accident and pension insurance (1884 and 1889, respectively).[105] Social security systems mushroomed in Western Europe after this time, though not modelled on the German example in every respect.

A good illustration of the speed with which the programs spread in Western Europe is that by 1901 each country in the region had some form of at least one of the occupational injuries, health or old age insurances and by World War I most of them had a program for all three risks.[106] In spite of this, it took decades until the first social security laws were passed in all three areas mentioned in all Western European countries. Switzerland, the country last in the line in Western Europe introduced old age insurance

[105] For legislation related to social security in Western European countries, see Ritter, Der Sozialstaat. 61-102; Flora and Alber, Modernization, Democratization and the Development of the Welfare States in Western Europe. 48-70; Detlev Zöllner, Landesbericht Deutschland, in: Köhler and Zacher (Hrsg.), Ein Jahrhundert Sozialversicherung. 83-92; Yves Saint-Jours, Landesbericht Frankreich, in: Köhler and Zacher (Hrsg.), Ein Jahrhundert Sozialversicherung. 209-212; Anthony I. Ogus, Landesbericht Großbritannien, in: Köhler and Zacher, (Hrsg.), Ein Jahrhundert Sozialversicherung. 334-342; Herbert Hofmeister, Landesbericht Österreich, in: Köhler and Zacher (Hrsg.), Ein Jahrhundert Sozialversicherung. 533-588; Alfred Maurer, Landesbericht Schweiz, in: Köhler and Zacher (Hrsg.), Ein Jahrhundert Sozialversicherung. 780-788.

[106] Alber, Vom Armenhaus zum Wohlfahrtsstaat. 28.

in addition to accident and health insurance only in the middle of the 20th century (1946) (Table 7). A pattern can also be identified in the *sequence* as social security programs were introduced.[107] Usually the first was industrial injury insurance, followed by health insurance and old age insurance. Nevertheless, there are deviations from the pattern: for example, France and Great Britain first introduced old age insurance before World War I. Unemployment insurance was usually introduced following the three programs already mentioned. It was established as a compulsory insurance type before World War I in Great Britain and after the war in other countries. However, in several countries it was established only well after the Second World War or not at all. Still, by 1920, there was some form of public support for the unemployed in 10 of the 13 countries examined (Table 7).

This temporal order was obviously influenced by the greatest degree of compatibility existing between accident insurance and traditional liberal views preferring individual responsibility and self-assistance. Even more so, because accident insurance was often introduced at the exclusive expense of employers' organisations, reconciliation was possible with the traditional principle of liability for damages caused. In addition, the establishment of health and pension insurance required greater administrative efforts and incurred greater costs than that of accident insurance, and presented a greater rift from liberal principles. The relative belatedness of unemployment insurance and benefits can also be explained by its great distance from liberal economic principles and liability laws.[108]

Nevertheless, the timing of the introduction in itself reveals little about the coverage and depth of a particular program. Early programs, as will be discussed later, progressed through a period of maturing, as it were. That is, they expanded with time to provide more comprehensive benefits. At the same time, there are examples, especially in Scandinavia, of programs launched relatively late with more extensive benefits, guaranteed for a wider circle of the citizens or those employed, from the beginnings than did earlier programs.

The programs mentioned (accident, health, pension and unemployment insurance), supplemented by family benefits, preserved their decisive importance in social security all through the period examined. Actually they gained prime significance among welfare services in Western Europe by the middle of the century. The reason behind this is that, though the formation of the social security system brought about the emergence of a welfare system functionally more differentiated than before, the programs themselves went through a *differentiation* process following their introduction. On the one hand, this meant increasing coverage of collateral risks associated with ones included before. On the other hand, new forms of benefits also appeared. The signs of differentiation

---

107 Saundra K. Schneider, The Sequential Development of Social Programs in Eighteen Welfare States, in: Comparative Social Research, 5 (1982), 195-219.

108 Manfred G. Schmidt, Sozialpolitik. Opladen 1988, 119-120.

were obvious already in the interwar period, and it accelerated after the Second World War.

This diverse process can be illustrated with examples from different fields. As regards *occupational injuries insurance*, the circle of covered risks was expanded in the interwar period to include, besides accidents themselves, certain occupational conditions, and then the range of these illnesses was gradually widened. The list of the illnesses grew after the Second World War, too, due to technological changes and other causes. In addition, damages were compensated in the cases of illnesses not on the list, as occurred in Denmark from 1976, and other countries also treated emerging cases with flexibility.[109] Furthermore, accidents occurring on the way to and from the workplace were included among insurance risks in some countries already in the interwar years (and in most countries after the Second World War).[110] In the area of *pension insurance* the expansion regarding different risk factors (age, disability and death of the bread-winner) was gradual. The parallel treatment of all three factors was present from the beginnings only in the Dutch regulation of 1919. By the beginning of World War II old-age pension insurance had already been established in all countries except Switzerland, but social security included disability pensions in only 11 countries and the case of the death of the bread-winner only in 8.[111] The decades after World War II, as will be discussed later, witnessed the liberalisation and expansion of pension programs in all respects. This transformation included the combination of different pension types as well as a decrease in the differences between them. Turning to *health insurance*, in the beginning this usually covered the costs of shorter illnesses. For example, in Germany access to hospital care was still rather restricted for workers in the interwar period and the 1911 law on health insurance in Great Britain did not cover hospitalisation or the services of specialists. That is, health insurances typically concentrated on cash assistance in the beginnings. With the exception of a few countries like Denmark, the rapid expansion of benefits in kind took place after World War II. Though cash benefits were also liberalised, the centre stage was gradually given to expenditures in kind, because the growth of accessibility and costs had a greater pace in the latter.[112] There was an especially strong tendency in health insurance to expand the list of covered risks, resulting in the inclusion of pregnancy, post post-natal maternity, and different forms of birth control, neither of which can be classified as an illness.[113] As regards *unemployment insurance*, very early on, before the Second World War everywhere except in France attempts were made to adjust services to the means of the families through benefits tied to the number of dependants. From the late 1960s the consideration of the causes of un-

---

109 Margaret S. Gordon, Social Security Policies in Industrial Countries. Cambridge 1988, 147.

110 Alber, Vom Armenhaus zum Wohlfahrtsstaat. 54.

111 Ibidem, 55.

112 Gordon, Social Security Policies in Industrial Countries. 199-204.

113 Peter A. Köhler and Hans F. Zacher, Sozialversicherung, Pfade der Entwicklung, in: Köhler and Zacher (Hrsg.), Ein Jahrhundert Sozialversicherung. 37.

employment in calculating the benefits was a characteristic trend. In the case of massive lay-outs resulting from market recession or technological modernisation, the benefits paid could have equalled former wages.[114]

Family allowance was first introduced in 1921 in Austria. Together with the other maternity and family benefits, family allowance had a special status among welfare benefits. Often assimilated with social security, it was given not so much as one of such provisions than a kind of acknowledgement of maternity, independent of the entitlement earned by contributions. Before the Second World War only 4 countries had some form of family allowance but by the mid-1950s all Western European countries had established it (Table 7).[115]

In addition to the above, good examples of emerging new benefits assimilated with social security include the establishment of the right to attendance for the aged in 1968 in the Netherlands or wages paid for the employees of bankrupt firms in Germany.[116] Other welfare services outside social security (and beyond the scope of the present discussion) also expanded, and among them new ones were also established and used widely. Examples of such are housing benefits, or study assistance.[117] Nevertheless, the differentiation and expansion of welfare programs ended in the mid-70s. Economic recession and demographic development, e.g. ageing populations, had a slowing effect on the pace of growth and even resulted in the termination or restructuring of some programs.

The process of expansion and functional differentiation, visible in all major areas of social security and all Western European countries did not entail the same significance of each specific program or the same dynamics of growth. At the same time, differentiation and expansion progressed in structures of growing similarity in Western European societies, at least after World War II. A good indicator of the significance of programs in social security and the change of their relative weights is their place in the social security budget.[118] Although, as shown above, *pension insurance* was not usually introduced as first among social security programs, after its establishment such expenditures generally soon exceeded that of other programs. The crucial importance of the pension system in the structure of social security expenditures, and, in general, in welfare expenditures, is shown in Table 8 which summarises the distribution of the major items in

---

114 Alber, Vom Armenhaus zum Wohlfahrtsstaat. 169-170.

115 Anne Héléne Gauthier, The state and the family. Oxford 1996, 52.

116 Detlev Zöllner, Landesbericht Deutschland, in: Köhler and Zacher (Hrsg.), Ein Jahrhundert Sozialversicherung. 157.

117 Kaelble, A Social History of Western Europe. 125; Jens Alber, Germany, in: Flora ed., Growth to Limits. Vol. 2. 42-47; Richard Perry, United Kingdom, in: Flora ed., Growth to Limits. Vol. 2. 183-188; Hans Günter Hockerts, Die Entwicklung vom Zweiten Weltkrieg bis zur Gegenwart, in: Peter A. Köhler and Hans F. Zacher (Hrsg.), Beiträge zur Geschichte und aktueller Situation der Sozialversicherung. Berlin 1983, 158-159.

118 Richard M. Coughlin and Philip K. Armour, Sectoral Differentiation in Social Security Spending in the OECD Nations, in: Comparative Social Research, 6 (1983), 175-199.

social security expenditures in the Western European countries examined in 1960 and in 1980 to characterise the main tendencies. Besides pension insurance, health services, unemployment benefits and family allowances are considered here and also a miscellaneous category is included, covering cash and in kind benefits in the cases of illness, occupational injuries and maternity. The ratio of pensions was already the highest among all items everywhere except France in 1960, amounting to about half of social security expenditures. This was approximately three times higher than the second item, family allowance (17.3% on the average), which in turn was still higher than expenditure on health services (15.4% on the average). It must be noted, though, that a slight statistical distortion is present in the latter because at that time the ILO-statistics did not include the expenditures of the public health care system of Great Britain and Ireland.[119] The indexation of pensions, introduced characteristically after World War II was associated with the expansion of such programs to cover the population more universally and with the gradual increase in the ratio of senior citizens. These three factors resulted in the expansion of pension expenditures, which in turn brought about a significant growth not only in social security, but also in welfare expenditures in general, i.e. this was one of the starting points of the expansion of the welfare state in the 1960s. (Table 8)

It does not contradict this trend that the most dynamic growth can be seen in the ratio of *health* expenditures in the 1960s and 1970s, reaching 30.3% of social security expenditures on the average in Western Europe in 1980. This growth affected pensions only to a small degree; it occurred rather at the expense of *family allowance* and *maternity benefits*. The ratio of the former dropped to less than half in this period. Besides the usual factors, i.e. the expansion of coverage and the increase in the ratio of the aged, there emerged a special cause, the price explosion of health services, that is, the higher than average growth of the prices in that sector.[120]

The emergence of mass *unemployment* in the 1970s and 1980s resulted in new and significant changes in the construction of welfare states. Though high unemployment did occur in the interwar period in industrial countries, the commitment of the state for income maintenance was not so high then as later. In some countries, as a result of this commitment, unemployment (growing demand for social benefits and fewer people who paid contributions) considerably affected the structure of the welfare budget and strengthened the stability of welfare expenditures even in the second half of the 80s in England, although debates over the deconstruction of the welfare state were fierce. Differences between countries, however, were considerable and, in sum, unemployment-related expenditures accounted for a relatively low ratio of social security expenditures in Western Europe (Table 8).

[119] The change in this respect occurred from 1978; ILO, The cost of social security. Eleventh international inquiry, 1978-1980. Geneva 1985, 2-3.

[120] Coughlin and Armour, Sectoral Differentiation in Social Security Spending. 195.

Due to reasons explained earlier, our analysis is limited to social insurance and social security. Here we can only note that most of the tendencies observed above are also tangible when examining the structure of a wider circle of welfare institutions. Applying the OECD definition of social expenditures, we can see that after World War II resources channelled to education, health care and pensions amounted to a major proportion of all welfare expenditures in Western Europe. The ratio of expenditures on education increased after World War II, but started to be more moderate in the total expenditures in the 1970s, with the exception of Finland. At the same time, the ratio of expenditures on health care and pensions grew steadily, though with fluctuations. The inertia of pension expenditures is shown by their increasing ratios even under the conditions of slowing economic and welfare growth after the mid-70s.[121]

The structural development of welfare institutions regarding the areas discussed above shows several phenomena that can be interpreted as convergences. Surfacing in the interwar years, this convergence became really apparent after World War II.[122] The major social security programs had been introduced before or immediately after World War I in most countries, and by the middle of the century in those few remaining. Differences in the introductions, amounting to decades, obviously increased diversity initially. The rapid spread of the programmes, however, soon decreased the differences already in interwar years.[123]

The functional differentiation and expansion of social security programs can both be observed in Western European societies. This process was associated with a growing structural similarity, especially after World War II. The number of risks covered by insurance gradually grew, especially as regards health insurance, but the same applies to occupational injuries, pension and unemployment insurance. The increasing similarity in the structure of social security benefits is also supported by the changes in the structure of expenditures.[124] Around the middle of the century there had been great differences between Western European countries with respect to the structure of social security expenditures. In 1960 the variance of unemployment benefit ratios was the highest, with considerable differences between health-related expenditures and forms of family

121 Colin Crouch, Social Change in Western Europe. Oxford 1999, 371-373, 482-487.

122 Kaelble, A Social History of Western Europe. 123-128; Hartmut Kaelble, Wie kam es zum Europäischen Sozialmodell?, in: Jahrbuch für Europa- und Nordamerika-Studien, 4 (2000) 41-46.

123 John B. Williamson and Jeanne J. Fleming, Convergence Theory and the Social Welfare Sector: A Cross-National Analysis, in: Alex Inkeles and Masamichi Sasaki eds., Comparing Nations and Cultures. Englewood Cliffs 1996, 351; originally in: International Journal of Comparative Sociology, 18 (1977) 3-4, 242-253; Pekka Kosonen, European Welfare State Models: Converging Trends, in: International Journal of Sociology, 4 (1995), 81-110.

124 Coughlin and Armour, Sectoral Differentiation in Social Security Spending. 175-199; Jerald Hage and Robert Hannemann and Edward T. Gargan, State Responsiveness and State Activism. London 1989, 95-96.

support. Expenditures on pensions showed the smallest variation (Table 8 and Appendix). Between 1960 and 1980 the coefficient of variation of the structural distribution of social security expenditures unambiguously decreased. That is, the Western European countries examined spent increasingly similar ratios of their welfare budgets on health care and unemployment benefits and the already modest differences regarding old-age pensions continued to fade (Appendix).

Naturally, the similarities observed in the major institutional characteristics do not exclude the continuance of significant differences between the social security systems at a lower level. Thus there is justification for the claim that the introduction and the spread of basic programs only partly demonstrates convergence.[125] Further characteristics of welfare systems will be selected for discussion in the following chapters.

* * *

In *Hungary*, Act III of 1875 was the first legislative move to treat social security considering the whole working population. This act obliged employers to cover costs related to medical treatment, sick-nursing and birth up to 30 days if the workers themselves or their parents or spouses were not able to do so.[126] This immediate legislative precedent for workers' social security was soon followed by the first social security programs. The introduction of these was relatively early in an international comparison, taking place well before World War I, though the sequence of the introductions was somewhat different from the Western European pattern. The above antecedents may have contributed to compulsory *health insurance* of industrial workers being the first to be established, in Act XIV of 1891. This also meant that only Austria and Germany had such regulations earlier than Hungary. In 1907, on the one hand, health insurance was organisationally re-regulated and, on the other hand, the compulsory *occupational injuries insurance* of industrial workers and commercial employees was introduced.[127] Also

---

125 Harold L. Wilensky et al., Comparative Social Policy: Theory, Methods, Findings. Berkeley, Calif. 1985, 11-12.

126 For the precedents of social security, see István Laczkó, A magyar munkás- és balesetbiztosítás története. Budapest 1968, 41-49; A munkásbetegsegélyezési törvény módosítása. I. kötet. Hazai anyag. Budapest 1905, 14-31; for early Hungarian social care and policy, see, Gyáni, A szociálpolitika első lépései hazánkban. 94-110; Gyáni, Könyörületesség, fegyelmezés. 57-84.

127 For pre-World War I social security legislature, see Ernő Lőrincz, A munkaviszonyok szabályozása Magyarországon a kapitalizmus kezdeteitől az első világháború végéig, 1840-1918. Budapest 1974, 186-213; a contemporary overview, Munkásbiztosítás a Magyar Szent Korona országaiban. Budapest 1911; Farkas Heller, Magyarország socialpolitikája. Budapest 1923; for the whole period before, see A magyar társadalombiztosítás ötven éve, 1892-1942. Budapest 1943; a detailed account of the interwar period, mainly from a legal standpoint, Lajos Esztergár, A szociálpolitika tételes jogi alapja. Pécs 1936, 319-375; Gusztáv Ladik, Jóléti intézményeink. Budapest 1940, 211-349; also see Társadalombiztosítási évkönyv. I. évf. Budapest 1930, and other volumes of the series.

relatively early was the introduction of *family allowance* (called child rearing supplement) for state employees. *Pension insurance* appeared in 1913, but only for public service employees and their relatives, in addition to special (army, local government and railways) pension programs. The old-age pension program for those not employed by the public was running from 1928, a late introduction in international comparison. At the same time, in the interwar period, and also following World War II, *unemployment insurance* already present in several Western European countries was missing in Hungary. Still, because of the low levels of unemployment benefits between the two world wars in Western Europe, this was not such a considerable difference in this period as later. In summary, at the end of the 19th century and in the first half of the 20th Hungary saw the introduction of social security programs and benefits similar in their principles (e.g. the pension of public employees) which became the main instruments of welfare policy in Western Europe in the course of the 20th century. Also, the timing of the introductions of Hungarian social security programs conformed to Western European trends.

After their introduction, a similar *differentiation* and expansion process affected social security programs in Hungary as in Western Europe in the first half of the 20th century. Health insurance is a good example here. Following the original regulation of 1892, the most important services were extended to family members from 1907. From 1 January 1918 the maximum period of services was raised and a government decree introduced new forms of care, e.g. nursing assistance for insured persons and maternity benefit for eligible family members.[128] A new regulation from 30 September 1919, after the fall of the Hungarian Soviet Republic, increased the period for sickness cash benefit, medical treatment, benefits for family members and other benefits from 20 weeks to 1 year, cash sickness benefit from 50% to 60% and 75% of the earnings, introducing pre-natal assistance, and raising maternity assistance.[129] At the beginning of 1928 there was another raise in a number of benefits for insured persons (pre-natal assistance). In addition, on the one hand, the range of eligible family members was expanded (to include siblings and stepchildren) and, on the other hand, family members became eligible for pre-natal and nursing assistance. During World War II, in 1941 smaller changes were introduced, partly tightening entitlements and partly contributing to their expansion. Then in 1942 the changes were pointing unambiguously to the expansion of benefits again.[130]

After its establishment in 1907, accident insurance also had its first major reform in 1927, defining illnesses resulting from employment as injuries, in accordance with international labour law agreements.[131] Pension insurance for non-public employees was

---

128 Rezső Hilscher, Bevezetés a szociálpolitikába. Budapest 1928, 94.

129 Dénes Bikkal, Betegségi biztosítás Magyarországon. Budapest 1932, 5-9; A magyar társadalombiztosítás ötven éve, 1892-1942. Budapest 1943. (Mellékletek – V. sz. táblázat)

130 A magyar társadalombiztosítás ötven éve, 1892-1942. Budapest 1943. (Mellékletek – V. sz. táblázat)

131 Hilscher, Bevezetés a szociálpolitikába. 98.

introduced relatively late and in a quite generous form in Hungary, thus its differentiation in the interwar period was not tangible. Family allowance was given only to public employees from 1912, but from 1939 those working in industry, commerce and mining received it as well.[132]

Between the two world wars, similarly to most countries in Western Europe, the greatest dynamic of growth was shown by social security expenditures on pensions, which, though starting from a very low base, multiplied in the 1930s. Furthermore, taking into account the programs for public employees outside social security, this used by far the greatest resources among welfare expenditures. For example, in 1932 304.57 million Pengős were spent on this, while only a fifth of this amount was allocated for health insurance (64.17 million P), and only a fraction of this for occupational injuries insurance (11.53 million P).[133] In this period, an important structural characteristic of pension expenditures was the high ratio spent on the programmes for public employees. In the year mentioned the total pension expenditure was 304.57 million Pengős; 70.1% of this, 213.6 million Pengős were pensions paid to public employees and their relatives or survivors.[134]

The political and social changes following the post-World War II communist takeover affected the social functions of the Hungarian welfare system profoundly, and, as such, that of social security, too. In this respect, the changes can be traced back to the loss of independence of social policy and social welfare institutions. In the new welfare system the principles of social policy were also applied to other areas of social and economic life which are considered autonomous in market economies. So considerations of social policy appeared in the price calculations of goods and services through subsidies or in the labour market through political efforts to maintain full employment, even at the price of so called hidden or latent unemployment, as it were, in certain periods and in certain economic branches. This relatively diminished the significance of social security in the whole welfare system. At the same time, however, social security did gain importance because social policy in the classical sense had been indeed restricted to social security, labour safety and social benefits offered at the workplace. As a sign of this transformation, from 1950 former important instruments of relieving poverty, such as assistance for the poor, disappeared almost completely. This in turn resulted in poverty on a more dire scale than before in the case of certain social groups, such as the aged or

---

132 József Botos, A magyar társadalombiztosítás kialakulása és fejlődése. Budapest 1998, 19.

133 The amounts indicate sum of contributions for the purposes specified and state contributions. Dénes Bikkal, Társadalombiztosítás Magyarországon, in: Közgazdasági Szemle, LVIII (1934) 6-8, 389; for the pension of public servants, see István Hollós, A közszolgálati alkalmazottak nyugdíjkérdése és a megoldási lehetőségek. Budapest 1940, 3-55.

134 Bikkal, Társadalombiztosítás Magyarországon. 374.

those unable to hold a job, because in the early communist period the coverage of social security was limited and because the level of benefits was low.[135]

The loss of the independence of social security as an institution and the direct political influence in that area lead to important consequences even beyond the above in a number of areas included in the scope of the present study. Although the *differentiation* and expansion of social security programs continued in Hungary just like in Western Europe, here, similarly to the other communist countries, economic, or, rather, production-related considerations exerted direct influence on these processes. It is not simply that social security benefits were strongly connected to paid work and, hand in hand with this, a job in the state-controlled sector of the economy.[136] Programs focused mainly on risks associated with the ability to work (e.g. accidents or illnesses). Risks not jeopardising growth in production, however (e.g. the poverty of the aged) were assigned a smaller role among insurances. Later in the communist period there was a significant change in this respect and from the 1970s this economic determination became less characteristic than before, or than in other communist countries. The transformation was reflected in the structural changes of expenditures as well.[137]

The *structure* of Hungarian social security expenditures diverged significantly from Western European patterns already fifteen years after World War II. Then the expenditures on pensions were especially low and funds allocated for family allowance were also way below Western European averages. For example, in 1960 38.7% of all expenditures were spent on pensions in Hungary compared to the Western European average of 50%, and 12.2% on family allowance compared to the average level of 17.3% in the West. In contrast with this, the ratio of health care expenditures was more than double the Western European average in this period (Table 8).

From the 1960s transformations reshaped the structure of Hungarian social security expenditures. First of all, while in Western Europe the ratio of resources allocated for cash and in kind benefits of *health insurance* significantly grew to reach 30.3% in 1980, doubling the ratio two decades before, in Hungary such expenditures were halved. These opposing tendencies can be explained primarily by the lack of price explosion in this sphere in Hungary, i.e. the more rapid rise in health care related costs than in other areas, mostly because of the introduction of new but expensive technologies took place in Western Europe but not in Hungary. In addition, the income levels of Hungarian health care workers relative to other occupational groups did not reach Western European standards, which also tempered expenditures. At the same time, situations of shortage resulting from the low level financing of health care urged the population to try to purchase higher quality health services within the officially free state health care

---

135 Ferge, Fejezetek a magyarországi szegénypolitika történetéből. 159.

136 Maltby, Social insurance in Hungary. 208.

137 For the expenditures in other communist countries, see Castles, Whatever Happened to the Communist Welfare State? 213-226.

system. This, paired with a decline in moral standards as a primary cause and with other factors, created institutionalised corruption in Hungarian health care, unknown in Western Europe. The sums channelled into heath care as a result of this practice are estimated to reach 5-10% of all official expenditures in the late 1980s.[138]

Parallel to the relative decrease of health expenditures, however, there is a convergence between Hungarian and Western European expenditures regarding *pensions*. While between 1960 and 1980 in Western Europe the ratio of pensions compared to other social security services changed only a little, in Hungary it grew steeply, approaching Western European levels (Table 8). In part, this structural shift resulted from a continuous rise and the introduction of the indexation of pensions in Hungary, and, more importantly, from the growth of the ratio of those eligible, which was related to the low retirement age even though negative mortality indices had an opposite effect.[139]

From the 60s the high ratio of *family and maternity benefits* among expenditures as compared to Western Europe became an important characteristic of the Hungarian welfare system. This was primarily the consequence of a major drop of amounts allocated to family allowance in Western Europe, while in Hungary such expenditures grew, even if only moderately. In addition to family allowance, maternity leave assistance ("gyes") was introduced in 1966, paid to mothers with infants in order to enable them to care for their children at home while preserving their job. Paid for the first two, then three years of the child's life, the level of the assistance was not insignificant, especially compared to the average income of women workers with lower qualifications. In sum, the ratio of family and maternity benefits grew from 12.2% to 13.3% in social security expenditures between 1960 and 1980 (Table 8).[140] A good illustration of the significance of these supports is that they amounted to 21% of all cash benefits, or one third of the amount paid on pensions in 1975. There is no similarly high ratio in the welfare programs of any Western European country.

Another characteristic of the communist welfare system was the virtual lack of *unemployment benefits*. Although unemployment benefits were nominally introduced in 1957, until their termination in 1988, such benefits were actually paid only in about 5000 cases.[141] This lack was partly related to job security becoming a constitutionally guaranteed right in Hungary. Even more important, however, under the conditions of planned economy labour was subject to shortages like any other resource. With the ex-

---

138 György Ádám, Az orvosi hálapénz Magyarországon. Budapest 1986; for a considerably higher data of 25% see Andorka and Kondratas and Tóth, A jóléti rendszer átalakulása Magyarországon. 45-46.

139 Rudolf Andorka and István György Tóth, A szociális kiadások és a szociálpolitika Magyarországon, in: Társadalmi riport. 1992. Budapest 1992, 413.

140 According to Zsuzsa Ferge the the ratio of family and maternity benefits among welfare expenditures increased from 14.1% to 18.6% between 1960 and 1981. Ferge, A szociálpolitika hazai fejlődése. 53.

141 Andorka and Tóth, A szociális kiadások és a szociálpolitika Magyarországon. 419.

ception of shorter periods and smaller settlements or regions, e.g. purely agrarian areas affected by collectivisation in the 1960s, those intending to take up a job could find one relatively easily and thus unemployment did not exist until the end of the 1980s, or at least not in the Western European sense. Full employment made the institution of unemployment benefits dispensable, but the lack of such benefits was obviously also meant to urge people temporarily unemployed (e.g. because of being between jobs) to start a new job as soon as possible. In other words, this structural characteristic also reflected production related considerations as shown in other social security programs. The lack of unemployment benefits meant significant structural differences in welfare expenditures compared to Western Europe from the 1970s, when mass unemployment appeared there, amounting to as much as 18% of social security expenditures in some countries. In Hungary, no such expenditures were present – or, rather, they were covered by other institutions, e.g. companies, in the form of hidden or latent unemployment.[142]

Though the present study follows welfare development through the example of social security and first of all its main component, social insurance, it seems necessary to highlight again a developmental trend beyond this. Compared to Western Europe, a significant structural difference in the realm of welfare resulted from the appearance of *price subsidies* in Hungary after World War II. This had not been unknown in Western Europe either, but, as shown earlier, in Hungary it amounted to a substantially higher proportion of welfare expenditures. While changes in the world economy resulted in the emergence of mass unemployment in Western Europe in the early 1970s, in Hungary the same changes, or, rather, the intention of shutting these out caused a significant rise of price subsidies. In the late 1980s, however, their sum steeply decreased, which now meant a greater role given to cash benefits, as well as to state subsidies for special housing loans with reduced interests and in kind benefits in health care and education.[143]

In summary, in the pre-World War II period the developmental direction of Hungarian welfare institutions coincided with Western European trends. On the one hand, the early introduction of social security in comparison with Western Europe and the timing of programs in accordance with Western European trends made social security and the assimilated schemes the most important instruments of welfare policy in Hungary, too. In addition, convergence, but at least similarity can be seen in the differentiation of social security programs and in the structure of social security. Although the pace of differentiation is difficult to measure, the maturing of health insurance in Hungary in the

---

142 David Fretwell and Richard Jackman, Munkaerőpiacok: munkanélküliség, in: Nicholas Barr ed., Munkaerőpiac és szociálpolitika Közép- és Kelet-Európában. Budapest 1995, 198-201.

143 Fraternité Rt., Jelentés a társadalombiztosítás reformjáról. 1991. Budapest 1991, 115; Tóth, A jóléti rendszer az átmenet időszakában. 317; István György Tóth, Welfare Programmes and the Alleviation of Poverty, in: Rudolf Andorka et al. ed., A Society Transformed. Hungary in Time-Space Perspective. Budapest 1999, 133-134.

first half of the century is obvious, which considerably expanded the types of services financed by social security even in a Western European comparison. Similarly to many countries in Western Europe, the growth of expenditures on pensions was the most rapid in Hungary, too, making it the most important among the programs.

Differences between Western Europe and Hungary started to be greater from the middle of the century. The changes in the functions of social security were specifically contradictory in communist Hungary. On the one hand, the elimination of the traditional institutions of poor relief increased the significance of social security programs, and, on the other, the influence of social policy in other areas, which have a relative autonomy in Western European societies, such as price mechanisms or the labour market, decreased the importance of social security within the whole welfare system. The differentiation of social security programs continued in Hungary but with priorities different than in Western Europe, with prime considerations related to the efficiency of production and the mobilisation of the work force. The differences in the relative significance of institutions are also shown by the structure of expenditures. In the first two postwar decades, the most important characteristic was the low ratio of pension-related expenditures and the relatively high ratio of those in health care in a Western European comparison. The changes observed between 1960 and 1980 signalled an advancement toward the Western European pattern only in the growth in the proportions of pension expenditures. As regards the other expenditure items, the trends were the opposite. In contrast to Western Europe, the relative decrease in health expenditures and the opposite process in family benefits represent especially strong divergences. As an important difference, we should mention the complete lack of unemployment expenditures in Hungary.

3 DEVELOPMENT OF SOCIAL RIGHTS

Though the survey of the important structural characteristics of social security has refined the picture of welfare development drawn in the analysis of expenditures, some further aspects need to be explored. Among these, it is worth devoting special attention to social rights, the examination of which began early, with the work of Thomas H. Marshall in 1950. He regarded social rights as the third set of important citizen rights beside civil rights and political rights. Since then research on social rights has been playing an important role in research on the welfare state.[144]

Based on the results of this research, several important aspects of the assertion of social rights can be distinguished. The present chapter focuses on the following dimensions: 1., the degree of coverage, that is, how extensive is the coverage of social security schemes among the population or active earners; 2., qualifying conditions for social security benefits, that is, what kind of conditions should be fulfilled to qualify for a benefit; and 3., the relative levels of benefits, that is, how generous are the benefits of the schemes in comparison to the previous earnings of the recipient or to the average earnings in the society.[145]

The first, pre-World War I forms of Western European social security were not comprehensive as regards the *degree of coverage*, since only a small proportion of the population or those employed received benefits. Perhaps the only exceptions are Germany and, in a certain respect, England and Denmark. In Germany the majority of the labour force had occupational injuries and pension insurance already at the turn of the century and the same applies to England with regard to occupational injuries insurance and Denmark to health insurance in 1910 (Tables 10, 11 and 12).[146]

In the development of social rights, one of the most characteristic tendencies of the following decades was the gradual growth in the ratio of those receiving social security benefits. This process greatly progressed in the interwar years, especially in Scandinavia, but development toward universality (the inclusion of the whole population in insurance schemes) accelerated especially after the Second World War. Complete cover-

---

144 Thomas H. Marshall, Citizenship and Social Class. Cambridge 1950; another distinguished publication in this area, Joakim Palme, Pension Rights in Welfare Capitalism. Stockholm 1990.

145 Ibidem, 26-28.

146 For the ratio of those eligible, see Peter Flora ed., State, Economy, and Society in Western Europe, 1815-1975. Vol. I. Frankfurt/M. 1983, 460-461; ILO, The cost of social security. Fourteenth international inquiry, 1987-1989. Geneva 1996, 201-216; ILO, Yearbook of labour statistics. 1995. Geneva 1996, 164-169.

age cannot be declared everywhere even at the end of the period examined but the levels reached were such by the late 1980s that Western European social security systems can be called mature in this respect, applying Peter Flora's terminology.[147]

With a closer look at individual insurance areas, three waves of expansion can be distinguished in *occupational injuries insurance*. In the years before the First World War, insurance previously applying to workers in the industries with the most dangerous working conditions was generally extended to occupational accidents in other industrial branches. Thus on the eve of the First World War there existed insurance schemes in all the countries examined covering the majority of industrial workers and one third of all employees on the average.[148] The next expansion phase took place in the interwar years, when other occupational areas were included (agriculture was left out only in Switzerland and Germany). This meant that occupational injuries insurance covered 53% of employees in Western Europe on the eve of the Second World War (Table 10, Appendix). Finally, in the decades after the Second World War in a long, outstretched process, economically inactive groups, such as students (Belgium, Germany, Norway) and housewives (the Netherlands) were also included, i.e. coverage was now independent of employment. As a result, in 1975 this type of insurance covered four-fifths of those employed and in 1990 almost 90% on the average (Table 10).[149] These data include active insured persons, but the proportion of those covered may have been even higher, considering the increasing ratios of insured family members and pensioners.[150]

The beginnings of *health insurance* also reach back to the period before the First World War, with the exception of the Netherlands and Finland. Still, at this time only 15% of employees were eligible for it, mostly industrial workers and the lowest paid employees. Between the two world wars, expansion gained momentum. As a result of the inclusion of agricultural workers and higher paid public employees, coverage in Western Europe was 57% on the average before the Second World War. Benefits were extended to the family members of the insured persons relatively soon, between 1930 and 1946. Another big social group, pensioners were granted the same relatively late, first in Germany in 1941 and last in Finland in 1963. Among large social groups, those self employed were targeted last, only from after the Second World War. Surprisingly, Germany acted late, extending compulsory health insurance to this group only in 1971.[151] This left Switzerland the only country without compulsory health insurance, although because of the high ratio of voluntary insurance it had belonged among the

---

147 Peter Flora, On the History and Current Problems of the Welfare State, in: S. N. Eisenstadt and Ora Ahimeir eds., The Welfare State and its Aftermath. London and Sydney 1985, 19.

148 Alber, Vom Armenhaus zum Wohlfahrtsstaat. 54. Data are presented regarding the countires examined by Alber. This group differs somewhat from those included in the present study.

149 Flora and Alber, Modernization, Democratization, and the Development of Welfare States in Western Europe. 52.

150 Alber, Vom Armenhaus zum Wohlfahrtsstaat. 54-58.

151 Ibidem, 55; Alber, Anhangtabelle 4.

countries with high coverage ever since the fifties. The greatest coverage of health insurance in the 1950s was characteristic of Norway, Denmark, Great Britain, Sweden and Switzerland; and in the 1980s of Scandinavia and Switzerland.[152] The Western European average was above 90% of employees by then (Table 11).

Of the three different risks involved, disability, old age and the death of the breadwinner, *pension insurance* first provided security against the most significant one, the loss of income due to old age. Similarly to health insurance, in the beginning it generally covered workers and low paid employees. However, in Germany widows and orphans were given a pension relatively early, in 1911. Most countries followed suit in the interwar period, though the legislation of several Scandinavian countries took this step well after the Second World War. Besides health insurance, between the two world wars it was the coverage of old-age pension insurance that grew in the greatest degree, including two thirds of employees on the eve of the Second World War on the average (Table 12). The highest ratios were found in the Scandinavian countries, practically reaching full coverage already at this point, or almost immediately after the war. After the Second World War the number of those eligible for benefits rose rapidly in the other countries as well, covering 90% of employees on the average by 1970. In this period some countries catched up (e.g. Italy, which started from the lowest level and progressed above the average), others dropped below the average (e.g. Ireland, Austria, Germany and the United Kingdom). The continuing rise of the next two decades meant that practically all employees had old-age insurance by 1990, with the only exception of the United Kingdom (Table 12).[153]

Unemployment had long been considered incalculable and thus non-insurable because of its connection to economic cycles. Furthermore, political decision makers were afraid that *unemployment insurance* would be used by slackers, and employers opposed it because they were afraid trade unions would be strengthened as a result of the intervention in the labour market.[154] Trade unions did organise insurance for unemployment in several countries and, in addition, communal (the Ghent system) and other forms also existed. However, compulsory unemployment insurance existed only in Great Britain before the First World War, and even there it covered just a small group of workers; besides there was voluntary, state supported insurance in Denmark, France and Norway.[155] After the First World War Great Britain (1920) extended compulsory unemployment insurance to cover the majority of workers, applying to 58% of employees by 1925. With the exception of Finland and Sweden, the other countries also introduced at least the voluntary form by 1930 but coverage remained significantly smaller there. By the late 1930s unemployment insurance covered about one-fourth (27%) of employees

152 Pekka Kosonenen, European Integration: A Welfare Perspective. Helsinki 1994, 54.

153 Palme, Pension Rights in Welfare Capitalism. 42-48.

154 Ritter, Der Sozialstaat. 111.

155 Gordon, Social Security Policies in Industrial Countries. 227.

in Western Europe as an average.[156] This coverage lagged behind the other major branches of social security even after the Second World War, even though its expansion was also obvious: in 1960 the Western European average was 47%, with an evident decrease of the differences between the countries. The growth slowed down somewhat after this point, to reach 63% in the mid-70s. By then, Germany, the Netherlands, Ireland and Norway joined the United Kingdom with respect to coverage ratios.[157]

These developments also shed light on some general characteristics of the expansion of social rights. On the one hand, the extension of social security eligibility progressed along two paths from the beginnings. One was the inclusion of ever widening groups of employees into insurance in their own right, the other was granting share for more and more people not in their own right as benefits were extended to relatives, primarily regarding health insurance, as well as to survivors, and the number of dependants was also considered in several other benefits. On the other hand, while political rights diffused principally top down in the social hierarchy in Western Europe, it was more or less the other way round regarding social rights.[158] Workers in the most dangerous occupations in the most important industries were first included in the programs, which were then extended to the other industrial workers, later to agricultural workers and to dependants, then to widows and orphans of the insured. The next step was extension to high earners and then those self-employed. The inclusion of the latter, especially farmers, was a complex process, partly because these groups themselves often rejected the burdens associated with social security. Finally other, non-employed social groups, e.g. students also became insured in their own right in several countries. Those living on the periphery of society were exceptions in this regard, sharing in these rights relatively late.[159] This type of gradual extension primarily effected countries which had a Bismarckian insurance system. As a result of continuous expansion, almost the whole population became insured in time in several of these countries, e.g. West Germany, Austria and France by the 1970s.[160] In contrast, in countries with the Beveridge type of welfare system, the growth of the coverage often took place abruptly. In the Scandinavian countries and Great Britain several social security schemes were extended to the

---

156 Ritter, Der Sozialstaat. 112; Flora ed., State, Economy, and Society in Western Europe. Vol. I. 461.

157 Ibidem.

158 Peter Flora, Solution or Source of Crises? The Welfare State in Historical Perspective, in: W. J. Mommsen ed., The Emergence of the Welfare State in Britain and Germany. London 1981, 358; Alber, Vom Armenhaus zum Wohlfahrtsstaat. 52.

159 The 1906 Austrian pension insurance is the most important exception in this respect, for a long time applying to employees (Angestellte) only. Though in theory it was extended to workers in 1927, this became practice only during the Nazi occupation. Alber, Vom Armenhaus zum Wohlfahrtsstaat. 52.

160 Hans Günter Hockerts, Die Entwicklung vom Zweiten Weltkrieg bis zur Gegenwart, in: Köhler and Zacher (Hrsg.), Beiträge zur Geschichte und aktuellen Situation der Sozialversicherung. 155.

whole population in one step in the interwar period and after the Second World War. Furthermore, in Switzerland, which did not belong to this category, the whole population was included in old-age and survivors' pension insurance in 1946/48.

Analysing the principles defining the *qualifying conditions* for welfare benefits, the dominance of two systems can be seen in the pre-Second World War period of social security: one determined by the type of work and depending on contribution; and another, a means-tested system. An example of the former is the benefits of pension insurance in Germany, for which only workers were eligible at first, and even then just in proportion to their contributions paid. In contrast, in several Scandinavian countries and Great Britain eligibility for state pension services depended on age and earnings. Such means tested state pension was first introduced in Denmark in the 1890s. Great Britain adopted a similar means-tested pension system, not tied to previous contributions in 1908.[161]

Later this double pattern of eligibility began to change. After the First World War the means-test temporarily gained ground but its importance started to fade in the interwar period and even more so in the second half of the century. For example, as regards old-age pensions in 1930, this principle was applied when determining eligibility in most of the countries, but after the war this practice was present only in about half, and then it was terminated everywhere by the 1980s, with the exception of supplementary pensions in Ireland, Switzerland and Italy (Table 18).[162]

In addition, the principle of citizenship as a factor guaranteeing eligibility for benefits emerged early. Sweden introduced a universal, contribution-based pension system in 1913. At this point it was rather of theoretical significance because it provided very low level services.[163] However, citizenship gained a considerable practical role a few decades later, in the interwar period and especially in the years after the Second World War in the assertion of social rights. A part of this process was the introduction of health and pension insurance covering all citizens in Denmark; another important step was the reforms following and based on the Beveridge report in Great Britain. Here the citizenship-principle was clearly applied in the transformation of health insurance, and the establishment of the National Health Service after the Second World War. In spite of this, the great expansion of welfare systems in the two decades after the Second World War seems to have been based on former eligibility principles. It was only in the 1960s or, in other interpretations, in the 1970s, that citizenship was beginning to be

---

161 Therborn, European Modernity and Beyond. 90.

162 Palme, Pension Rights in Welfare Capitalism. 52; for conditions of eligibility between the world wars and in the 1980s, see also, ILO, International Survey of Social Services. Studies and Reports. Series M., No. 11. Geneva 1933, 42-618; U.S. Department of Health and Human Services ed., Social Security Throughout the World. 1981. Washington D.C. 1982, 12-261.

163 Ritter, Der Sozialstaat. 152.

considered as a determining factor in eligibility.[164] This especially applies to the Danish, Swedish and Finnish systems, which belong to the welfare model often referred to as social democratic, in essence open to all relevant social groups. For example, in Denmark those self-employed could join voluntary unemployment insurance, just like they were eligible for the basic state pension having reached a certain age and on condition of being resident in the country for a defined period. Nevertheless, the supplementary state pension was tied to being actively engaged and paying contributions even here.[165]

An increasing application of the citizenship principle in welfare eligibility does not mean, however, that the equality of social rights in every aspects would have been even approximately full in Western Europe in this period. On the contrary, in most countries benefits were tied to contributions paid and were also determined by occupational type. For example, in France social security systems gradually expanded and merged, and the level of their services became more similar – but still, considerable differences remained all through the period between insured groups regarding the conditions for eligibility, with 12 occupationally distinct public pension schemes. At the end of the period examined, Germany was another typical example of the welfare type referred to as conservative or corporatist, where different social security systems existed for different occupational groups. Those employed in the private sector had their own insurance schemes, but, within this sector, there were separate systems for, e.g., agriculture, mining, or the self-employed. Belonging to a distinct social security scheme was part of the benefits of public employees.[166]

At the same time, a convergence can be observed between the different eligibility systems. In the countries where universal and unified insurance existed, benefits were somewhat differentiated in relation to incomes, i.e. the contributions paid. This was the case in the United Kingdom and in Scandinavia between 1959 and 1966, where an earnings-related supplementary pension was introduced besides the flat-rate state pension. In contrast, in countries where an earning-related pension system was in operation, flat-rate elements were introduced, e.g. in the Netherlands (1956), Italy (1965) and Germany (1972).[167] Later in the 1980s, the convergence continued, but rather on the basis of the "workfare state" model, which implied an emphasis on entitlements tied to labour market position rather than citizenship.[168]

As regards the actual eligibility conditions of individual benefits, the means-test has already been discussed in relation to pensions. With respect to other conditions, only surprisingly small changes can be seen between 1930 and 1980. The other qualifying

---

164 Therborn, European Modernity and Beyond. 92.

165 Hans Hansen, Elements of Social Security. Copenhagen 1998, 9-11.

166 Esping-Andersen, The Three Worlds of Welfare. 70.

167 Alber and Flora, Modernization, Democratization. 53; Harold L. Wilensky, The Welfare State and Equality. Berkeley 1975, 39.

168 Kosonen, European Welfare State Models. 100.

condition for old-age pension, the age limit was lowered only slightly and primarily only for women. In 1930 the average age limit was 64.9 years and in 1981 64.3, with small variations and 65 years being specified in the majority of the countries. In the mid 1980s the highest retirement age existed in Denmark and Norway, at 67 for both sexes. The age limit was the lowest in Italy, 60 for men and 55 for women. With the exception of some Scandinavian countries where no such requirement existed, the waiting period required for eligibility for pension grew in the fifty years following 1930. This was mostly due to the maturing process of the programs, because in the period following the introduction of schemes shorter waiting periods were in effect. Later this became unnecessary because the majority of those retiring did have the contribution period necessary (Tables 15 and 18).[169] There is a slight decrease in the compulsory waiting time regarding accident and health insurance but altogether no marked change occurred by 1980 compared to the interwar period (Tables 13, 14, 16 and 17). This trend in the changes of waiting periods and age limits supports the argument about the prevalence of the insurance principle.

The *level of the benefits* provided by early social security programs were rather modest and also quite static, because they were not connected to price changes or to the growth of earnings and economic output. This was even more the case because roughly until the Second World War it was not supposed that the beginning of the payment of pension benefits would coincide with retirement and therefore the pension in itself would enable the insured to live off it alone.[170] However, as an important development of social security, the benefits were approaching earnings levels, a process beginning on a small scale in the interwar period and then growing after the Second World War.[171] Thus these relieved not only the most serious emergencies, but could increasingly contribute to the maintenance or approximation of the living standard and the relative social status of the insured. An instrument of this was the adjustment of benefits to growth in economic output and/or the income of the active population, thus offering a share of economic growth to inactive generations and those eligible for benefits. Denmark introduced this principle in the pension system as early as 1933, but the other Western European countries adopted for it only between 1955 and 1965, the exceptions being Switzerland (1968) and Great Britain (1975).[172] In the terminology of the 1957 German pension reform this meant the "dynamisation" of pensions, being significant mostly because of its long term effects, but it also resulted in the immediate and radical rise of pensions, by 65.3% for workers and 71.9% for employees.[173] In the next decades the

---

169 Palme, Pension Rights in Welfare Capitalism. 52.

170 Christoph Conrad, The Emergence of Modern Retirement: Germany in an International Comparison (1850-1960). Population. An English Selection, 3 (1991), 191; Hockerts, Die Entwicklung vom Zweiten Weltkrieg. 156-157.

171 Conrad, The Emergence of Modern Retirement. 192.

172 Alber, Vom Armenhaus zum Wohlfahrtsstaat. 55.

173 Ritter, Der Sozialstaat. 160.

same principle was applied to the other benefits in Germany (the latest being sick pay in 1974) and other countries followed suit, though using different methods.[174]

The changes in the levels of the two most significant cash benefits, pension and sick pay can be presented as good examples of the changes in the relative levels of benefits. Before the Second World War pensions were relatively modest amounts, afterwards, however, they increased rapidly, both regarding the minimum pension and the average worker pension. The average of minimum pension in 18 OECD countries, expressed in the percentage of wages in the manufacturing industry, was 10% in 1930, 19% in 1950, 25% in 1965, and 37% by 1985. It first reached 40% in Austria in 1960, and exceeded 50% in 1970 in the Netherlands and Denmark. By the 1980s this ratio was even surpassed by France and the other Scandinavian countries.[175] The other index examined, the average worker pension amounted to 14% of the net average wages in the processing industry in this group of countries in 1930. This ratio doubled by 1950 to reach 43% by 1965, 50% by 1975 and 58% by 1985.[176] There was no significant variation in this regard in the development of the Western European countries included in the present study, where in 1939 the average pension was about 12% of the average income of workers.[177] In the 1930s the relative level of German and Italian average pensions was the highest. In 1950 pensions amounted to 20-30% of the average income of workers in Western Europe (1/3 in Denmark, 1/5 in Sweden, and 1/6 in Norway), and there were only a few countries where they exceeded its half (Austria and France). First in this regard since the Second World War, Austria was joined by Belgium only in the 1970s. In 1985 the average levels of pensions exceeded two-thirds of incomes in Austria, Belgium, Italy, Finland, Norway and Sweden. The lowest level (slightly below 50%) was found in Ireland. Altogether by then the Western European average itself was well above 50%.[178] In parallel with this, the relative levels of pensions also converged in these countries. J. Palme finds convergence in the case of OECD countries as regards the levels of pensions after 1930. Exceptions were the 50s, when the coefficient of variation temporarily grew, and the period between 1975 and 1985, when no considerable change occurred in this respect.[179]

Similarly to pensions, a dynamic growth can be observed in the levels of cash benefits of health insurance relative to wages, which nearly tripled between 1930 and 1985. In the latter point in time 90 to 100% of wages were paid as sick leave in a number of Western European countries including Austria, Finland, Germany, Norway and Sweden. The lowest ratio of sick pay was given in Belgium, Great Britain and France.[180]

---

174 Hockerts, Die Entwicklung vom Zweiten Weltkrieg. 157-158.

175 Palme, Pension Rights in Welfare Capitalism. 48.

176 Ibidem, 48.

177 Our own calculation based on Esping-Andersen, Three Worlds of Welfare Capitalism. 99.

178 Palme, Pension Rights in Welfare Capitalism. 49.

179 Ibidem, 68.

180 Comission of the European Communities, Comparative Tables of the Social Security

Several researchers claim that trends observed in the development of social rights support the existence of a convergence in Western Europe in the development of social security, first of all in the post-Second World War period.[181] Hartmut Kaelble regards the systems of the 1980s as "highly uniform".[182] In accordance with this, our results also show a steady decrease in the differences in the coverage of the population in Western European countries over the 20th century (Appendix). In the early, pre-World War I period Germany, Denmark and the United Kingdom had a great advantage over the other countries, but already in the interwar years cross-country differences were significantly reduced. In this period the Northern countries (the United Kingdom, Sweden, Denmark and Norway) had the highest growth rate in coverage, while Finland, Switzerland, France, Belgium and Italy stayed well below the average. After the Second World War Western European social security systems reached or approximated universality as regards the degree of coverage. In the mid 70s the majority of the whole work force did belong to social security systems almost in all Western European countries. This especially applies to health and pension insurance. The exceptions were Germany, Austria, Ireland and, regarding health insurance, the Netherlands, where 10-20% of the work force, mostly those self employed were still not insured. Undoubtedly less important, occupational injuries insurance covered the majority of employees by a later period. After the Second World War convergence continued in the coverage: By the late 80s the coefficient of variation dropped to a very low level in health and pension insurance, signalling only slight differences in Western Europe in these areas (Appendix).[183] The decrease of differences took place on a smaller scale in occupational injuries insurance, and was even less pronounced in unemployment insurance. This latter progressed through the slowest development and J. Alber did not find convergence in this regard.[184] Moreover, in interpreting the processes it must be taken into consideration that there was complete coverage in certain types of insurance in several countries in the 60s, thus the smallest increase in the others could result in convergence.[185]

Schemes in the Member States of the European Communities. Luxembourg 1989, 46-47.

181 Ritter, Der Sozialstaat. 183; Kaelble, A Social History of Western Europe. 127; Schmidt, Sozialpolitik. 137; Heikki Niemelä and Kari Salminen and Jussi Vanamo, Converging Social Security Models? The Making of Social Security in Denmark, France and the Netherlands. Helsinki 1996, 43.

182 Kaelble, A Social History of Western Europe. 127.

183 Palme, Pension Rights in Welfare Capitalism. 67.

184 Jens Alber, Government Responses to the Challenge of Unemployment: The Development of Unemployment insurance in Western Europe, in: Peter Flora and Arnold J. Heidenheimer eds., The Development of Welfare States in Europe and America. New Brunswick 1981, 177.

185 A somewhat different dynamics is indicated in Flora and Alber, Modernization, Democratization, and the Development of Welfare States in Western Europe, in: Flora and Heidenheimer eds., The Development of Welfare States in Europe and America. 57; Flora and Alber weigh individual insurances in their calculations: pension insurance is given a weigh of

As regards the qualifying conditions for welfare services, in the interwar period no clear tendency of convergence or the opposite can be seen in Western Europe, but after the Second World War forces pointing to growing similarity dominated. On the one hand, means tested services gradually faded to give ground to benefits granted on the basis of the insurance or the citizenship principle everywhere. Besides, the systems based on these two defining principles approached each other. The cash benefits of insurances universal for all citizens, most of all pensions, were differentiated relative to incomes, thus moving closer to the principles of the traditional Bismarckian social security system. At the same time, in countries where the level of benefits depended on contributions, new, flat-rate elements were introduced for all who qualified. However, in the 1980s, the convergence of systems was realised rather on the basis of the insurance principle and the citizenship principle had smaller importance in this process.

It was a new objective in the post-Second World War development of social security in Western Europe not only to relieve the most dire poverty, but to maintain the level of income of the insured.[186] Accordingly, the level of services rapidly improved in all areas examined and, at least till the 70s, after which no clear trends emerge, the services insurances provided in different countries became increasingly similar. Besides the changes in the structures of expenditures, this is evidenced by the development of individual areas of social security, especially pensions.

* * *

As shown before, basic social security programs were introduced early in *Hungary* in a Western European comparison. However, at that time and for a long period following, these lagged behind the pioneering Western European countries considerably in their *degree of coverage*.[187] This can be explained primarily by two factors. On the one hand, early programs applied to fewer social groups than in Western Europe. The benefits of the first schemes were applied to workers in the industry, commerce and groups of public employees. The considerable body of agricultural workers was excluded completely, as were private white-collar employees. On the other hand, social groups first to be insured in Western Europe and in Hungary, especially workers, represented a significantly smaller proportion of society in the latter.

1.5-health insurance 1, unemployment insurance 1, and occupational injuries insurance 0.5, corresponding to the significance attributed to them.

186 Ritter, Der Sozialstaat. 219.

187 For the ratios of the eligible in the first half of the 20th century, see Statisztikai Havi Közlemények, (1925) 1, 119; ILO, Compulsory Sickness Insurance. Geneva 1927, 105; Magyar Statisztikai Évkönyv. 1930. Budapest 1931, 30; ILO, International Survey of Social Services. Studies and Reports. Series M., No. 11. Geneva 1933, 363-370; Statisztikai Negyedévi Közlemények, XLIII (1940), 204; ILO, Compulsory Pension Insurance. Studies and Reports. Series M., No. 10. Geneva 1933, 106-107; Time series of historical statistics. 36, 97.

The earliest data are available on the degree of coverage in health insurance. In 1924, approximately one-fourth (24.8%) of active earners were eligible for sick pay in Hungary, while the ratio of those entitled to in kind benefits may have been somewhat higher.[188] This rose only slightly by 1930 (26.5%). At this point 39.3% of active earners had occupational injuries insurance and 16.1% had old-age insurance (Tables 10, 11 and 12).[189]

Though the extension of eligibility progressed in the interwar years and during the Second World War, reforms did not point primarily in this direction. Instead of significant improvements in coverage, the level of benefits was raised and, especially with the introduction of pension insurance, additional risks were covered for groups already insured. Thus all the elements of the Hungarian social security system (accident, health and pension insurance) applied only to industrial, mining, commerce and transportation workers and domestic servants even after the 1927 and 1928 reforms. It must be noted, though, that the family members of the insured also enjoyed relatively extensive rights. Near relations (wife and children), the woman keeping the household of the insured or siblings without independent earning were also qualified for the benefits of compulsory health insurance, and the orphans' allowance was paid generously up to age 24 in case the orphan was engaged in studies.[190] By the Second World War compulsory occupational injuries insurance was extended to apprentices. Health insurance now covered them as well as domestic servants but not higher paid members of specific occupational groups. Old-age and disability pensions covered even smaller numbers. In this case, although the earning limit of private white-collar employees was different, which mandated membership for a higher proportion of this group, for other important occupational categories (e.g. public employees, railway employees with company insurance, etc.) it was not compulsory to join the scheme.[191]

In several Western European countries certain benefits of social security had already been extended to agricultural workers before, during or immediately after the First World War (e.g. health insurance in Germany in 1886 and 1911, in Great Britain and

188 Susan Zimmermann and, partly relying on Zimmermann's data, Dorottya Szikra report considerably lower coverage. Their data, however, contradict both the ILO surveys and the compulsory official Hungarian statistics. Cf. Zimmermann, Geschützte und ungeschützte Arbeitsverhältnisse. 91; Szikra, Modernizáció és társadalombiztosítás a 20. század elején. 18-19; for the ILO-data and that of the Hungarian Statistical Office, see ILO, Compulsory Sickness Insurance. 105, 106-107; ILO, International Survey of Social Services. 363-370; Statisztikai Havi Közlemények, (1925) 1, 119; Magyar Statisztikai Évkönyv, 1930, 30; Magyar Statisztikai Évkönyv, 1940, 47, 56-57.

189 Excluding welfare benefits for public employees based on non-contributory schemes.

190 For the favourable and less favourable conditions of Hungarian social security system in the interwar period in international comparison, see Béla Kovrig, A munka védelme a dunai államokban. Kolozsvár 1944, 279-282.

191 Béla Kovrig and József V. Nádujfalvy, Társadalombiztosítási kézikönyv. Budapest 1938, 9-22.

Ireland in 1911, in Norway in 1915 and Austria in 1921).[192] This makes it especially striking that in Hungary agricultural workers, who significantly outnumbered those in the industry, were only partly covered by social security, moreover, for certain agricultural groups even this was completely missing.[193] In this respect farm labourers and some agricultural workers were in the most favourable position, for whom there were legal guarantees regarding *occupational injuries insurance* already before the First World War (1900, 1912 and 1913), which was later (in 1928 and 1939) extended to other agricultural employees. In contrast, there was no compulsory *health insurance* at all even for this group, though there existed a limited obligation for employers to cover expenses of medical and hospital care as well as medication for the majority of agricultural workers, farm labourers and their immediate family members.[194] Still, this was not an insurance-type benefit and was clearly below the level of such, e.g. it included only a 30 day coverage of hospital care and no sick pay. Other groups of agricultural workers (e.g. farm labourers working at their domicile, etc.) could not receive similar benefits, thus having to rely on poverty assistance. Therefore in their case the government decrees of the early 1930s brought advancement, guaranteeing medication and hospital care for the poor, even if outside social security. Although the idea of introducing *old-age insurance* and widows' assistance in the case of agricultural employees came up already in the late 1920s, at the time when similar social security benefits were instituted for industrial and commerce employees, such regulation took place only in 1938 and 1939. Thereafter, agricultural workers over 65 qualified for the old-age pension after a 15 year waiting period, which was similar to that of industrial workers. The sum paid as pension was also similar. One insured all through his career received an annual flat-rate of 60 Pengős and 20% of the total amount of his contributions. However, this did not include disability pension or orphans' allowance, and the law applied only to men who did not own landed property (2 cadastral acres).[195]

With these changes, only the number of those covered by pension insurance increased dynamically in Hungary in the interwar period. On the eve of the Second World War health insurance was available for about 1/4 of the active population, while pension insurance covered slightly less than one third, and occupational injuries insurance somewhat more. These figures appear low in a Western European comparison, though ratios were similar in Finland, Belgium and Switzerland (Tables 10, 11 and 12). Therefore the changes in the population covered by insurance followed the Bismarckian pattern until the Second World War regarding both the groups insured first and the dynamics of extension. Similarly to Germany, in Hungary it was workers who first

---

192 ILO, Compulsory sickness insurance. 35-36.

193 Gyáni, A szociálpolitika múltja Magyarországon. 14; Béla Kovrig, Magyar társadalompolitika. II. kötet. Társadalompolitikai feladatok. Kolozsvár 1944, 384-389.

194 Kovrig, Magyar társadalompolitika. 130-132.

195 Ibidem.

received the benefits of social security and expansion was a process spanning several decades.

As shown above, regarding the *qualifying conditions* for social security benefits in the first half of the century it was clearly the type of occupation and the contribution paid that played a definitive role in Hungary. Means-test hardly existed, either in the earliest programs or after the 1928 pension reform. Table 15 shows that the conditions for pensions in 1930 (the age limit and the waiting period) largely corresponded to the Western European policies, though the latter cannot be labelled unified.[196] Exceptions include the regulation applied to the blind, which was more favourable than the average and the unfavourable payment conditions of old-age pensions and widows' allowances. The latter was unfavourable because it required a relatively long, 20 year waiting period, consequently, considering the introduction of 1928, no payments were made in this program between the wars. In addition, the prospective amount of pensions strongly depended on the length of the contribution period in Hungary, more markedly than elsewhere. At the same time, in contrast to most Western European countries, there was no waiting period required for health insurance in Hungary (Tables 14 and 15).

For industrial workers, health and occupational injuries insurance guaranteed rather high *level of services* in Hungary already from 1891 and 1907, respectively. Although in the period of economic disorganisation and inflation following the world war social rights were difficult to realise, the 1927 social security legislation reinforced them. The 1928 pension insurance law introduced similarly high level benefits for industrial and commercial employees.[197]

The relative level of the benefits is well illustrated by the regulation of health insurance and *sickness payments*. In the early 1930s Hungarian industrial workers received 60% of their wages as sick pay from the fourth day of their illness, or, if their scheme could afford it, this could rise to 75%.[198] Consequently, as shown in Table 14, sick pay exceeded the German, French and Belgian levels, and only in the Netherlands can a more favourable service be found.[199] Furthermore, Béla Kovrig's surveys indicate that the interwar Hungarian regulation was considerably better than the conditions guaranteed by the 1948 British social security legislation with regard to health benefits.[200] Of course, all this concerns the relative level of benefits, as compared to wages, and not the absolute level of services. In an international context further features of the conditions of payment appear pioneering. The insured were entitled to receive cash sickness benefits up to 52 weeks and no waiting period was required to qualify (Table 14). Another positive characteristic of the Hungarian regulation was the entitlement for 1 year of

---

196 ILO, Compulsory Pension Insurance. 106-107.

197 Cf. Kovrig, A munka védelme a dunai államokban. 211-294.

198 Országos Társadalombiztosító Intézet, A magyar társadalombiztosítás tíz éve, 1919-1929. Budapest é.n., 153.

199 ILO, International Survey of Social Services. 368.

200 Kovrig, Magyar társadalompolitika. 126-129.

medical, hospital and sanatorial care. Members of the insured's household were also entitled for 6 weeks of hospitalization in addition to medical care and medication. However, the services provided for agricultural labourers were fairly limited. E.g. medical and medicine costs were covered only for 45 days for farm labourers, and the employer was obliged to meet hospital expenses only for 30 days, a regulation which did not apply for sanatorial care, and hospitalisation for family members also fell outside the scope of benefits.[201]

In 1930 in Hungary an insured person becoming incapacitated due to *occupational injuries* received free medical and hospital care as well as medication, and was entitled to 60% of the basic wages for the first 10 weeks, which then could be raised to 75%. Although the complexity of Western European and Hungarian regulations result in difficulties regarding detailed international comparisons, the ILO data provide a firm basis to establish that the Hungarian level of benefits of occupational injuries insurance equalled, and, in certain respects, surpassed that of several Western European countries. Only the Dutch and Irish regulations can be considered clearly more favourable for the insured (Table 13).[202] The same applies to other conditions of occupational injuries insurance, the permanent disability, partial disability, and total disability benefits, and also in kind benefits, including medical care and medication.

As mentioned before, the pension reforms of the late 1920s made the insured entitled to *old-age pension* after a 400 week waiting period, thus the first payments were made from 1932.[203] After the introduction old age benefits comprised of several components: an annual flat benefit of 120 Pengős, a yearly 25% of the former total contributions for workers and 19% for white-collar employees, and a 15% supplement for each child under 15.[204] As regards old-age pension, regulation was even more complex than for sick pay and occupational injuries insurance in Europe, thus it is not possible to give a systematic comparison of their relative levels. A contemporary calculation suggests that around 1930 Hungarian old-age pensions and disability benefits, based on 30 years of contributions, would be 477 Pengős, equalling the Austrian level converted into Pengő. Taking 40 years into account (596 Pengős) it significantly exceeded Austrian and Italian levels, equalled Czechoslovakian services but was under the English and especially the German level.[205] The international comparison also accentuates the high levels of

---

201 Kovrig, A munka védelme a dunai államokban. 281.

202 ILO, International Survey of Social Services. 363-370.

203 Győző Vígh, Az öregségi, rokkantsági, özvegységi és árvasági biztosítás szolgáltatásainak megindulása. Budapest 1933, 9.

204 During the Second World War old-age benefits comprised of several components: an annual 120 Pengős flat amount, a 30 P supplement, a component dependent on the length and sum of contributions paid and a supplement tied to the rise of the lowest wages.

205 Emerich von Dréhr, Die soziale Arbeit in Ungarn. Budapest 1930, 60.

maternity assistance and funeral assistance, and the relatively unfavourable level of the widows' pensions.[206]

The development of social rights in Hungary between the Second World War and 1990 was determined by a combination of different factors, such as the Bismarckian traditions of the previous periods, political discrimination, and solidarity or the principle of citizenship. These elements gained different weights from time to time and their significance also varied in different areas of welfare, influencing both the relationship to the previous period and to Western European trends.

The extension of *coverage* was almost continuous in the post-Second World War period, though three major waves can be distinguished, the first following the war, the second in the late 50s and early 60s, and the third in the mid- and late 70s.[207] As a result, the pattern of growth of coverage occupied a mid-position: it was not so abrupt in Hungary as had been earlier in several Scandinavian countries or in Great Britain, but was not so gradual either as in the majority of countries following Bismarckian traditions.

After the war, but predating the communist takeover, there was a significant rise in the number of those included in the social security schemes. Health insurance was extended to agricultural workers (1945, 1947), all private white-collar employees, and in the late 40s and early 50s to other groups as well (college/university students, artists, etc.). Certain categories of relatives previously excluded from the schemes also became eligible for health insurance, e.g. those mothers, sisters and daughters of working women (from 1947) or either of working spouses (1950) who ran their household.[208] The most significant change regarding pension insurance was its extension to all wage-workers in agriculture from 1945 in case they did not have landed property larger than one cadastral acre.[209] As a result, in 1950 about half of the Hungarian population participated in compulsory occupational injuries, health and pension insurance, which then were operated in essence by a unified system. Although this ratio still lagged considerably behind several Western European countries (Germany, the United Kingdom and Scandinavia), the remarkable growth, exceeding 50% over only a few years, closed the gap somewhat between Hungary and Western Europe in the coverage of social security schemes (Tables 10, 11 and 12).[210]

---

206 ILO, International Survey of Social Services. 363-370; Kovrig, Magyar társadalompolitika. 126-129.

207 The coverage ratios are our own computation based on the following publications A társadalombiztosítás fejlődése számokban, 1950-1985. Budapest 1987, 52-59; Statisztikai Évkönyv. 1990. Budapest 1991, 17; Time series of historical statistics, 1867-1992. Vol. I. Budapest 1993, 36.

208 A magyar társadalombiztosítás húsz éve. 16.

209 Laczkó, A magyar munkás- és társadalombiztosítás története. 167.

210 A magyar társadalombiztosítás húsz éve. 16-28; Gál et al., Szociálpolitikánk két évtizede.

As the first sign of a new wave of expansion, non-working members of agricultural and industrial cooperatives, pensioners and students were granted compulsory health insurance in 1955 and then in 1958 the compulsory pension insurance of agricultural cooperatives was instituted. Thus in the wake of the second big wave of collectivisation, in the late 50s and early 60s the majority of farmers become insured, and in a few years other social groups followed them, e.g. the self-employed in 1962 and 1964.[211]

Even though members of cooperatives and the self employed did not receive full social security benefits, their inclusion can be interpreted as a significant move towards universality even in international comparison. While in 1960 the coverage was under the Western European average, in a few years' time it exceeded the Western European level. In 1963 in all the schemes discussed Hungarian coverage was 97%, except for eligibility for sick pay, where it was considerably lower (Tables 10, 11 and 12). The remaining small social groups were granted benefits by the 1975 social security law. The degree of coverage created as a result was in essence complete (again with the exception of sick pay), equalled in Western Europe only by Scandinavian countries in health and pension insurance.

In the development of the qualifying conditions of social security there are discontinuities between the interwar and the post-Second World War periods in several respects. As an element of this, the political discrimination of certain social groups had already appeared immediately after the war, which affected qualifying conditions and existed for decades, even though it was gradually losing its weight. The infamous "B-lists" and other measures aiming at restructuring the state apparatus, the police, and the armed forces meant that former government employees, soldiers and police officers as well as their relatives lost their previous qualifications for pensions in large numbers. In addition, the extension of eligibility applied only to employees, equalling a status of state employment as a result of nationalisations. The self-employed in industry and commerce, a relatively small strata after the nationalisation, were still excluded from the benefits of social security. Discrimination, however, primarily affected the agricultural population. From the late 50s the agricultural population also became insured, but was not granted rights equal to those who worked in the state sector. With regard to health insurance, this surfaced primarily in the lack of qualification for sick pay. In addition, farmers in agricultural cooperatives could retire only 5 years later than state employees and there were great differences in the qualifying conditions for family allowance as well. However, the divide in social rights was not only drawn between the self- and the state employed. There were privileged categories within the latter group as well, depending on what importance rulers attributed to them with regard to the production process or to the preservation of their own power. Consequently, certain occupations

34-38; A magyar társadalombiztosítás húsz éve. 16-17.

211 Gál et al., Szociálpolitikánk két évtizede. 34-38; A magyar társadalombiztosítás húsz éve. 16-28.

(e.g. soldiers and miners) enjoyed benefits much more advantageous than others in the 50s; and several of these privileges had been maintained for decades (e.g. age limits in pension qualifications). The loss of social rights secured previously and other forms of discrimination were in sharp contrast with the practice of the interwar period as well as with contemporary Western Europe, where the inclusion of the self employed in insurance was slow but the extension of social rights did not take place at the expense of any other group.[212]

At the same time, from the very beginnings of the communist transformation of the welfare system, the unification of *qualifying conditions* on the basis of solidarity was a clear tendency. First these applied only to or within certain groups, primarily in the case of state employees, and thus, paradoxically, they coexisted with the discrimination of certain other groups. In time, however, state employment and coverage increased, leading to the loss of ground for discrimination. The gradual unification of qualifying conditions also provided the basis for granting benefits on the citizenship principle.

In health insurance, the unification of benefits for those covered took place relatively early, in the 1950s as regards in kind benefits, with partial qualifications remaining only with respect to sick pay. The 1951 law on pension insurance divided contributors into 6 groups, providing in every group the same benefits independent of former contributions. In this decade further laws were passed, each by the name of "unified pension law", but the intention of unification was to be found only with regard to those employed by the state. At the same time, as discussed earlier, new groups were continually included in the schemes. This process, as well as its limits that existed for a long time, is illustrated by the payment of family allowance. Farmers in cooperatives were granted this benefit in 1953, but until 1970 they qualified only with the birth of their third child and, until as late as 1975, received a smaller amount than did workers or employees.[213]

The mid 1970s can be seen as a turning point in the regulation of qualifications, principally because in 1975 health care and the assimilated occupational injuries insurance become citizenship rights. This meant the realisation of universality in the broadest sense in health care, with not only insurance coverage for the whole society but also theoretically the same levels of services with the exception of the cash benefits already mentioned.[214] This was obviously a favourable change compared to the interwar period, even though the elimination of the waiting period in health and industrial occupational injuries insurance as well as the unlimited period of the payments could be regarded universal in Western Europe, too, at this time (Tables 14 and 17).

---

212 For the discrimination in other communist countries, see Jack Minkoff and Lynn Turgeon, Income Maintenance in the Soviet Union in Eastern and Western Perspective, in: Irving Louis Horowitz ed., Equity, Income, and Policy. Comparative Studies in Three Worlds Development. New York and London 1977, 178-180.

213 Ferge, Fejezetek a magyar szegénypolitika történetéből. 160-161; Népesség- és társadalomstatisztikai zsebkönyv. 1985. Budapest 1986, 211.

214 Botos, A magyar társadalombiztosítás kialakulása és fejlődése. 30-31.

Also by this time, the differences between employees and other insured groups had disappeared with regard to qualifying for pension. The 5 year higher age limit for retirement in the case of members of agricultural cooperatives and their widows was lowered from 1975, over a 5-year transitory period, to meet the limit for other employee groups, and the method of pension calculations was also unified. Thus by the early 1980s differences between insured groups regarding qualifying conditions for social security completely disappeared. In this regard, Hungary approached the Scandinavian countries with the exception of maintaining lower age limits in certain occupations (e.g. miners) justified by unfavourable work conditions.

Besides the signs of discontinuity, i.e. the ideologically rooted discrimination and the introduction of benefits based on the citizenship principle, continuity with the interwar period is also clear in the area of qualifying conditions. On the one hand, similarly to the earlier period, the means-test principle was not given a significant role after the Second World War in state welfare provisions, and its significance further diminished with the dissolution of voluntary charity organisations and other non-state welfare institutions.[215]

On the other hand, though benefits were paid increasingly by the same principles for the whole population, among which citizenship as a source of rights was clearly gaining ground in some welfare areas, these principles also showed unambiguous continuity with the pre-1945, Bismarckian traditions based on individual insurance. A proof of this is that for decades the precondition for all social security benefits was the payment of contributions, or, rather, being employed. The inclusion of great numbers of farmers in social security schemes from the late 1950s was possible because they had ceased to be self employed and became employees of state farms or joined agricultural cooperatives. Universality with regards to the in kind benefits of health insurance emerged also at the time when the private sector virtually disappeared and the distinction between cooperative and state ownership became insignificant. This provides further support for the important role of the workplace and especially the status of state employment in qualifying for social rights.[216]

In contrast to health insurance, the pension system preserved such important features of the Bismarckian insurance system as compulsory contribution, relatively long waiting periods and, consequently, the differentiated calculation of pensions until the end of the period examined. The regulation of the early 50s, disregarding the length of the period through which contributions were paid and establishing only a few pension categories proved to be transitory. Afterwards the contribution principle was stressed again more strongly in determining qualification. Of crucial importance in another regard, the

---

215 Endre Sik, New Trends in the Hungarian Welfare System, in: A. Evers and H. Wintersberger eds., Shifts in the Welfare Mix. Frankfurt/M. 1990, 283.

216 For similar observation, see Endre Sik and Ivan Svetlik, Similarities and Differences, in: Evers and Wintersberger eds., Shifts in the Welfare Mix. 276.

1975 reform did not bring about changes in this area, requiring a period of minimum 10 years of contributions for old-age pension from social security. Moreover, for those retiring after 1990 this was gradually increased to 20 years, which strengthened the contribution principle and which appears to be a strict condition for qualification in a Western European comparison. In contrast, the age limit (60 years for men, 55 for women) seemed rather favourable not only in relation to the interwar Hungarian situation but also in comparison to Western Europe, where similarly low age limits could be found only in Italy (Table 18). Other benefits of social security, e.g. sick pay were also associated with contributions and calculated on the basis of one's income. In addition, family benefits, which played an important role in the Hungarian welfare system, also depended on employment and contributions. These characteristics are similar to those appearing in the conservative Western European welfare systems of Germany, Austria and the Benelux countries.

With respect to the *level of benefits*, efforts in the post-Second World War years seem to have been principally directed at a strong levelling off, rather than a general improvement of standards. This meant, for example in the case of pensions, evening out differences between public employees and other occupational groups. A procedure springing from strong political motivations used the assessment of political reliability as a pretext and employed administrative means to decrease or nullify qualifications already secured in the case of those formerly in public service and their relatives. In addition, financial measures were taken to eliminate differences in benefits which were regarded as excessive. Thus the sums of higher pensions were not raised and the pensions in the different categories were re-regulated, for which the economic disorganisation of the post-war years created a good opportunity. In theory, the 1952 pension reform gave a unified regulation for the level of benefits of those employed. However, politically motivated discrimination was also tangible because the modest base amount (15-30% of the average wage) was supplemented by an annual 2% only based on time spent in employment after 1 January 1945. In a few years (1954) the ratio of the base amount was raised to 50% but the annual 1% supplement was still calculated from 1945. Then in 1959 this borderline was pushed back to 1929 and the elimination of the disproportionate relationships between old and new types of pensions was also attempted at this point.[217]

In spite of the politics of levelling off, employment and the corresponding social security contribution was decisive in the determination of the level of benefits in this period, and later the moderation of the differences in benefits was attributed no priority at all. The most important elements of cash benefits were linked to earnings even at the end of the period examined, as shown by the calculation methods of pensions and sick pay. While before the war pensions included a flat-rate component, in the 1980s they were set on the basis of the earnings in the few years immediately preceding retirement,

---

[217] A magyar társadalombiztosítás húsz éve. 24-25.

i.e. as 35% of the average earnings, which could rise to 75% in case of 42 years of contribution payments. This method was obviously designed to press people to stay on the labour market in an economy with labour shortages. It must be noted that this is somewhat contradictory to the retirement age limit both for women (55 years) and men (60 years), which was quite low in Western European comparison. The contradiction is partial, though, because the pension system clearly encouraged working beyond the retirement age, as the low absolute level of pensions could be significantly improved with additional years of work. Sick pay was calculated also exclusively in relation to income, e.g. in 1981 65% of it was paid in case of illness (Table 17). In a Western European comparison these figures do not appear favourable and also indicate that improvement with respect to the relative level of benefits was of a smaller scale in the communist Hungary regarding the degree of coverage.

The emphasised role of work and employment in the benefits of social programs was reflected in the more generous regulation of benefits of occupational injuries insurance, which compensated accidents directly resulting from work. In the early 1980s occupational injuries insurance did not require a waiting period and guaranteed a 100% income replacement (Tables 16, 17 and 18).

Considering the low retirement age limit it is noteworthy that the relative levels of Hungarian pensions increased significantly by the early 1980s compared to the very low post-Second World War levels. The 57% ratio in 1982 practically equalled the average of OECD countries (58%) and was considerably above that of communist countries, e.g. the GDR (30%) and even Czechoslovakia (45%).[218] An obvious explanation here is that, unlike other communist countries, pensions in Hungary were continuously raised (indexed) from the 1960s on. This raise was a fixed amount for a long time, e.g. 2% p.a. and a minimum 70 Forints between 1972 and 1986 (Table 18). The galloping inflation of the 80s, however, made this increasingly insufficient. Therefore repeated ad hoc measures were taken to preserve the purchasing power of pensions, with less and less success and with consequences to the relative level of average pensions.[219]

The comparison of the social security development of interwar Hungary and Western Europe in the area of social rights reveals a dichotomy. On the one hand, the available data indicate that the ratio of those covered by social security schemes was rather low in Hungary, and diverged from the Western European level. On the other hand, however, the relative level of benefits, especially as regards state employees largely approached the conditions in Western Europe and with the maturing of the generous 1928 pension insurance further convergence could be expected. Interwar Western European trends

---

218 Therborn, European Modernity and Beyond. 94.

219 Gabor Hegyesi, Anna Gondos and Eva Orsos, Hungary, in: John Dixon and David Macarov eds., Social welfare in socialist countries. London and New York 1992, 113; Andorka and Tóth, Szociális kiadások és szociálpolitika Magyarországon. 415.

were also reflected in the changes of the qualifying conditions for social security benefits. The means-test principle was assigned a secondary role behind the insurance principle and the specific qualifying conditions such as the age limits and waiting period of pension insurance, or the waiting period of the health insurance also approached Western European standards (Tables 14 and 15). At the same time, the pattern of coverage with high benefit levels conforms to the Bismarckian tradition, and constitutes the application of the Bismarckian principles to a dominantly agrarian society with a relatively small working class.

After the Second World War the degree of coverage increased at a significant pace in Hungary, with ratios close to the Western European average even in the first decades. In contrast, the politically motivated discrimination of certain social groups, most of all, farmers, in the 1950s meant more of a divergence from Western Europe regarding qualifying conditions, even if these could not have been regarded unified for all walks of social security in the given period either. The marked equalization of the level of benefits, even eliminating rights obtained earlier, is another characteristic of the early communist welfare system that had no parallel phenomenon in the West. The level of benefits relative to earnings was also low in comparison to Western Europe. However, the crudest forms of discrimination were eliminated in Hungary in the second half of the 1950s and the growing significance of the solidarity principle of the 1960s and 1970s in the area of qualifying conditions, paired with the rapid increase of the coverage can be regarded as moves toward universality in accordance with Western European processes. Moreover, in Hungary the whole population was covered by social security sooner than in most Western European countries. The relative level of benefits does not turn out so favourably in a Western European comparison, although the ratio of pensions relative to earnings corresponded to the Western average in the early 1980s. By the 1980s in Hungary an increasing number of benefits were granted on the basis of citizenship, and from the mid-1970s all in kind benefits of health care belonged to this category, similarly to the British or Swedish systems. At the same time, other important social security services, e.g. pensions or sick pay were closely tied to the contributions paid, regarding both their qualifying conditions and their levels, which is similar to the Western European welfare type called conservative or corporatist. These similarities to different type of Western European welfare regimes suggest that by the 1980s the Hungarian social security system applied a combination of elements customary in Western Europe as qualifying conditions. Although this is not a distinct feature compared to the interwar period, in this area it signals a new convergence to Western Europe in contrast to the 1950s (Appendix).

4 ORGANIZATION AND CONTROL

In contrast with the areas analysed above, the issues of who and in what arrangement administers the social security system and who exerts the final control over it have drawn little attention in international welfare research. The fact that the communist transformation of the welfare system brought about considerable changes in this area justifies the inclusion of these aspects in our inquiry. Also, this is the way to meet our objective to include in our comparative analysis not only important aspects of the West European development but those which are highly relevant in the Hungarian context as well.

Accordingly, the following aspects will be discussed in the present chapter: 1. the organizational forms of social security, with special emphasis on the role of the state; and, closely related to this, 2. the functioning of control mechanisms, that is, what scope of control the organizational framework offered over clients, and vice versa, what means those who were eligible had at their disposal to control the operation of social security.

At the end of the 19th and the beginning of the 20th century, a period hallmarked by the dissolution of the traditional forms of social protection, mutual insurance associations, independent of state intervention were real alternatives to state welfare systems in Western Europe.[220] The emergence of the German *Hilfskassen auf Gegenseitigkeit*, the English *Friendly Societies*, the French *mutualités* and their Belgian, Swiss and other counterparts preceded the first governmental welfare measures. In the 1870s these types of voluntary associations had more than 1.25 million members Great Britain, and in 1870 in France there were about 825,000 workers insured by them.[221]

These voluntary institutions had several shortcomings, though. In terms of their organisation, being fragmented in nature, they were too small to share risks effectively. Moreover, the service they provided covered only a small circle of risks (e.g. they provided no old-age pension), the standard of services was low, and only available for more well-to-do members of the workers' elite, those who did have the capacity for advance savings.

The intervention of the welfare state was a response to these problems. It unfolded at a different pace and in diversified ways in the Western European countries, resulting in considerable differences regarding the *organizational forms* of the early, pre-First World War social security systems. One of the major types was referred to as *compul-*

---

220 Gerhard A. Ritter, Social Welfare in Germany and Britain. Origins and Development. Leamington Spa and New York 1986, 134.

221 Kaelble, A Social History of Western Europe. 80-81; Ogus, Landesbericht Grossbritannien. 299; Saint-Jours, Landesbericht Frankreich. 204; Maurer, Landesbericht Schweiz. 764.

sory insurance, where the state mandated membership in a specific form of insurance without prescribing the actual company that the client was to take out the insurance policy with. Thus in this type the state had a great role in developing and enforcing the basic principles governing the operation of insurance, it was also involved in the operation of the insurance schemes but had only a modest role in financing. Beside Germany, this arrangement was characteristic of the Austrian and Norwegian systems in the pre-First World War period, and it can also be detected in the British social security system from 1908 onwards. Both the German and the British systems integrated voluntary insurance institutions (which existed in great numbers by then) but, respected their independence.[222]

The other type, state subsidised *voluntary insurance* was typical of Belgium, France, Italy, Sweden, Denmark and Switzerland initially. Here the state played a much less dominant role, limited to defining the operational framework of the social security system, controlling and subsidising its operation. The right to define the scope of benefits, other conditions of payment, and the amount of contributions was left with the individual insurance fund. Benefits were proportionate to contributions paid. Vertical re-distribution between social strata was modest, however, unlike with private insurance, contributions were calculated irrespective of individual risks, that is, solidarity prevailed in this regard.[223]

Between the two world wars the economic intervention of the state became more extensive throughout Western Europe, which also affected the role the state undertook in welfare provisions. Mostly as a result of governmental and legislative initiatives, compulsory insurance became more widespread at the expense of voluntary insurance schemes. On the one hand, already existing voluntary, state subsidised social security schemes were transformed into compulsory ones and newly introduced programs were compulsory from the start. It was only the less widespread unemployment insurance that continued as voluntary for a long time. Beside compulsory insurance thus becoming dominant, in most countries (Belgium, France, Ireland, Italy, etc.) a new type, national insurance also appeared on the scene. This type of insurance covers the whole population and is administered by the state, thus gaining a more central role here than in earlier types of social security programs. The national programs are co-financed by the clients similarly to insurance schemes. However, there is only a weak relationship between the contributions or special taxes paid and the benefits received. The Swedish social security system was the first one to have been organised along these lines in 1913, followed by other Scandinavian countries introducing national pension schemes between the two world wars.[224] Beyond Scandinavia there were new benefits introduced

222 Alber, Vom Armenhaus zum Wohlfahrtsstaat. 47.

223 Ibidem, 43.

224 Ibidem, 45; Gordon, Social Security Policies in Industrial Countries. 203; Kaelble, A Social History of Western Europe. 124.

in several other countries, exclusively financed by the state, such as family allowance and unemployment benefit in Germany in the 1930s. Although these were not direct compensations for contributions paid, often only members of social security programs were eligible for them. Besides these forms of increasing involvement, the social security activity of the state was further amplified by the extension of the eligibility of various schemes to include non-employed people who, consequently, paid no contribution. However, with the exception of a few Scandinavian countries and Great Britain, contributions by the state still did not dominate the social security budget.[225]

After the Second World War different types of compulsory or national insurance requiring a considerable state involvement were introduced even in countries and for risk groups that had only voluntary insurance up to that point. Compulsory occupational injuries schemes were set up in France (1946), Great Britain (1946), Ireland (1966) and Belgium (1971), compulsory health insurance in Belgium (1944), Sweden (1953) and Finland (1963) and compulsory pension insurance in Ireland (1960). Following in the wake of Scandinavian countries, national pension insurance was introduced in Great Britain, the Netherlands and Switzerland. Great Britain, Italy and the Scandinavian countries also restructured their health insurance along the principles of national insurance. By the beginning of the 1980s, the various types of voluntary occupational injuries, health and pension insurance were superseded, Switzerland was the only to maintain such forms in the first two areas. Unemployment insurance still remained an exception to this trend, as compulsory forms did not become widespread in this area in Western Europe.[226]

These social security systems, especially national insurance, shifted more responsibility to the state in terms of both administrative operation and control. The spreading of national insurance schemes, however, was not a steady process. As pointed out above in another context, the model sometimes referred to as continental started gaining ground at the expense of state-administered systems from the 1970s. In this, social security systems were increasingly constructed along the principles of insurance and it was overwhelmingly financed by the contributions of employers and employees.[227] The prevalence of the insurance principle is supported by the fact that state contributions to the expenditures of social security were rather limited in most of the countries in the period after the Second World War. Our calculations suggest that the average state contribution to the financing of social security remained unchanged in Western Europe between 1960 and 1980, being 39.7% and 40% in the opening and the closing year, respectively (Appendix).[228] True, the average evens out significant differences between

---

225 ILO, Financing social security: The options. An international analysis. Geneva 1984, 7-10.

226 Kaelble, A Social History of Western Europe. 126; Alber, Vom Armenhaus zum Wohlfahrtsstaat. 28, 44-48, 232-235; Gordon, Social Security Policies in Industrial Countries. 203.

227 Kosonen, European Welfare State Models. 81-110.

228 Own computations based on the following publication ILO, The Cost of Social Security. Eleventh international inquiry. Geneva 1985, 46-51.

the individual countries: in Great Britain, Ireland and the Scandinavian countries it was well above the mean, as in these countries an average of 60% of social security expenditures were financed from state resources not only in the above discussed period but also between 1949 and 1974 (Table 9).[229] Although our calculations reveal neither convergence nor divergence in the sample as regards the ratios of contributions between 1960 and 1980, other studies highlight the similar methods of financing and diagnose convergence for the 1980s.[230] The state also provided incentives for forms of private insurance to expand, for example, in the form of tax breaks,[231] however, its role increased more in terms of providing the legal framework and administration and not in terms of financing social security in Western Europe in the decades after the Second World War.

The emergence of social security was a great move compared to 19th century poor laws in that it was free from their repressive and stigmatising features. Nevertheless, the operation of social security was characterised by mechanisms of discipline and *control* as well. The aim of these mechanisms was to motivate clients to pay the contributions on the one hand and, on the other, to detect those who wanted to take advantage of the benefits but had not qualified for them.

These control mechanisms became obviously more relaxed on the long run. For example, the various time limits loosened up: waiting periods became shorter, maximum periods of entitlements became longer or were eliminated altogether. In Germany, for example, for all the four major social security programs waiting periods decreased or were abolished between the time of their introduction and the mid-1970s. The periods of benefits increased: from 13 weeks to 78 in the case of health insurance from its introduction (1884) by the middle of the 1970s, from 26 to 52 weeks for the unemployment insurance (1927), and basically the same happened in the case of pension insurance (1891) when the age of retirement was lowered from 70 to 65 years.[232] However, the trend of decreasing control, as pointed out in the previous chapter, holds primarily for the beginning and the middle of the century, after which it stopped, to give way again to the trend of stricter control of receiving services which prevailed alongside with the establishment of a new, extensive organizational network of this control in welfare states (Tables 13 to 18). The term "welfare crime" illustrates the link between the welfare state and the institutions of state control. This became a central theme of the

---

229 Peter Flora, On the History and Current Problems of the Welfare State, in: S. N. Eisenstadt and Ora Ahimier eds., The Welfare State and its Aftermath. London and Sydney 1985, 20.

230 Hansen, Elements of social security. 14-16; Robert Hagfors, The Convergence of Financing Structure, 1980-1995, in: Juho Saari and Kari Välimäki eds., Financing Social Protection in Europe. Helsinki 1999.

231 The level of tax benefits was significant in some countries: At the end of the 1980s with regard to the pension insurances accounted for 1% of the GDP in Denmark and 0.7% in Great Britain. Esping-Andersen, The Three Worlds of Welfare Capitalism. 101-102.

232 Alber, Vom Armenhaus zum Wohlfahrtsstaat. 64.

public discourse on the welfare state in the 70s and 80s, when there was less of a social consensus on welfare programs than before. The lack of consensus, as shown e.g. in the case of the Netherlands, in tandem with the increase of tax burdens and the increasing complexity of fiscal legislation resulted in greater inclinations for tax avoidance.[233] Legal offences included the abuse of unemployment benefit rights, social security contribution frauds by employers and the accounting frauds of health institutions. Moreover, the state at this stage was already facing problems fulfilling its extensive welfare responsibilities, therefore, it made more efforts to fight "welfare crime", which manifested itself in the establishment of a number of new institutions of inspection and control.[234]

The increased engagement of the state in the security schemes, and in welfare services in general did not necessarily limit the citizens' scope of action, as it is not so much the degree of state participation than its nature that is of major importance. It is not only that the prerequisite for exercising the social rights requires the reliable and transparent operation of social security and other welfare organisations, which state measures aimed at in often not transparent insurance markets. It is also that states directly intervened to help the insured to exert control over the schemes. Laws passed at the early stage of development institutionalised the participation of contributors in the management in several countries, which was a major claim of the workers' movement, too.[235] In Germany the insurance system of the 1880s incorporated the already existing Hilfskassen, which gained autonomy in the new system and both the workers and the employees had control over them. In like manner, employers and employees of other countries obtained a major role not only in financing but also in operating welfare institutions.[236]

Participatory administration, however, did not become the dominant and effective means of control in Western Europe either in the first half of the century or after the First World War. In Austria the original regulation of social security self-governments, which was in force until the Nazi occupation, provided even more autonomy than the post-Second World War regulations: the clients had a more direct representation on the one hand, and self-governments' rights to self-regulation were less limited by the state on the other.[237] Especially in the second half of the century, in parallel with the increas-

233 Uriel Rosenthal, Welfare State or State of Welfare? Repression and Welfare in Modern State, in: Richard F. Tomasson ed., The Welfare State, 1883-1983. Greenwich, Connecticut and London 1983, 279-297.

234 Rosenthal, Welfare State or State of Welfare? 294.

235 Göran Therborn, Classes and States: Welfare State Developments, 1881-1981, in: Wallace Clement and Rianne Mahon eds., Swedish Social Democracy: A Model in Transition. Toronto 1994, 27-28.

236 Franz-Xaver Kaufmann, The Blurring of the Distinction 'State Versus Society' in the Idea and Practice of the Welfare State, in: Franz-Xaver Kaufmann et al. ed., Guidance, Control, and Evaluation in the Public Sector. Berlin and New York 1986, 133.

237 Herbert Hofmeister, Landesbericht Österreich, in: Köhler and Zacher (Hrsg.), Ein Jahrhun-

ing coverage of the population by social security, i.e. the increasing complexity of the systems, the indirect control of the clients over welfare programs through the institutions of political democracy became of great importance beside, or, rather, instead of the direct control of social security institutions. A significant body of the welfare research literature consider the institutions of political democracy as crucially important in the emergence and expansion of the welfare state, maintaining that this development directly resulted from left-wing parties articulating the interests of the working class assuming power.[238] Even if a direct connection cannot be clearly found between the expansion of welfare services and specific political forces, mass democracy can obviously be regarded a determining factor of this process in Western Europe. This issue will be elaborated in the next chapter.

The organizational forms of social security became more alike in Western Europe in the course of the 20th century. There were considerable differences at the beginning of the century and between the two world wars ranging from state supported voluntary to compulsory and national schemes. Convergence began in the interwar period, then it gathered momentum after the Second World War. As part of this process, voluntary schemes were transformed into compulsory ones in an increasing number of countries, and national systems also took shape in Great Britain, Ireland, Italy, and Scandinavia. Consequently, voluntary insurances shrank by the 1970s and only the other two types operated. On the other hand, the growth rate of national schemes and state subsidies came to a limit, which is also illustrated by the trends in the sources of financing. After this point Beveridge-type systems introduced more elements of the insurance principle thus converging to the structure of the continental welfare model.

The increasing role of the state in welfare did not exclude the right of the clients to exercise control, what is more, from the very beginnings state regulation often aimed at transparency and providing contribution payers with opportunities to protect their own interests. Although there is no empirical research available in this area, several signs indicate that throughout the 20th century there were considerable differences between the institutionalisation of direct control of the clients in Western European countries. With the expansion and growing complexity of the welfare systems after the Second World War, direct control lost importance and indirect control became of increasing importance through the converging institutions of political democracy.

* * *

The first social security laws in Hungary openly relied on German and Austrian models, which also manifested itself in the regulation of organizational issues. Social security programs took the form of *compulsory insurance* already at the initial stage of devel-

---

dert Sozialversicherung. 723.

[238] Korpi, The Democratic Class Struggle. 198.

opment regarding health and occupational injuries insurance for industry workers (1891: XIV.tc.; 1907: XIX.tc.) and the same form was applied to the pension insurance set up between the two world wars (1928: XL.tc.). Agricultural workers were an exception to this, regulations introducing voluntary insurance for them (1900: XVI.tc., 1902: XIV.tc.), which was modified before the Second World War when compulsory insurance for this social group had been partially established (1938: XII.tc.).[239]

The compulsory health insurance of 1891 created a fragmented system along the principles of self-government, features that the Hungarian social security system shared with its German counterpart. In 1892 there were 92 legally acknowledged health benefit funds, their number growing to 409 by 1906.[240] Moreover, there were various forms of funds to choose from, such as district, crafts union, mine, company, and others. The high costs due to the fragmented nature of the system and the lack of transparency that caused hitches in the operation of the system resulted in the Health and Accident Insurance Act (1907) that made attempts to centralise the institutions of social security. The various types of funds were merged and only the operation of three types of funds was allowed: that of mine mutual funds, company and district funds. Moreover, the OMBP (Országos Munkásbetegsegélyező és Balesetbiztosító Pénztár, National Fund for the Aid of Sick Workers and Accident Insurance) was established, which administered the operation of district and company funds in accordance with national standards. The costs of its operation were covered by the state as well as the costs of administration of the controlling body, the ÁMH (Állami Munkásbiztosítási Hivatal, State Office of Workers' Insurance). However, not only the individual funds but also the OMBP continued under their respective self-governments.[241]

Further legislation was also hallmarked by centralisation, and by 1930 all industrial workers and domestic servants belonged to the same institution of health and pension insurance (OTI: Országos Társadalombiztosító Intézet, National Social Security Institute) which provided equal rights for them. There were only a few sectors (the railways, the post, the tobacco industry and mining) that managed to preserve their own, independent institution of social security. Therefore, at this stage the organizational form of Hungarian social security was considerably different from the German system, which continued to be decentralised.

In the first half of the century the state in Hungary had the role of the organiser and supervisor of welfare programs, while the direct role of the state as provider of welfare services was less significant. In accordance with the Bismarckian tradition, social security was subsidised by the state to a small extent. 2.4 million Pengős p. a. were allotted in the budged for contributing to the operational costs of the OTI and the other major

[239] For social security legislation, see Gyáni, A szociálpolitika múltja Magyarországon. 11-14; Laczkó, A magyar munkás- és társadalombiztosítás története. 151-155.

[240] Bikkal, A társadalombiztosítás Magyarországon. 344-345.

[241] Dréhr, Die soziale Arbeit in Ungarn. 42-44; Lőrincz, A munkaviszonyok szabályozása Magyarországon. 192-204.

fund, the MABI (Magánalkalmazottak Biztosító Intézete, Institute of Insurance for Private Employees), which sum accounted for less than 2% of their total expenditures in 1930. The social security act of 1928 proposed a higher percentage of support, continuously increasing by 5% p. a. for social security regarding the old-age pension and the disability allowance but the dissolution of the Ministry of Welfare and Labour in 1932 prevented the launch of this project.[242]

The first Hungarian act of social security already created self-governments of social security funds and these institutions were heavily relied on by laws passed later. Although self-governments were temporarily abolished after the 1918-19 revolutions, the need for them re-emerged when drafting the reform of social security in the second half of the 1920s, supported not only by József Vass, the Minister of Welfare and Labour but also by Prime Minister István Bethlen.[243] Act XXI of 1927 therefore reintroduced the self-government of social security funds by insured employees and their employers. They elected self-governments in the OTI, the MABI, the latter operating in Budapest and its environs, the Magyar Hajózási Betegség Biztosító Intézet (Hungarian Health Insurance Institute for Shipping) and the miners' mutual funds.

The election processes in the new regulations were in many respects more democratic than before. In the first election taking place in 1929 employees and employers delegated members to national and district self-government bodies by a secret and direct ballot.[244] These bodies of self-government had a real control over social security in the 1930s, making decisions regarding contributions of insurance, qualifying conditions for social security benefits and supervised the work of the administration. The state, however, had considerable control rights, too. The constitution was to be approved by the minister of domestic affairs, who supervised the self-governments and had the right to dissolve them in the case of any legal offence. The administrative body comprised of public servants, who, therefore, were entitled to appropriate protection and were responsible to the minister. The government had the right to veto the budget of the self-government, its investment policy, the operation of health and other institutions of the self-government.[245] The government had a similar but more limited control over the company pension funds.[246]

---

242 Kovrig, Magyar társadalompolitika. 124.

243 For self-governance, see A magyar társadalombiztosítás ötven éve, 1892-1942. Budapest 1943, 66-76.

244 Béla Kovrig, A társadalombiztosítási választások eredményei, in: Társadalombiztosítási Közlöny 1929. május-június. 3; Béla Kovrig, A társadalombiztosítási önkormányzati választások eredményéről, in: Munkaügyi Szemle, 1935. 5. szám, 1-22.

245 Kovrig, Magyar társadalompolitika. 123; Kovrig, A munka védelme a dunai államokban. 218-219, 238-239, 258-260; for the self-governance see the reports of the National Social Security Institute, Az Országos Társadalombiztosító Intézet jelentése az 1940. évi működéséről. Budapest 1941, 10-19.

246 For state supervision, see Gusztáv Ladik, Jóléti intézményeink. Budapest 1940, 265-277, 298-300.

In sum, self-governments of social security funds in Hungary exercised their control function just as effectively as their Western European counterparts in the 1930s. Self-governments could even do some actual work for some time during the Second World War, assessing qualifications and the amount of benefits and participating in the definition of the funds' investment policies.[247]

The communist takeover brought about fundamental changes in the *organizational form* of the Hungarian social security system. The most striking difference in terms of organizational transformation was the fast and practically complete centralisation of the social security system, rather concentrated between the two world wars anyway. The first step was the unification of OTI and MABI in 1949, followed by the merger of other independent institutions such as the OTBA (Országos Tisztviselői Betegsegélyezési Alap, National Clerk's Health Insurance Fund), company pension funds, etc., with the exception of the social security institutions of the railways.[248] And, more importantly, in accordance with the exclusive responsibility of the state, a fundamental principle of the communist welfare system, social security, as the major welfare program, had been taken under state control already by the end of the 1940s. From 1950 onwards social security funds were administered by the SZOT (Szakszervezetek Országos Tanácsa, National Council of Trade Unions) and the SZTK (Szakszervezeti Társadalombiztosítási Központ, Social Security Centre of Trade Unions), the latter fulfilling its task with through local branches. The SZOT had practically no authority to make decisions and was only an administrative executive body. The social security budget was incorporated in the national budget, that is, contributions and expenditures were not administered separately.[249]

The organizational form of social security had been restructured many times. In 1964 the SZOT Társadalombiztosítási Főigazgatósága (SZOT Central Administration for Social Security) was established, taking over the responsibilities of the SZTK alongside with some governmental tasks, such as the drafting of social security laws or supervision. In 1984, social security related responsibilities of trade unions were taken over by Országos Társadalombiztosítási Főigazgatóság (National Central Administration for Social Security), now a formally governmental body. However, despite all these changes, social security was kept under exclusive state control until the fall of the communist regime. Social security expenditures were separated again from the national budget only

247 See the statement of Dr. Oswald Stein, ILO delegates, in his introductory lecture at the First International Social Security Congress at Budapest in 1936, as reported by Kovrig, Magyar társadalompolitika. 123; Kovrig, A munka védelme a dunai államokban. 238-239, 258-260, 273-274.

248 A magyar társadalombiztosítás húsz éve. 6.

249 For the social security after the years following the Second World War, see Laczkó, A magyar munkás- és társadalombiztosítás története. 156-176.

as late as 1989, and a year later the national health service was also financed by the social security schemes.

The increasing role of the state after the Second World War is reflected by the distribution of social security revenues. As we showed earlier, prior to the Second World War only a small percentage of these came from the national budget, which then increased to 37.1% and 43.6% by 1960 and 1980, respectively. This basically conforms to Western European figures. However, with the role of the state as an employer also taken into account, Hungarian figures will significantly surpass Western European ones. The change in the contributions paid by employees is another sign of the new welfare concept of the state. Prior to 1945, with the exception of accident contribution, which was completely covered by employers, half of the contributions was paid by the employees, which dropped to 13-15% in the coming years and both in 1960 and 1980 their level was lagging well behind West European figures in proportion to the total revenues of social security schemes (Table 9, Appendix).[250]

At the end of the 1940s, the communist Gleichschaltung eliminated all types of control over social security by self-governments, and these institutions were not restored again in the communist era. The central role assigned to trade unions in the operation of the welfare system meant, by definition, the violation of the self-government principle, as qualification for social security and trade union membership did not necessarily coincide. Although trade unions and their local branches could have represented the interests of social security clients, acting as a "transmission belt" of the communist party, they were incapable of fulfilling this task. Regarding the control rights of the clients of social security, it was even of higher importance than the lack of self-governments that the state operating the system was not subject to democratic control either, a distinctive feature as compared to the practices of Western European countries. Although the communist regime obviously made efforts to consider the interests of those eligible, no democratic mechanisms were institutionalised to articulate these interests. The communist leadership was hostile even in the era of soft dictatorship to all initiatives that questioned its monopoly – or, rather, its claim to monopoly – in welfare in any way. Authorities, for example, deployed police forces in the 70s to isolate and eliminate the SZETA (Szegényeket Támogató Alap, Fund Aiding the Poor), a civic initiative.[251]

In tandem with the organizational merging of social security into the party state bureaucracy, control mechanisms of the social security system over the clients also took new forms, moreover, social security became part of the mechanism of control and discipline of the one-party state.[252] "Sick pay tricksters" and "pretenders", those not quali-

---

250 A magyar társadalombiztosítás húsz éve. 12; Maltby, Social Insurance in Hungary. 209-210.

251 Deacon, Social policy and socialism. 155.

252 For the broader control functions of the welfare system, see Philip K. Armour and Richard M. Coughlin, Social Control and Social Security: Theory and Research on Capitalist and Communist Nations, in: Social Science Quarterly, 66 (1985) 3, 770-788; Pierson, Beyond the Welfare State? 53-56.

fying for social security benefits and still obtaining them had been fought against already at an early stage, from the speech of Mátyás Rákosi at the Third Congress of the Communist Party in 1948. The intervention of authorities resulting in a long sequence of prosecutions intensified in the following years, with more than 6,000 prosecutions of social security frauds initiated by the authorities in 1952 alone. After 1954 the system became less repressive and prosecutions became scarce but the problem of welfare frauds reappeared on the agenda of the regime from time to time in the next few decades.[253]

Before the Second World War the organizational features of Hungarian social security programs resembled those of the countries following Bismarckian principles. Similarly to Germany and Austria, programs were introduced in the form of compulsory insurance. The specific feature of the Hungarian development is the centralisation that took place within the framework of this system. Moreover, several types of schemes had self-governments before the First World War and in the 1930s, which operated just as democratically as many of their Western European counterparts.

After the Second World War divergence can be observed between Hungary and Western European societies in the organizational forms of social security. These decades saw the state strengthen its role in the operation of social security in most Western European countries. At the same time, the complete nationalisation of social security in Hungary opened up considerably greater influence for the state in this area than anywhere in Western Europe and resulted in an organizational construction unknown there. Until the mid 1980s the operation of social security was in the hands of trade unions, themselves an organic part of the power structure of the party state. In addition, there was no democratic control of any kind over social security schemes. Elected self-governments did not exist and the lack of democratic control over the state administration made even indirect monitoring by clients impossible, thus turning this aspect of social security into the welfare area where divergence from Western Europe was the greatest degree.

---

253 Ferge, Fejezetek a magyar szegénypolitika történetéből. 162-167; Tibor Huszár, Gondolatok a munkaerkölcsről. Budapest 1982, 126-127.

5 DETERMINANTS OF WELFARE DEVELOPMENT

As discussed above, the welfare state not only appeared in all countries of Western Europe in the course of the 19th and 20th centuries, but the expansion of welfare services also took place, sometimes as a rather rapid phenomenon. Several explanations in the international social research have targeted this universal presence of the welfare state. A number of other publications endeavoured to reveal the causes of differences between welfare states, i.e. why welfare institutions were introduced at different times and worked through different mechanisms in Western European countries and why these progressed along different developmental paths. In the following we also turn to the most important determinants of welfare development as well as their interpretations, although regarding the latter it is not possible to give a detailed discussion. Here we may but briefly survey the most important trends and most characteristic arguments in welfare research. Corresponding to our original objective, the most appealing for us to consider is the extent to which the characteristics of Hungarian welfare development support models constructed of the genesis of welfare systems on the basis of Western European findings. Furthermore, we shall also examine the implications of the determinants of welfare development regarding the validity of convergence theories.

Several authors view the emergence of welfare institutions as an international *diffusion* process.[254] It is remarkable how rapidly social security based on the Bismarckian principles diffused to other countries and what advanced forms it took in the proximity of Germany even in less developed countries, more so than in highly developed ones far from it. There are also signs that political decision makers in several countries devoted considerable attention to the developments in Germany in this regard. Moreover, a certain institutionalised form of diffusion is signalled by the visits of several foreign delegations to Germany with the purpose of studying social security programmes.[255]

At the same time, it can be stated that, although ideas of social policy did cross borders, their presence in itself is obviously insufficient for the emergence of welfare programs. The diffusion hypothesis cannot explain why the ideas came to reality in one society and why not in another. To put it more sharply, accepting the existence of diffu-

---

254 David Collier and Richard Messick, Prerequisites versus Diffusion: Testing Alternative Explanations of Social Security Adoption, in: American Political Science Review, 69 (1975), 1299-1315; Harold L. Wilensky et al., Comparative Social Policy. Berkeley 1985, 12-15.

255 Stein Kuhnle, The Growth of Social security Programs in Scandinavia: Outside Influences and Internal Forces, in: Flora and Heidenheimer eds., The Development of Welfare States. 125-150; Hugh Heclo, Modern Social Politics in Britain and Sweden. From Relief to Income Maintenance. New Haven 1974.

sion still leaves the question unanswered: Why was the German example followed early on in some Scandinavian countries for example and why not in Great Britain?[256]

Another characteristic line of interpretation, often referred to as *functionalist*, attributes the emergence and development of the welfare state to socio-economic changes, to the "logic of industrialism".[257] Representatives of this approach argue that, on the one hand, growing needs of populations emerging as a result of industrialisation, required the introduction of state supported welfare institutions from the late 19th century and, in turn, the resources created by industrialisation made this possible. In this respect, social change refers primarily to the decrease in agricultural employment, widespread urbanisation, a separation of labour and instruments of production, and the emergence of a working class, owing no property and concentrated in towns. In the wake of industrialisation, individual and family income were separated, family and kinship ties loosened up and, at the same time, there occurred a growth in the ratio of elderly age groups. Therefore the state helped to address the needs of the social strata more vulnerable to different risk factors through welfare programs. Later, in the course of the 20th century social deprivation was moderated. Then, however, a demand for a well trained, reliable and mobile labour force emerged, the supply of which was greatly facilitated by pension and other welfare programs. Resources brought about by industrialisation included first of all ones created by economic growth, the centralisation and professionalisation of state bureaucracies and thus the increase of their efficiency. In addition, the improving channels of communication could be utilised by both the state bureaucracy and the social classes/groups which were in the process of organising themselves.[258] Some authors stress that the primary mediators of economic development to welfare systems are demographic factors, because both mortality and birth ratios decrease as a result of industrialisation and the ageing population creates ever growing demands for welfare services. It has also been proposed that program duration or program experience is positively correlated with coverage, because once created, programs have a momentum that propels their expansion as a rule. Program duration as a determinant can also be regarded as a bureaucratic correlate of economic development.[259]

It is obvious that there exists a connection between socio-economic development and state welfare activities. In the course of modernisation problems emerged which elicited state social policy as a possible solution and countries more advanced economically

---

256 Wilensky et al., Comparative Social Policy. 1985, 15; Heclo, Modern Social Politics in Britain and Sweden; Kuhnle, The Growth of Social Security Programs in Scandinavia. 126-131.

257 Harold L. Wilensky, The Welfare State and Equality: Structural and Ideological Roots of Public Expenditures. Berkeley 1975; Frederick Pryor, Public Expenditure in Capitalist and Communist Nations. Homewood/Ill. 1968.

258 Harold L. Wilensky, The Welfare State and Equality. Berkeley 1975, 47.

259 Wilensky et al., Comparative Social Policy. 8; Philips Cutright, Political Structure, Economic Development, and National Social Security Programs, in: American Journal of Sociology, 70 (1965), 537-550.

may have had more resources at their disposal for such purposes. At the same time, although a thorough consensus is out of the question, international research on the history of the welfare state seem to refute arguments which attribute the emergence and development of the welfare state directly to social and economic transformations, hypothesising that welfare programs appear at a certain level of modernisation and expand if economic development is continuous, and in contrast, when economic development is hindered, the need for the reduction of welfare systems emerges.[260]

Empirical studies have proven that, although social security laws were indeed introduced in almost all countries of Western Europe between 1880 and 1914, this took place at different levels of socio-economic development. Furthermore, Jens Alber and Gosta Esping-Andersen rightly point out that the first modern welfare, that is, social security systems in the 1880s appeared not in the most industrialised and urbanised England, but in Germany and Austria, then significantly less developed countries.[261]

In addition, while the dates of introduction are concentrated in the three decades prior to First World War, the social security laws passed in each country were different. The creation of social security systems handling similar risks in similar ways could have been, at times, decades apart. These time differences cannot be explained by socio-economic differences, either, as shown empirically with regard to urbanisation and industrialisation levels and the introduction of social security systems in Western Europe.[262]

Differences in the level of modernisation cannot explain differences present at a later stage in welfare policy and welfare institutions. In the interwar period it was the then relatively less advanced Scandinavia where the most dynamic welfare development occurred. Countries at similar levels of economic development would spend different ratios of their domestic product on welfare even after the Second World War and their welfare institutions were also partly different.[263]

Another aspect from which economic determination proves not valid is that the advanced nature of welfare systems becomes a burden for economy in time, which elicits a demand for restrictions. After one hundred years of welfare expansion, the controversy over state welfare systems was greatest not in Scandinavia, where they were the most expanded, but in Great Britain, where welfare expenditures had been relatively low.[264]

Several empirical studies support the secondary role of economic factors and their hypothesised derivates in welfare development. Of these, here we refer to the decomposition analysis of the OECD regarding the largest expansion period, 1960-1975. Ac-

---

260 Cf. Peter Baldwin, The Politics of Social Solidarity. Cambridge 1990, 288-299.

261 Esping-Andersen, The Three Worlds of Welfare Capitalism. 32.

262 Alber, Vom Armenhaus zum Wohlfahrtsstaat. 120-125.

263 Arnold J. Heidenheimer and Hugh Heclo and Carolyn Teich Adams, Comparative Public Policy. New York 1990, 223-224.

264 Esping-Andersen, The Three Worlds of Welfare Capitalism. 32.

cording to the report, in this period, from among the demographic components of growth, the expansion of the population covered by programs and the improvement of the level of services, the latter was the decisive factor in the growth of social expenditures in OECD countries. This explains approximately two thirds of the growth of health expenditures and half that of pension and unemployment insurance. The remaining can be attributed to demographic factors and, to an even smaller extent, to the expansion of the number of those qualified for benefits.[265] This means that the increasing expenditures occurred not in an economically or demographically determined manner but as a result of political decisions aiming to increase benefits, at least between 1960-1975 and in the whole OECD region.[266]

The decisive role of political factors is emphasised in another school of interpretation, called *conflict or class mobilization theory*. This holds that social movements, collective political actors (labour movements, political parties, interest groups) were decisive in the introduction of the first welfare programs as well as in their development. Social problems will enter the state of consciousness only as a result of social struggles and their solution is also possible to such an extent as it is in the interest of the social group which can win on the political battlefield against the other social groups. Naturally, the outcome of this struggle depends on political power relationships, in which a definitive change has been induced by the accomplishment of political democracy, or, more specifically, the expansion of parliamentarism and franchise. The neo-Marxist line of this view holds that this enlivened the political and unionist movements and it were these organisations of the strengthened working class and especially the social democratic movement that forced welfare development to happen.[267] Several researchers belonging to this paradigm argue that the levels of welfare expenditures also depend primarily on whether social democratic parties gain power, because these grow dynamically under such government. One possible political consequence to draw is that the working class is able to abolish exploitation gradually through the reformist politics and welfare programs of its parties and organisations.[268]

The view attributing a determining role to social movements has a wider version that may be regarded as pluralist. This views the political role of social classes and groups besides the workers' movement as also significant. From this viewpoint, democratisation transforms the ability of political groups to assert their interests, but it is not only

---

265 OECD, Social Expenditure, 1960-1990. Problems of Growth and Control. Paris 1985, 29-44.

266 Alber comes to the same conclusion regarding unemployment assistance. Cf. Jens Alber, Government Responses to the Challenge of Unemployment: The Development of Unemployment Insurance in Western Europe, in: Flora and Heidenheimer eds., The Development of Welfare States. 177.

267 Walter Korpi, Social Policy and Distributional Conflict in the Capitalist Democracies, in: West European Politics, 3 (1980) 3, 296-316; Michael Shalev, The Social Democratic Model and Beyond, in: Comparative Social Research, 6 (1983), 315-351.

268 Walter Korpi, The Democratic Class Struggle. London 1983.

the working class that steps forward to gain new social rights, and for redistribution through the welfare system, but other classes, too, or even groups impossible to describe within the class framework, e.g. pensioners. In addition, it was not only workers' parties but conservative ones as well that greatly contributed to the expansion of the welfare state.

There are arguments supporting the importance of political factors in the emergence and development of the welfare state. These factors, however, cannot be narrowed down to the social democratic movement. The creation of the first social security laws conspicuously coincided with the period of the emergence and institutionalisation of the socialist workers' movement, as well demonstrated by the example of Germany. However, the circumstances of the introduction of social security programs in different countries seem to refute any possible simple causal relationship with the demands of the workers' movement surfacing in related laws. On the one hand, it is true in this case, too, that the programs emerged at rather different levels of development regarding social democratic parties and other workers' organisations and unions. There were countries where workers' parties were altogether lacking votes and ones where they had more than half the votes at the time of the introduction of the first social security program.[269] On the other hand, the introduction of social security programs generally took place not as a result of the demands of the socialist workers' movement, but, often, despite its objections.[270] Germany is a case in point: the introduction of the Bismarckian social security laws were opposed by the social democrats because they saw in them an attempt to put off revolutionary ambitions.

J. Alber found that the developmental level of trade unions, important instruments for mobilising workers, had no effect on the introduction of social security programs. Such relationship can be observed as regards the formation of workers' parties, but its validity is strongly curtailed by the lack of correlation between franchise and the first social security laws mentioned above.[271]

In another sense the empirical correspondence between the type of government and early social security laws is obvious. Authoritarian, or, rather, non-parliamentary systems (Germany, Austria, Denmark before 1901, Finland and Sweden) introduced these laws earlier than parliamentary democracies (e.g. France, Belgium, the Netherlands, Norway and the United Kingdom). The difference was remarkably great regarding compulsory insurance schemes. The former countries introduced seven times as many compulsory systems in Western Europe by 1900 than the latter.[272] These non-parliamentary systems, or, to be more exact, their political elites struggling with legitimisa-

[269] Flora and Alber, Modernization, Democratization, and the Development of Welfare States. 65-68.

[270] Christopher Pierson, Beyond the Welfare State? Cambridge 1991. 35.

[271] Alber, Vom Armenhaus zum Wohlfahrtsstaat. 126-133.

[272] Ibidem, 132-133; Gaston Rimlinger, Welfare Policy and Industrialization in Europe, America and Russia. New York 1971.

tion deficits, felt it necessary to legitimate themselves through social security. Moreover, the strong bureaucracies of these countries enabled them to carry out the related organisational and administrative tasks with high efficiency. Legitimisation objectives are also revealed by a high ratio of social security programs being introduced in authoritarian countries immediately before not entirely legitimate elections.[273]

However, it cannot be justified that social democracy or other major political forces would have had a leading role in the development of the welfare state either during the emergence of social security or in later periods. In the period between the turn of the century and First World War democracies with liberal dominance showed the most dynamic development in this respect. Between the two world wars, the situation changed again. In this period development was most rapid when and where social democratic parties were successful at the elections. The most obvious example can be found in Scandinavian countries which, as shown above, were taking large steps in the field of welfare legislation at this time.

After the chronologically successive conservative-liberal-social democratic leadership in welfare development, in the decades following Second World War at least until the mid 1970s, the largest growth period of the welfare state, no leadership by any major political force can be shown in this regard in Western Europe.[274] For a long time in this era, social policy was not among the debated political or ideological issues. It was not only social democrats ascending to governmental positions that supported the expansion of welfare services but conservative parties as well, as shown by the example of the Netherlands or France.[275] Moreover, there are signs that permanent left wing exercise of power was plainly restraining the growth of welfare efforts. In contrast, when parties of the left operated in a very competitive political context, characterised by frequent changes of power with Christian democratic parties, the expansion of welfare programs increased.[276]

Several facts become interpretable when the scope of examination is enriched with a political angle and the focus is extended from the working class and social democracy to all the political forces behind the welfare state and to the nature of their relationships. Esping-Andersen argues that the welfare state could only appear and could only remain solid to this day where, besides workers' groups most in need of social policy, it was possible to include the new middle class (i.e. those parts of the middle strata who did

---

273 Alber, Vom Armenhaus zum Wohlfahrtsstaat. 126-133.

274 For the role of catholic forces in welfare development, see Harold L. Wilensky, Leftism, Catholicism, and Democratic Corporatism: The Role of Political Parties in Recent Welfare State Development, in: Flora and Heidenheimer eds., The Development of Welfare States. 356-358, 368-370; for the same in the Netherlands, see Robert H. Cox, The Development of the Dutch Welfare State. Pittsburgh 1993, 58-95.

275 Hugh Heclo, Toward a New Welfare State?, in: Flora and Heidenheimer eds., The Development of Welfare States. 383-406.

276 Wilensky, Leftism, Catholicism, and Democratic Corporatism. 345-382.

not make their living from their property) among those benefiting from, and thus supporting the welfare system. The middle class was completely incorporated in the social democratic welfare state in Scandinavia. In the conservative welfare model found in its most characteristic form in Germany as well as in France and Austria, the loyalty of the middle class was ensured by separate social security schemes designed for it.[277] Occasionally the behaviour of the rural classes also significantly influenced the development of the welfare state. In Sweden, the rural classes were won very early, in the first half of the century, to be supporters of the welfare state by making it possible for them to receive welfare benefits, quite an unusual move in the era. In contrast, where the often complex conditions of political coalition formation were not present, such as in Great Britain, and where only the lowest income groups received most of the benefits, support for welfare systems was weak and, especially in the last third of the 20th century, welfare programs were questioned.[278]

Based on his empirical study of the post-Second World War era Alber concluded that the leading governmental position of social democratic parties resulted in a somewhat greater degree of increase in welfare expenditures than in the case of other parties.[279] However, this extra contribution was small and it is not enough to provide a basis for the consideration of this political force as the motor of welfare development. Therefore, also considering the findings regarding earlier periods, we can state that social democratic or conservative influences did not determine the emergence and expansion of welfare states. At the same time, it is obvious that different political forces had different welfare preferences. While social democratic parties strongly supported the expansion of coverage, resulting generally in lower benefits, conservatives opted for providing higher level services for smaller segments of societal groups.

Despite all their persuasive powers, interpretations concentrating on political movements cannot appropriately explain all phenomena related to welfare development. One of the most important critical points may be that from the outset there are economic and social transformations behind political processes. For example, the number of voters interested in the increase of state social benefits obviously rose in part because of the growth in the ratio of employees. Also, the influence of individual political parties was greatly affected by societal changes. In addition, there are welfare programs which, though initially related to political decisions, were later more driven by economic and social development. For example, demographic factors operated as a kind of automatism: if, indeed as a result of political decisions, a pension program covered the whole population, pension expenditures automatically increased with the ageing of the popula-

277 Esping-Andersen, The Three Worlds of Welfare Capitalism. 31-33.

278 Ibidem.

279 For the positive role of left wing parties in the development in health insurance in the OECD area between 1930 and 1980, see Walter Korpi, Power, Politics, and State Autonomy in the Development of Social Citizenship: Social Rights during Sickness in Eighteen OECD Countries since 1930, in: American Sociological Review, 54 (1989) 3, 309-328.

tion.[280] Similarly, the introduction of unemployment benefits can be regarded as the outcome of political struggles, but once established, such expenditures increased with the rise of unemployment.[281]

In summary, we can say that the universality of the emergence and the expansion of the welfare state can be best explained by the functionalist interpretation, which concentrates on socio-economic development. However, it is the approaches focusing on political and institutional factors that can grasp the causes of the differences in welfare development in the Western European countries.[282] Therefore it is not surprising that efforts at synthesis do surface in the literature. Perhaps the most significant attempt to bring together different views is presented by Peter Flora. In his integrated pluralist model, constructed in part together with Jens Alber, Flora attempted to find an appropriate place for both socio-economic development and political factors in the interpretation of welfare development.

In this view, the European welfare state emerged as a manifestation of modernisation and as a result of social differentiation as well as social and political mobilisation, based on a developing mass democracy and growing capitalist economy, in sovereign nation states. This is because the social problems accompanying industrialisation and urbanisation will appear to governments as phenomena eliciting action depending on the way they are presented by the activities of parties and other interest groups due to improving communication channels and a growing concentration of the working class.[283] Governments act depending on the developmental characteristics of the given society and especially of state and nation formation. These factors determine the way workers can have their values accepted and also the possibilities for the governments to act.[284]

* * *

The determining factors of the emergence and development of welfare systems in *Hungary* have hardly attracted any attention in research. The only systematic interpretation of the determinants is based on a starting point profoundly different from ours – it argues for the increasing divergence of Hungary from Western Europe in the first half of

---

280 W. J. Mommsen ed., The Emergence of the Welfare State in Britain and Germany, 1850-1950. London 1981; Franz-Xaver Kaufmann and Lutz Leisering, Demographic Challenges in the Welfare State, in: Else Oyen ed., Comparing Welfare States and their Futures. Aldershot 1986, 96-113.

281 Crouch, Social Change in Western Europe. 370.

282 Schmidt, Sozialpolitik. 147.

283 Peter Flora and Jens Alber, Modernization, Democratization, and the Development of Welfare States in Western Europe, in: Flora and Heidenheimer eds., The Development of Welfare States in Europe and America. New Brunswick and London 1981, 42; Peter Flora, Solution or Source of Crises? The Welfare State in Historical Perspective, in: W. J. Mommsen and Wolfgang Mock eds., The Emergence of the Welfare State in Britain and Germany. London 1981, 343-389.

284 Alber, Vom Armenhaus zum Wohlfahrtsstaat. 84-85.

the 20th century.[285] In addition to this, only such Hungarian studies can be mentioned from the past decades that put emphasis on the destitute conditions of the labour force on a mass scale, and also on the importance of the struggle of the working class, and point to the organised power of the working class (or the lack of it) to explain the successes and failures of Hungarian social policy in the pre-Second World War era.[286] As regards the period following, these studies usually take the stance that one of the inherent characteristics of the communist regime is the expansion of social benefits, although Zsuzsa Ferge has highlighted the conflicts between economic objectives and social policy.[287] In contrast, the scarce Western literature on the welfare development of the communist era in general attributes a decisive role to economic factors. The basis of these arguments, however, is the analysis of aggregated data series including several other communist and capitalist countries, thus these studies cannot really contribute to the present discussion.[288] The lack of previous research partly explains why some of the following propositions will be only hypothetical, calling attention to future research tasks rather than giving definitive answers.

In the analysis it seems expedient to pay special attention to the factors surfacing most often among the determinants of Western European welfare development in the literature and debates reviewed above. These can be defined as follows: (1) the level of economic and social development; (2) the age structure of the population; (3) program durations; (4) diffusion processes; and (5) the character of the political system. Of these, the age structure of the population and program duration are often defined as intervening factors between the economy and the welfare sector.

There is undoubtedly a correlation between economic and welfare development also in Hungary in the broad sense, that is, with economic development welfare programs with ever growing scopes were introduced. The ways through which the economy influenced the welfare sector can be traced in several respects. One such important intervening factor was employment structure, the transformation of which had long term consequences in the growth of welfare programs. In the interwar period this was effected primarily by the restratification between industrial employees who qualified for social security benefits and agricultural employees who did not. In addition, in the two decades following the Second World War a similar effect resulted from the decrease in the ratio of the self-employed who did not qualify or did so at a lower level compared to employees. Nevertheless, from the mid 1960s the stratum of the self-employed almost disappeared in Hungary, so from this time on this latter factor cannot be considered as a cause of expansion. Later, however, the transformation of the employment structure

[285] Szikra, Modernizáció és társadalombiztosítás a 20. század elején. 20-23.

[286] Katalin Petrák, A szervezett munkásság küzdelme a korszerű társadalombiztosításért. Budapest 1978.

[287] Zsuzsa Ferge, Társadalompolitikai tanulmányok. Budapest 1980, 68-75.

[288] Pryor, Public Expenditure in Capitalist and Communist Nations; Wilensky, The Welfare State and Equality; Castles, Whatever Happened to the Communist Welfare State? 224-225.

received a special role again, namely as a result of the emergence and growth of the so-called "second economy". From the 1970s, a growing ratio of economic output was produced by this sector, balancing on the borderline of legal and black economy but being more part of the latter in Western terms. No social security benefits were offered by this sector, nor did its performance appear in official economic statistics.

The timing of the emergence and the dynamics of welfare development seems to contradict any closer relationship, however. In the literature on welfare development several indices are used to assess economic and social development and there is no consensus on which can be regarded as most appropriate for this purpose. Still, choosing either per capita GDP or the ratio of agricultural workers, or the degree of urbanisation, the level of socio-economic development does not give a satisfactory explanation for the timing of social security programs. The first programs appeared in Hungary rather early in a Western European comparison, before countries with high industrialisation and urbanisation such as Belgium or Great Britain. Actually, the industrialisation of Hungary was lagging behind all Western European countries in this period, thus the early timing of the welfare programs is an anomaly from the point of view of socio-economically oriented interpretations. In addition, the growth of the welfare sector was not the most rapid when industrialisation and the related transformation of the employment structure progressed at the highest pace, i.e. in the 1950s and 1960s. The correlation was even negative in several periods: the greatest increase of expenditures occurred when the economic development slowed down in the 1970s and 1980s.

An important field related to socio-economic factors is demographic development, which, as shown above, is often considered to be an intervening factor between the economy and the welfare sector. The transformation of the age structure of the population influences the demand for welfare services, as is obvious in the case of pensions or family allowances, where qualification is directly related to age.

Because in most of the period under examination pension expenditure was the major item in the Hungarian social security budget, it may be useful to reveal the components of growth. For this, there is a decomposition analysis available for the period between 1960 and 1989, constructed with methods similar to those used in the OECD statistics referred to above. The results of this analysis show that the increase in pension expenditures was primarily (60.4%) due to the increase in the ratio of those covered, i.e. more and more people became qualified for pension benefits in the age group concerned. This was the result of partly the maturing of earlier qualifications and partly the expansion of rights in the given period, that is, in both cases it was the consequence of political decisions. A significantly lower contribution to the rise in pension expenditures, 22.4% came from the average increase of pension levels relative to the per capita economic output. An even smaller effect can be attributed to the growth of the pensioner-age population (16.7%), while the change in the ratio of the active and inactive population effected only 0.5% of the increase.[289] This shows that, though demographic factors did contribute to the rise in pension expenditures in the period examined, their influence was lagging far behind the consequences of the political decisions aiming at the expansion of rights, similarly to Western Europe. Besides this similarity, however, there is an outstanding difference in comparison with the OECD countries mentioned. While in the latter, over a somewhat shorter period, the improvement of the quality of services contributed approximately to the rise of pension expenditures by half, in Hungary this explained approximately only one quarter of the increase.

In addition, in Hungary the effects of demographic factors was special. On the one hand, while it is usual to consider the changes in the ratio of the old age population almost exclusively as the demographic determinant of welfare expenditures in Western Europe, in Hungary it is not the only factor deserving attention. As shown in one of the previous chapters, in Hungary the relative significance of family and maternity benefits was considerably above Western European levels from the mid 1960s. This had obvious demographic causes, because the birth rate in Hungary in the early 60s was the lowest in the world. The catastrophic demographic situation elicited pronatalist measures, one of the key elements of which was the expansion of cash benefits related to child rearing and maternity. There were political causes responsible for the decline of the birth rate, such as the retributions following the suppressed revolution and the forced collectivisation. Consequently, as another Hungarian characteristic, demographic factors mediated the effects of political and not only economic transformations to the welfare sector.

A further possible intervening factor between the economy and the welfare sector discussed in the literature is program duration, i.e. the number of years a nation has had a program or programs in operation in any important field of social security or considering these fields together. On the one hand, program duration might have an effect on welfare schemes because the bureaucracy of already existing programs is interested in the expansion of benefits. On the other hand, the duration and maturing of programs could contribute to expansion in the case of programs tied to a waiting period, and especially pension insurance. In Hungary, this occurred two decades after the introduction of pension insurance, from the years following the Second World War. At the same time, program durations were already considerable in Hungary in the second half of the century even in a Western European comparison, therefore the modest achievements in welfare reveal the small – or, at least, the fading – significance of this factor, in conformity with several research findings related to Western Europe.

Thus, confirming the research findings of Flora, Alber and others, economic and social factors – such as the ratio of industrial employment and the level of urbanisation – do not explain the beginnings of welfare development in Hungary, either. Although it is obviously not an easy task to weigh the importance of different factors, everything points to the necessity of attributing a more significant role to the demonstration effect

289 Andorka and Tóth, A szociális kiadások és a szociálpolitika Magyarországon. 412-413.

or diffusion in the early emergence of Hungarian welfare programs than what it played in the Western European countries mentioned above. An obvious sign of the transfer of welfare institutions is that the first Hungarian law of social security almost completely adopted the text of the corresponding German law.[290] The influences of German and, later, Austrian legislature may have been enhanced by the close political and traditionally strong cultural ties with the Western parts of the Habsburg empire. Nevertheless, diffusion alone cannot explain the emergence of social security programs and especially the characteristics of later development in Hungary, the same way it was not plausible enough regarding Western Europe. Other factors must be taken into account for a full explanation.

Hungary conforms to the group of those constitutional monarchies that were first to introduce social security laws (Germany, Austria, Denmark and Sweden). This system had a propensity to paternalism, and the extensive state bureaucracy could also greatly help the operation and control of social security systems. Besides, the opponents of market intervention were weak because of the lacking influence of liberal ideology. Political and ideological characteristics help to explain not only the introduction of social security programs but also the nature of early programs. Besides the relatively underdeveloped state of voluntary forms of insurance, the weakness of liberalism also facilitated the introduction of the compulsory form of insurance.

At the same time, Hungarian development contradicts the decisive role the workers' parties – usually characterised by union development and the extension of franchise – would have played in the timing of social security laws. Although early social security legislation focused on workers, this cannot be attributed to their great political influence or high degree of mobilisation. This especially applies to the parliamentary representation of social democracy, which was non-existent in this period. The trade unions and the social democratic party were even in the defensive during the social security legislature of the 1920s. Moreover, at this time there was a retreat in the enfranchisement.[291]

Nevertheless, the political organisation and mobilisation of the workers could have had an indirect influence on welfare development. Although these organisations could not influence legislature directly, they could have inspired the ruling elite to find new ways to legitimate its domination. Social security could be undoubtedly appropriate for this purpose, because it ensured considerable new rights for workers. In addition, despite the small ratio of workers in Hungary as compared to Western Europe, it gained special importance from the marked Hungarian economic emancipation efforts vis-à-vis Austria which concentrated primarily on industrial development.

The peculiarities of political development also explain important features of the welfare system in the interwar period, such as the relatively high welfare expenditures or

---

290 Szikra, Modernizáció és társadalombiztosítás a 20. század elején. 11.

291 For the decisive role of labour movement in the growth of social security, see Petrák, A szervezett munkásság küzdelme a korszerű társadalombiztosításért.

the privileged position of public employees and workers. The Christian parties in power were influenced by the social teaching of the Catholic church, and this was reflected in their welfare efforts. In addition, those in power defined themselves against liberalism and left wing political forces. Opposition to liberalism might explain the considerable welfare tasks the state undertook toward its own employees (also reflecting paternalist traditions) and the state's responsibility in running and controlling social security programs. On the other hand, the objectives of pushing left wing parties into the background and the social integration of the working class were reflected in the relatively high welfare benefits given to the working class. The marked assertion of the greatest landowners' interests in politics can be a major factor of the slow expansion of coverage to agricultural employees.

While in several Western European countries, impending parliamentary elections had tangible effects on the increase of welfare benefits, most of all, pensions, in Hungary this type of electorate cycle was lacking all through the century, rather, some kind of "crisis cycle" can be seen in its place.[292] The appearance of the electorate cycle was hindered from the outset. In addition to the limits of parliamentarism between the world wars, hardly any benefits were paid in the pension program because of the considerable waiting period, and the government could not influence the amount of pensions on the short run as a consequence of the contribution principle. After the Second World War, the elections were mere formal events, which obviously could not play any role in this regard. As early as the first half of the century there were signs that the increase of social benefits were related to political cataclysms. Immediately after the post-First World War revolutions, social security qualifications were re-regulated and certain social security benefits were expanded to cover selected strata of the rural population on the eve and in the first years of the Second World War. Immediately after the Second World War coverage was again increased, and the same occurred in the years following the 1956 revolution. The same pattern is repeated in social expenditures, the highest growth dynamic of which occurred under expressly critical economic and political conditions in Hungary in the late 1980s.

Ideological factors played an important role in the formation of the communist welfare system. As we have seen, this did not mean in the least the dominance of collectivist or egalitarian principles in welfare practices. These notions had been in conflict with other objectives of the regime, such as the privilegisation of certain social strata or the increase of economic output. In addition, in the explanation of post-Second World War welfare development dynamics a considerable role must be attributed to political constraints with which the system was confronted in different forms from time to time, such as the overt opposition of the population in 1956 or the eroding legitimisation of the regime in the late 1980s.

---

292 Maurizio Ferrera, Italy, in: Peter Flora ed., Growth to Limits. Vol. 2. Berlin 1986, 446.

One of the most important lessons learnt from the study of Hungarian welfare development is that neither economic nor other factors are able to explain the characteristics of the emergence and development of welfare programs in themselves, that is, there is no single-cause explanation of the emergence and development of the welfare state. Moreover, the determinants of development changed over time and individual determinants had altered relevance in different periods. On the one hand, it is indubitable that there existed a correlation between socio-economic development and the development of welfare systems in Hungary, too. Economic development and, in its wake, the changes in demographic factors and the maturing of programs contributed to the long term development of social security programs. On the other hand, however, the emergence of welfare programs or their timing is not explained in the least by the level of socio-economic development. In contrast, diffusion, i.e. the demonstration effects of German and Austrian welfare legislature and practice could have had an important role in this. Political factors such as the constitutional monarchy, the legitimisation claims of the elites, the relative weakness of liberalism and national emancipatory efforts promoting industrial development are additional factors influencing the expansion of social security programs to workers at an early date and in a compulsory form. In the interpretation of the interwar development the political constellation, i.e. the political influence of Christian parties and the assertion of landowners' interests, can also be attributed greater weight than economic and social conditions. The welfare system of the communist era was not simply defined by economic and social development, either. The dynamics of the changes were influenced to a much greater degree by ideological and political factors, the inherent contradictions of the communist ideology, crises, and legitimisation efforts. Moreover, at this time even the age structure, a factor traditionally considered as economically and socially determined, transmitted to the welfare system the effects of political decisions and processes.

All this discussed above can have important consequences regarding the study of social convergences. The convergence theory of the 1960s claimed that important features of societies will become increasingly similar in the process of modernisation, independent of political regime and cultural or other characteristics, merely as a result of needs and possibilities created by technological and economic development. However, if economic and social factors do not fully explain Western European welfare development, as shown above, there may have been other factors behind the convergence apparent in the 20th century and especially in its second half in Western Europe. The maturing of social security programs lead to convergence in itself, as demonstrated by the case of coverage: after a period, more and more countries achieved full coverage and afterwards even small rises elsewhere resulted in convergence. This yields a more general consequence for the study of European social convergence, namely, that some important social institutions may have a life cycle: increasing diversity when emerging, because they are not introduced at the same time in every country, and leading to convergence when, in time, more and more countries adopt them. Even more important, though, convergence may have had causes originating in post-Second World War political development. The political systems of Western European countries became more similar than ever before, which promoted a convergence in itself in a field as sensitive to political influence as welfare.

Hungarian welfare development supports this argument, because differences in this area were diminishing in the first half of the 20th century, to be on the rise in the second between Western European societies and Hungary. As regards demographic and family development, discussed elsewhere, convergent and divergent processes were even more pronounced.[293] These trends reflected the changes of the political system, especially its strong divergence from Western Europe following the Second World War. Although Western European and Hungarian welfare development as presented here does not necessarily contradict that economic and technological development may bring about social convergence, it calls attention to the circumstance that convergence can be hindered by differences in political conditions.

293 Béla Tomka, Családfejlődés a 20. századi Magyarországon és Nyugat-Európában: konvergencia vagy divergencia? Budapest 2000; Béla Tomka, Social Integration in 20th Century Europe: Evidences from Hungarian Family Development, in: Journal of Social History, 35 (2001) 2, 327-348; Béla Tomka, Demographic Diversity and Convergence in Europe, 1918-1990: The Hungarian Case, in: Demographic Research, 6 (2002) 2, 17-48.

SUMMARY AND CONCLUSIONS

In this study we examined the development of welfare systems in Hungary and Western European societies in the course of the so-called "short 20th century" (1918-1990) from a long term comparative perspective. An effort was made to incorporate important characteristics besides the changes in expenditures most frequently analysed in the literature and to focus on aspects of analysis allowing for long term investigations as well as the assessment of the dynamics of changes and not biased regarding any welfare system. Accordingly, the most important areas of study included the relative levels of social expenditures, the basic structural characteristics of welfare institutions, social rights, the organisational forms of welfare programs and the realisation of the right to control by the clients of welfare schemes.

Convergent and divergent processes between Hungary and Western European societies were in the focus of our comparison. In addition, largely due to practical considerations, such as the availability of data, it was not the whole of the welfare sector we analysed. Rather, we primarily compared the development of social security systems. Although this may lessen the validity of the results regarding the whole welfare systems, we believe that the central significance of the areas targeted makes them appropriate to show major tendencies of the development of the welfare sector.

The comparison we carried out was asymmetrical in its nature. As a result we could study individual Western European societies to a considerably lesser degree than Hungary. The comparison, however, made it possible to refine some of the existing notions of 20th century Hungarian welfare development and might contribute to a new interpretation of welfare both in the interwar and the communist period.

One result of such significance is related to the level of welfare expenditures in the first half of the 20th century. Due to the lack of appropriate data and methodological problems both in the case of Hungary and Western Europe, considerable difficulties arise in the comparison of welfare efforts. Still, based on the definitions of welfare services most often applied by international organisations (ILO and OECD) and in international research, it can be stated that although Hungary did lag behind Western Europe in welfare expenditures relative to the GDP all through the period examined, the difference is smaller between the world wars – and greater in the second half of the century – than has been supposed in the scarce literature on the subject. Furthermore, when also taking into account the benefits of those in public employment, expenditure levels appear high even in a Western European comparison in the interwar period.

Nevertheless, due to the lack of long-term data sets it is hard to make any definitive statements about the first half of the century regarding the convergence/divergence of

Western European and Hungarian welfare expenditures. Considering trends in Germany, intensifying Hungarian welfare legislation in the late 1920s and in the 1930s as well as the welfare programs launched in this period provide sufficient grounds only to formulate the hypothesis that social insurance and social security expenditures in Hungary converged to those of Western Europe in the 1930s.

In the pre-Second World War period the developmental direction of Hungarian welfare institutions coincided with Western European trends. On the one hand, the early introduction of social security in comparison with Western Europe and the timing of programs in accordance with Western European trends made social security and the assimilated schemes the most important instruments of welfare policy in Hungary, too. In addition, convergence, but at least similarity can be seen in the differentiation of social security programs and in the structure of social security. Although the pace of differentiation is difficult to measure, the maturing of health insurance in Hungary in the first half of the 20th century is obvious, which considerably expanded the types of services financed by social security even in a Western European comparison. Similarly to many countries in Western Europe, the growth of expenditures on pensions was the most rapid in Hungary, too, making it the most important among the programs.

The comparison of the social security development of interwar Hungary and Western European societies in the area of social rights reveals a dichotomy. On the one hand, the available data indicate that the ratio of those covered by social security schemes was rather low in Hungary, and diverged from the Western European patterns. On the other hand, however, the relative level of benefits, especially as regards state employees largely approached the conditions in Western Europe and with the maturing of the generous 1928 pension insurance further convergence could be expected. Interwar Western European trends were also reflected in the changes of the qualifying conditions for social security benefits. The means-test principle was assigned a secondary role behind the insurance principle and specific qualifying conditions such as the age limits and waiting period of pension insurance, or the waiting period of health insurance also approached Western European standards. At the same time, the pattern of coverage with high benefit levels conforms to the Bismarckian tradition, and constitutes the application of the Bismarckian principles to a dominantly agrarian society with a relatively small working class.

Before the Second World War the organisational features of Hungarian social security programs resembled those of the countries following Bismarckian principles. Similarly to Germany and Austria, programs were introduced in the form of compulsory insurance. The unique feature of Hungarian development is the centralisation that took place within the framework of this system. Moreover, several types of schemes had self-governments before the First World War and in the 1930s, which operated just as democratically as many of their Western European counterparts.

Turning to development in the second half of the century, in welfare expenditures the most striking feature of the communist regime just establishing itself was the moderate nature of welfare efforts both compared to Hungary in the interwar period and in international comparison. In terms of social insurance expenditures, social security expenditures and social expenditures relative to the GDP, Hungary diverged from Western Europe until the end of the 1970s. Moreover, in 1980 Hungary was still more behind the West than it had been in 1930.

Regarding the relative levels of Western European and Hungarian welfare expenditures, the 1970s and the 1980s may be seen as the beginning of a new era. In terms of social insurance and social security expenditures the gap was narrowing from the 1970s, a process accelerating at the end of the 1980s. The latter was due to, first, the recession in Hungary that was reflected in the stagnation of the GDP, and, secondly, also the relative stagnation of Western European expenditures. This dynamic does not hold for total social expenditures, as these also show divergence between Hungary and Western Europe in the 1970s and 1980s, with the exception of the last few years of the observed period, mainly due to an increasing uniformity of the countries of Western Europe.

In the realm of institutional features, differences between Western Europe and Hungary began to increase from the middle of the century as well. The changes in the functions of social security were specifically contradictory in communist Hungary. On the one hand, the elimination of traditional institutions of poor relief increased the significance of social security programs, and, on the other, the influence of social policy in other areas, which enjoyed relative autonomy in Western European societies (such as price mechanisms or the labour market), decreased the importance of social security within the whole welfare system. The differentiation of social security programs continued in Hungary but with priorities different than in Western Europe, the prime considerations being related to the efficiency of production and the mobilisation of the work force. The differences in the relative significance of institutions are also shown by the structure of expenditures. In the first two postwar decades, the most important characteristic was the low ratio of pension-related expenditures and the relatively high ratio of those on health care compared to Western Europe. The changes observed between 1960 and 1980 signalled an advancement toward the Western European pattern only in the growth in the proportions of pension expenditures. As regards other expenditure items, the trends were opposite. In contrast to Western Europe, the relative decrease in health expenditures and the opposite process in family benefits represent especially strong divergences. As a significant difference, it is also important to mention the complete lack of unemployment expenditures in Hungary.

After the Second World War the degree of coverage increased at a significant pace in Hungary, resulting in coverage ratios close to the Western European average even in the first decades. In contrast, the politically motivated discrimination of certain social groups, most of all, farmers in the 1950s meant more of a divergence from Western European societies regarding qualifying conditions, even if these could not have been regarded unified for all walks of social security in the given period either. The marked equalization of the level of benefits, even eliminating rights obtained earlier, is another characteristic of the early communist welfare system that had no parallel phenomenon in the West. The level of benefits relative to earnings was also low in comparison to Western Europe. However, the crudest forms of discrimination were eliminated in Hungary in the second half of the 1950s. The growing significance of the solidarity principle of the 1960s and 1970s in the area of qualifying conditions, paired with the rapid increase of the coverage, can be regarded as moves toward universality in accordance with Western European processes. Moreover, in Hungary the whole population was covered by social insurance sooner than in most Western European countries. The relative level of benefits does not turn out so favourably in a Western European comparison, although the ratio of pensions relative to earnings corresponded to the Western average in the early 1980s. By the 1980s in Hungary an increasing number of benefits were granted on the basis of citizenship, and from the mid 1970s all in kind benefits of health care belonged to this category, similarly to the British or Swedish systems. At the same time, other important social security services, e.g. pensions or sick pay were closely tied to the contributions paid, regarding both their qualifying conditions and their levels, which is similar to the Western European welfare type called conservative or corporatist. These similarities to different types of Western European welfare regimes suggest that by the 1980s the Hungarian social insurance system applied a combination of elements customary in Western Europe as qualifying conditions. Although this is not a distinct feature compared to the interwar period, in this area it signals a new convergence to Western Europe, in contrast to the 1950s.

Thus, besides the characteristics discussed earlier (for example the structure of expenditures, the functions of social insurance and the principles of qualification) the Hungarian welfare – or, rather, social security – system shared features both with the Scandinavian social democratic and the continental Western European conservative models by the end of the period under examination. At the same time, after the Second World War a strong divergence began to appear between Hungary and Western European societies with regards to organisational issues in social security and such differences basically persisted all through the communist period. In most Western European countries the state commanded an increasing role in the operation of social security in the decades following the Second World War. However, the complete nationalisation of social security in Hungary allowed considerably greater influence for the state than anywhere in Western Europe and resulted in an organisational construction unknown there. Until the mid 1980s the operation of social security was in the hands of trade unions, themselves an organic part of the power structure of the party state. In addition, there was no democratic control of any kind over social security schemes. Elected self-governments did not exist and the lack of democratic control over the state administration made even indirect monitoring by clients impossible, thus turning this aspect of social security into the welfare area where divergence from Western Europe was of the highest degree.

Furthermore, the historical study of Hungarian welfare systems suggests that there is no single-cause explanation of the rise and evolution of the welfare state. That is, in themselves, neither economic nor other single factors are able to explain the emergence and development of welfare programs. In addition, the determinants of development changed over time as a result of which individual factors had various relevance in different periods. On the one hand, just like in Western Europe, socio-economic development influenced the development of welfare systems in Hungary, too. Economic development and, in its wake, the changes in the demographic structure along with the maturing of social security schemes contributed to the long term development of welfare programs. On the other hand, however, the emergence of welfare programs or the timing of their introduction cannot be attributed to the level of socio-economic development. In contrast, diffusion, i.e. the demonstration effects of German and Austrian welfare legislature and practice could have had an important role in the interpretation. Political factors such as the existence of constitutional monarchy, the legitimisation efforts of the elites, the relative weakness of liberalism and national emancipatory strains vis-à-vis Austria promoting industry are also important elements influencing the introduction of social security programs at an early date, to workers and in a compulsory form. In the interwar period the political constellation, i.e. the political power of Christian parties and the assertion of landowners' interests, can also be attributed greater weight than economic and social conditions. The communist welfare system was not simply determined by economic and social development, either. The dynamics of the changes were influenced to a much greater degree by ideological and political factors, social and political crises, and the legitimisation efforts of the ruling elites.

Evidence discussed above gives at least some ground for considering generalizations regarding the study of social convergences. The convergence theory in its classical formulation of the 1960s suggested that major features of societies become increasingly similar in the process of modernisation, independent of political regime and cultural or other characteristics, merely as a result of needs and possibilities created by economic, and, in particular, technological change. The comparative analysis of welfare development in Hungary and Western European societies contradicts this assumption, because differences were diminishing in the first half of the 20th century, to be on the rise in the second between Western Europe and Hungary. In demographic and family development, discussed elsewhere, convergent and divergent processes in the respective periods appear even more obviously. These trends reflected the changes of the political system, especially its marked divergence between Hungary and Western European societies after the Second World War. Although the evidence presented above does not necessarily contradict the notion that economic and technological change may cause social convergence, it corresponds with the argument that convergence can be hampered by differences in the political system.

Tables

Table 1. Social insurance expenditures in Hungary and Western Europe, 1900-1990 (as % of GDP)

	1900	1910	1920	1930	1940	1950	1960	1970	1980	1990
Hungary “A”				5.2		3.2	5.0	7.5	11.5	14.5
Hungary “B”				1.6	2.7					
Austria				4.4		6.5	8.6	11.9	13.6	16.2
Germany/FRG	1.0	2.6		5.2	4.3	7.3	10.0	12.0	17.4	17.2
France						4.8	6.0	12.2	15.9	17.6
Netherlands				1.5		3.7	7.3	13.9	20.2	20.9
Belgium						6.1	8.6	11.1	17.3	
Switzerland				1.4		4.0	5.4	8.2	10.4	11.4
United Kingdom				4.6		7.1	7.9	9.6	10.0	9.9
Ireland				2.8		5.5	6.6	8.5	15.9	15.7
Sweden				1.1		5.2	7.8	13.8	21.7	28.6
Denmark				2.6		5.9	8.1	11.5	17.9	17.4
Finland				0.7		1.9	4.6	8.7	11.6	12.1
Norway				1.0		3.6	6.6	11.7	15.9	
Italy						3.3	6.5	11.5	13.1	18.5

Notes: Hungary “A”: with pensions of public employees; Hungary “B”: without pensions of public employees. Expenditures on the four major social insurance programmes (occupational injuries, health, old age pension and unemployment insurance) and public health expenditures in Western Europe between 1950 and 1970. The expenditures of Western European countries exclude the special benefits of public employees, war victims benefits and public assistance; Hungary 1950-1990: total current health care expenditures, including public health, but excluding investments in the health care sector; Western Europe 1980-1989: excluding public health expenditures; Germany from 1950: FRG; Germany 1913: including public assistance; Germany 1930-1940: own computation based on the following publication: Statistisches Bundesamt (Hrsg.), Bevölkerung und Wirtschaft, 1872-1972. Stuttgart 1972, 219-224, 260; data of the United Kingdom, Ireland and Denmark referring to the budget year between April 1. and March 31. expressed as percentage of the GDP in the previous year; Western Europe 1989: own estimates based on the following publication: ILO, The cost of social security. Fourteenth international inquiry, 1987-1989. Geneva 1996, 107, 163 (Austria), 108, 164 (Germany), 107, 164 (France), 108, 165 (Netherlands), 109, 165 (United Kingdom), 109, 164 (Switzerland), 108, 165 (Ireland), 109, 164 (Sweden), 107, 163 (Denmark), 107, 164 (Finland), 108, 165 (Norway), 108, 165 (Italy); other dates: Germany 1910: 1913, 1940: 1938; France 1950: 1952, 1970: 1972; Switzerland 1950: 1951; United Kingdom 1980: 1979-80; Ireland 1930: 1929, 1950: 1953; Western Europe 1990: 1989; Hungary 1940: 1939, 1990: 1989.

Sources: Table 2 (Hungary 1930-1990); Peter Flora, Solution or source of crises?, in: W. J. Mommsen ed., The Emergence of the Welfare State in Britain and Germany, 1850-1950. London 1981, 359 (Germany 1913); Statistisches Bundesamt (Hrsg.), Bevölkerung und Wirtschaft, 1872-1972. Stuttgart 1972, 219-224, 260 (Germany 1930-1938); Jens Alber, Vom Armenhaus zum Wohlfahrtsstaat. Frankfurt/M. 1987, 60 (Germany 1900, Western Europe 1930); Peter Flora ed., State, Economy and Society in Western Europe, 1815-1975. Vol. I. Frankfurt/M. 1983, 456 (Western Europe 1950-1970); Wolfram Fischer (Hrsg.), Handbuch der europäischen Wirtschafts- und Sozialgeschichte. Bd. 6. Stuttgart 1987, 217 (Western Europe 1980); ILO, The cost of social security. Fourteenth international inquiry, 1987-1989. Geneva 1996, 107, 163 (Austria 1989), 108, 164 (Germany 1989), 107, 164 (France 1989), 108, 165 (Netherlands 1989), 109, 164 (Switzerland 1989), 109, 165 (United Kingdom 1989), 108, 165 (Ireland 1989), 109, 164 (Sweden 1989), 107, 163 (Denmark 1989), 107, 164 (Finland 1989), 108, 165 (Norway 1989), 108, 165 (Italy 1989).

Table 2. Social insurance expenditures in Hungary, 1930-1990 (billion P and Ft)

	1930	1940	1950	1960	1970	1980	1990
1. Pensions financed by social insurance	0.004	0.062	0.927	4.427	12.985	55.979	156.4
2. Pensions including benefits for public employees	0.229	...	0.927	4.427	12.985	55.979	156.4
3. Cash sickness benefits	0.081	0.083	0.249	1.656	3.750	8.534	21.4
4. Work injury benefits	0.017	0.014					
5. Health care benefits	...	...	0.595	3.782	8.329	17.8	71.0
6. Unemployment benefits	-	-	-	-	-	-	0.8
2+3+4+5+6 Together (1)	0.327	-	1.771	9.865	25.064	82.313	249.6
1+3+4+5+6 Together (2)	0.102	0.158	1.771	9.865	25.064	82.313	249.6
GDP (current prices) (3)	6.304	5.913	55.8	196.7	332.5	718.5	1722.8
(1)/(3)x100	5.2	...	3.2	5.0	7.5	11.5	14.5
(2)/(3)x100	1.6	2.7	3.2	5.0	7.5	11.5	14.5

Notes: Expenditures of the four basic social insurance programmes (work injury, health care, old age, unemployment insurance) and between 1950-1990 the total health care expenditures including public health, but excluding investments in the health care sector; pensions: old age, invalidity and survivors benefits; 1950-1980: including public contributions to the costs of medicines; Pre-WWII expenditures include public employees' benefits only in 1930 and as indicated; Post-WWII social insurance schemes include benefits for public employees; other dates: 1939 (Trianon borders); 1989; 1950 GDP is own estimation based on: United Nations, Statistical Yearbook. 1961. New York 1961, 486 (for methods of estimation, see text); 1930-1940: Net National Product.

Sources: Alexander Eckstein, National Income and Capital Formation in Hungary, 1900-1950, in: Simon Kuznets ed., Income and Wealth. Series V. London 1955, 165 (NNP 1930-1940); Magyar Statisztikai Évkönyv. 1940. Budapest 1941, 59 (social insurance expenditures 1939); Statisztikai Évkönyv. 1970. Budapest 1971, 74-75 (GDP 1960), 419 (social insurance and health care expenditures 1950-1970); Népesség- és társadalomstatisztikai zsebkönyv. 1985. Budapest 1986, 208 (social insurance expenditures 1950-1980); Magyar Statisztikai Évkönyv. 1980. Budapest 1981, 89 (GDP-data 1970-1980), 387 (social insurance expenditures 1980); ILO, International Survey of Social Services. Studies and Reports, Series M., No. 11. Geneva 1933, 361-390 (social insurance expenditures 1930); A magyar állam zárszámadása az 1930-31. évről. Budapest 1932, 60-153 (public employees' pensions 1930); Magyarország nemzeti számlái. Főbb mutatók. 1991. Budapest 1993, 4 (GDP 1989); A Világbank szociálpolitikai jelentése Magyarországról, in: Szociálpolitikai Értesítő, 1992. 2. szám. 54 (social insurance data 1989).

Table 3. Government social spending in Hungary and Western Europe, 1890-1930 (as % of GNP)

	1890	1900	1910	1920	1930
Hungary					0.64
Austria					1.20
Germany/FRG	0.53	0.59			4.96
France	0.54	0.57	0.81	0.64	1.08
Netherlands	0.30	0.39	0.39	1.10	1.15
Belgium	0.22	0.26	0.43	0.52	0.56
Switzerland					1.17
United Kingdom	0.83	1.00	1.39	1.42	2.61
Ireland					3.87
Sweden	0.85	0.85	1.03	1.14	2.60
Denmark	1.11	1.41	1.75	2.71	3.40
Finland	0.71	0.78	0.90	0.85	2.97
Norway	0.95	1.24	1.18	1.09	2.39
Italy					0.10

Notes: Government spending on health care, pensions, unemployment benefits and housing; excluding pensions and other benefits of public employees; Hungary 1930: own computation based on method and sources used by Peter H. Lindert (see in sources).

Sources: Peter H. Lindert, The Rise of Social Spending, 1880-1930, in: Explorations in Economic History, 31 (1994), 10 (Western Europe 1890-1930); Peter H. Lindert, The Rise of Social Spending, 1880-1930. Agricultural History Center, University of California, Davis. Working Paper, No. 68. 1992, 50-84 (methodological and technical details).

Table 4. Social security expenditures in Hungary and Western Europe, 1950-1990 (as % of GDP)

	1950	1960	1970	1980	1990
Hungary	3.8	5.8	8.9	14.2	18.4
Austria	12.4	13.8	18.8	22.4	24.8
Germany/FRG	14.8	15.0	17.0	23.8	22.7
France	12.6	13.4	15.3	26.8	27.1
Netherlands	7.1	11.1	20.0	28.6	28.5
Belgium	12.5	15.3	18.1	25.9	25.6
Switzerland	6.0	7.5	10.1	13.8	14.4
United Kingdom	10.0	11.0	13.8	17.7	17.3
Ireland	8.9	9.6	11.6	21.7	18.9
Sweden	8.3	11.0	18.8	32.0	35.9
Denmark	8.4	11.1	16.6	26.9	28.4
Finland	6.7	8.7	13.1	18.6	21.4
Norway	5.7	9.4	15.5	20.3	
Italy	8.5	11.7	16.3	18.2	23.4

Notes: Social security expenditures based on the ILO definition (see text); data of Denmark, Ireland and the United Kingdom referring to the budget year between April 1. and March 31. expressed as percentage of the GDP in the previous year; other dates: Austria: 1989; Germany: 1989; France: 1952, 1989; Netherlands: 1989; Switzerland: 1951, 1989; United Kingdom: 1974/1975, 1979/1980, 1989; Ireland: 1953, 1989; Sweden: 1989; Denmark: 1974/1975, 1989; Finland: 1989; Italy: 1989.

Sources: Table 5 (Hungary 1950-1990); Peter Flora ed., State, Economy, and Society in Western Europe, 1815-1975. Vol. I. Frankfurt/M. 1983, 456 (Western Europe 1950-1970); ILO, The cost of social security. Eleventh international inquiry, 1978-1980. Geneva 1985, 57-58 (Western Europe 1980); ILO, The cost of social security. Fourteenth international inquiry, 1987-1989. Geneva 1996, 74-75 (Western Europe 1989); ILO, World Labour Report 2000. Income Security and Social Protection in a Changing World. Geneva 2000, 313 (Belgium 1990).

Table 5. Social security expenditures in Hungary, 1950-1990 (billion Ft)

	1950	1960	1970	1980	1990
Cash sickness benefits	0.249	1.656	3.750	8.534	21.4
Unemploym. benefits	-	-	-	-	0.8
Pensions	0.927	4.427	12.985	55.979	156.4
Family allowance	0.303	1.391	2.810	13.561	52.8
Maternity benefits	0.070	0.179	1.952	5.808	15.1
Health care	0.595	3.782	8.329	17.800	71.0
Total (A)	2.144	11.435	29.826	101.68	317.5
GDP (B)	55.8	196.7	332.3	718.5	1722.8
(A)/(B)x100	3.8	5.8	8.9	14.2	18.4

Notes: Social security expenditures based on the ILO definition (see text); total current health care expenditures including public health, but excluding investments in the health care sector; 1950-1980: including public contributions to the costs of medicines; other date: 1989; pensions include not only old age benefits but also invalidity and survivors benefits; cash sickness benefits and health care costs also include work injury benefits; maternity benefits: pre-natal, post-natal and maternity assistance, maternity leave ("gyes" and "gyed"); 1950 GDP is own estimation based on: United Nations, Statistical Yearbook. 1961. New York 1961, 486 (for methods of estimation, see text).

Sources: Statisztikai Évkönyv. 1970. Budapest 1971, 74-75 (GDP 1960), 419 (health care expenditures 1950-1970); Magyar Statisztikai Évkönyv. 1980. Budapest 1981, 89 (GDP data 1970-1980), 387 (health care expenditures 1980); Népesség- és társadalomstatisztikai zsebkönyv. 1985. Budapest 1986, 208 (cash sickness benefits, pension benefits, family allowance, maternity benefits 1950-1980); A Világbank szociálpolitikai jelentése Magyarországról, in: Szociálpolitikai Értesítő, 1992. 2. szám. 54 (Orig. English: International Bank for Reconstruction and Development, Hungary: Reform of social policy and expenditures. Washington DC 1992) (total expenditures 1989); Magyarország nemzeti számlái. Főbb mutatók. 1991. Budapest 1993, 4 (GDP 1989).

Table 6. Social expenditures in Hungary and Western Europe, 1950-1990 (% of GDP)

	1950	1960	1970	1980	1990
Hungary		11.3	13.9	19.6	27.8
Austria		20.4	24.8	32.6	29.2
Germany/FRG	19.2	21.7	24.7	31.0	27.4
France		13.4	16.7	28.3	31.4
Netherlands	13.3	18.9	28.7	40.2	35.1
Belgium		18.3	23.4	36.0	31.6
Switzerland	7.4	8.8	12.5	19.7	22.5
United Kingdom	14.8	15.1	20.0	24.5	24.6
Ireland	14.7	14.0	19.8	29.0	24.3
Sweden	11.3	15.2	25.9	37.9	40.1
Denmark	10.4	14.4	22.6	32.8	35.3
Finland	10.5	12.7	17.2	24.8	31.4
Norway	9.2	13.7	21.1	26.1	34.0
Italy		16.5	21.3	27.0	26.2

Notes: Social expenditures based on the OECD definition (see text): income maintenance (cash sickness benefits, pensions etc.), education and housing expenditures; Western Europe 1950-1990: excluding social benefits specifically designed for public employees; Hungary 1960-1989: including social benefits for public employees; Hungary 1960: excluding housing expenditures; other dates: Hungary: 1989; Denmark: 1951/1952, 1960/1961, 1970/1971; Hungary 1970, 1980, 1989: own computations.

Sources: Gács Endre, Szociális kiadásaink nemzetközi összehasonlításban, in: Statisztikai Szemle, 63 (1985) 12, 1228 (Hungary 1960); Magyarország nemzeti számlái. Főbb mutatók. 1991. Budapest 1993, 85 (social benefits in Hungary 1970); Beruházási Évkönyv. 1980. Budapest 1981, 18 (investments in the welfare sector in Hungary 1970); Népgazdasági mérlegek, 1949-1987. Budapest 1989, 66 (capital depreciation in the welfare sector in Hungary 1970); A lakosság jövedelme és fogyasztása, 1960-1980. Budapest 1984, 21 (social benefits in Hungary financed by companies and cooperatives 1970); A Világbank szociálpolitikai jelentése Magyrországról, in: Szociálpolitikai Értesítő, 1992. 2. szám. 54 (Hungary 1980-1989); Wolfgang Weigel and Anton Amann, Austria, in: Peter Flora ed., Growth to Limits. The Western European Welfare States Since World War II. 4. Berlin and New York 1987, 584 (Austria 1950-1980); Jens Alber, Germany, in: Flora ed., Growth to Limits. Vol. 4. 325 (Germany 1950-1980); OECD, Social Expenditure, 1960-1990. Paris 1985, 80 (France, 1960-1990); Joop Roenbroek and Theo Berben, Netherlands, in: Flora ed., Growth to Limits. Vol. 4. 720 (Netherlands 1950-1980); Jos Berghman and Jan Peeters and Jan Vranken, Belgium, in: Flora ed., Growth to Limits. Vol. 4. 815 (Belgium 1950-1980); Peter Gross and Helmut Puttner, Switzerland, in: Flora ed., Growth to Limits. Vol. 4. 648 (Switzerland 1950-1980); Richard Parry, United Kingdom, in: Flora ed., Growth to Limits. Vol. 4. 393 (United Kingdom 1950-1980); Maria Maguire, Ireland, in: Flora ed., Growth to Limits. Vol. 4. 464 (Ireland 1950-1980); Sven Olsson, Sweden, in: Flora ed., Growth to Limits. Vol. 4. 42 (Sweden 1950-1980); Lars Norby Johansen, Denmark, in: Flora ed., Growth to Limits. Vol. 4. 234 (Denmark 1950-1980); Matti Alestalo and Hannu Uusitalo, Finland, in: Flora ed., Growth to Limits. Vol. 4. 167 (Finland 1950-1980); Stein Kuhnle, Norway, in: Flora ed., Growth to Limits. Vol. 4. 110 (Norway 1950-1980); Mauricio Ferrera, Italy, in: Flora ed., Growth to Limits. Vol. 4. 517 (Italy 1950-1980); OECD, Social Expenditure Statistics of OECD Members Countries. Labour Market and Social Policy Occasional Papers. No. 17. Paris 1996, 19 (social expenditures, Western Europe, 1990); UNESCO, Statistical Yearbook. 1993. Paris 1993, 416-418 (public expenditures on education, Western Europe, 1990); OECD, National Accounts. Main Aggregates, 1960-1997. Vol. I. Paris 1999. (GDP, Western Europe 1990).

Table 7. Introduction of major social security programmes in Hungary and in Western Europe

	Work injury		Health		Old age pension		Unemploy-ment		Family allowance
	Vol.	C.	Vol.	C.	Vol.	C.	Vol.	C.	
Hungary		1907		1891		1928		1957	1938
Austria		1887		1888		1927		1920	1921
Germany/FRG	1871	1884		1883		1889		1927	1954
France	1898	1946	1898	1930	1895	1910	1905	1967	1932
Netherlands		1901		1929		1913	1916	1949	1940
Belgium	1903	1971	1894	1944	1900	1924	1920	1944	1930
Switzerland	1881	1911	1911			1946	1924	1976	1952
United Kingdom	1897	1946		1911	1908	1925		1911	1945
Ireland	1897	1966		1911	1908	1960		1911	1944
Sweden	1901	1916	1891	1953		1913	1934		1947
Denmark	1898	1916	1892	1933	1891	1922	1907		1952
Finland		1895		1963		1937	1917		1948
Norway		1894		1909		1936	1906	1938	1946
Italy		1898	1886	1928	1898	1919		1919	1936

Legend: Vol.: Publically supported voluntary insurance or compulsory insurance with partial benefits; C.: Compulsory insurance; the nominally functioning unemployment insurance scheme ceased to be exist in Hungary in 1988.

Sources: Gábor Gyáni, A szociálpolitika múltja Magyarországon. Budapest 1994, 11-13; Jens Alber, Vom Armenhaus zum Wohlfahrtsstaat. Analysen zur Entwicklung der Sozialversicherung in Westeuropa. Frankfurt/M. 1987, 28 (work injury, health, pension, and unemployment insurance, Western Europe); Christopher Pierson, Beyond the Welfare State. Cambridge 1991, 108 (family allowance, Western Europe).

Table 8. Distribution of social security expenditures in Hungary and Western Europe, 1960-1980 (%)

	1960					1980				
	H.	P.	U.	F.	O.	H.	P.	U.	F.	O.
Hungary	33.1	38.7	-	12.2	16.0	17.5	55.1	-	13.3	14.1
Austria	21.4	49.4	5.1	15.3	8.8	16.3	55.0	3.5	15.4	9.8
Germany/FRG	20.6	59.6	1.8	3.0	14.9	27.9	51.5	7.4	6.2	7.0
France	21.6	30.8	0.2	35.0	12.4	29.7	41.3	6.5	14.4	8.1
Netherlands	19.8	46.5	2.1	18.0	13.6	25.0	51.2	5.0	9.5	9.3
Belgium	16.1	33.2	10.3	21.9	18.5	22.5	32.9	17.8	13.1	13.7
Switzerland	22.2	55.1	0.6	1.2	20.9	22.6	68.9	0.6	0.4	7.5
United Kingdom	-	66.6	4.0	11.5	17.9	35.7	44.4	3.3	12.0	4.6
Ireland	0.6	46.5	13.6	22.5	16.8	43.3	29.4	11.2	5.7	10.4
Sweden	8.4	55.3	2.2	17.7	16.4	31.7	41.4	1.7	7.0	18.2
Denmark	14.8	66.2	8.1	7.3	3.6	29.1	42.0	16.9	4.3	7.6
Finland	2.2	56.7	0.2	34.1	6.8	35.7	48.9	4.3	5.3	5.8
Norway	30.0	42.4	4.1	11.0	12.5	37.3	43.9	2.2	5.8	10.8
Italy	22.3	41.5	3.8	26.2	6.2	37.3	47.1	3.5	5.4	6.7

Abbreviations: H.: health care; P.: pensions; U.: unemployment benefits; F.: family benefits; O.: others.

Notes: Own computations based on the following ILO publication; other dates: United Kingdom 1959-1960; Denmark 1959-1960; Norway 1959-1960; Germany 1960: costs of health care services and in-kind health care benefits together; France 1980: pensions include costs of special family allowance programmes.

Sources: Table 5; Magyar Statisztikai Évkönyv. 1970. Budapest 1971, 419 (Hungary 1960), Népesség- és társadalomstatisztikai zsebkönyv. 208 (Hungary 1980); ILO, The cost of social security. Eleventh international inquiry, 1978-1980. Geneva 1985, 99 (Austria, Belgium), 100 (Denmark, Finland, France, FRG), 101 (Ireland,

Italy, Norway, Netherlands), 102 (Switzerland, Sweden, United Kingdom), 105 (France).

Table 9. Distribution of social security revenues in Hungary and in Western Europe, 1960-1980 (%)

	1960						1980					
	E.	Em.	T.	P.	C.	O.	E.	Em.	T.	P.	C.	O.
Hungary	13.1	49.2	-	37.1	0.1	0.4	14.6	41.1	-	43.6	-	0.6
Austria	23.1	55.8	-	19.0	0.8	1.4	31.3	48.5	-	16.8	0.7	2.7
Germany/FRG	25.9	44.4	1.4	25.0	2.2	1.0	34.0	34.2	-	28.9	0.8	2.0
France	15.6	62.9	2.9	17.7	0.2	0.7	21.0	53.4	1.9	22.2	1.0	0.6
Netherlands	40.8	40.3	-	12.2	6.6	-	33.2	33.2	-	24.7	8.9	-
Belgium	18.5	41.6	0.4	31.2	2.5	5.8	18.3	43.3	0.7	34.6	2.3	0.9
Switzerland	32.9	23.8	-	27.4	9.9	6.1	41.2	25.5	-	25.5	6.0	1.8
United Kingdom	20.0	17.9	-	58.7	1.8	1.6	15.8	26.5	-	54.9	2.8	-
Ireland	5.0	21.2	-	72.8	1.0	-	11.6	26.3	-	61.0	0.2	0.8
Sweden	20.5	11.0	-	66.9	1.6	-	1.0	45.9	-	45.3	7.8	-
Denmark	14.9	10.6	-	74.0	0.5	-	1.8	5.9	-	90.2	2.1	-
Finland	8.9	36.5	-	47.4	7.2	0.1	7.9	44.9	-	41.4	5.8	-
Norway	31.7	26.5	-	40.0	1.5	0.2	21.0	34.6	0.2	42.6	1.4	-
Italy	12.3	59.0	-	23.9	2.6	2.1	10.8	54.8	-	31.9	1.1	1.4

Abbreviations: E.: employees' contributions; Em.: employers' contributions; T.: special taxes; P.: public contributions; C.: capital revenues; O.: others.

Notes: The definition of public health changed in the ILO computations from 1978, with some minor effects on the reporting on sources of revenues; other dates: Hungary 1961; United Kingdom 1959-1960; Denmark 1959-1960; Norway 1959-1960.

Sources: ILO, The cost of social security. Eleventh international inquiry, 1978-1980. Geneva 1985, 52-53 (Hungary), 46-47 (Austria, Belgium, Denmark, Finland), 48-49 (France, FRG, Ireland, Italy), 50-51 (Norway, Netherlands, Switzerland, Sweden, United Kingdom).

Table 10. Coverage of employment injury insurance in Hungary and Western Europe, 1900-1990 (members as percentage of the labour force)

	1900	1910	1920	1930	1940	1950	1960	1970	1980	1990
Hungary				39	35	47	85	97	100	100
Austria	18	26	32	49		53	93	94	97	(100)
Germany/FRG	71	81	72	75	88	92	95	95	97	(100)
France	10	(20)	(20)	52	(53)	(61)	63	85		
Netherlands	-	28	36	51	44	57	66	73		
Belgium		29	32	32	37	55	59	80		
Switzerland	16	(19)	32	39	34	42	52	(56)	55	54
United Kingdom	39	70	80	68	(71)	90	92	94		
Ireland	-	-	-	(65)	(65)	(65)	(65)	74	83	(100)
Sweden	-	20	56	55	62	71	76	79	88	(100)
Denmark	(15)	(40)	(57)	57	(60)	(65)	(80)	81	90	(100)
Finland	7	8	15	31	33	43	53	71	85	69
Norway	13	16	33	29	35	40	73	77	86	88
Italy	(5)	11	(53)	(53)	(53)	56	63	57		

Notes: Numbers in parentheses refer to estimates partly based on legislative regulations and to coverage ratios exceeding 100 per cent of the labour force. For international comparisons the coverage is estimated at 100 per cent; national insurance scheme coverage is estimated at 100 per cent; Hungary 1940: estimates, based on sources indicated below; Hungary 1950-1990: as percentage of total population; data for Western Europe in 1980 are results of interpolation from data for 1975 and 1987; other dates: Hungary 1939, Austria 1989, Germany 1989, France 1955, Switzerland 1989, United Kingdom 1937, Ireland 1989, Sweden 1989, Denmark 1989, Finland 1989, Norway 1989, Italy 1901.

Sources: ILO, International Survey of Social Services. Studies and Reports. Series M., No. 11. Geneva 1933, 363. (Hungary 1930; own computation); Magyar Statisztikai Negyedévi Közlemények, XLIII (1940) 204; Statisztikai Évkönyv. 1940. Budapest 1941, 47 (Hungary 1939; own computation); A társadalombiztosítás fejlődése számokban, 1950-1985. Budapest 1987, 59 (Hungary 1950-1980); Statisztikai Évkönyv. 1990. Budapest 1991, 17 (Hungary 1990); time series of historical statistics, 1867-1992. Vol. I. Budapest 1993, 36 (Hungary; active earners); Peter Flora ed., State, Economy, and Society in Western Europe, 1815-1975. Vol. I. Frankfurt/M. 1983, 461 (Western Europe 1900-1975); ILO, The cost of social security. Fourteenth international inquiry, 1987-1989. Geneva 1996, 202 (Austria 1987, 1989), 203 (Denmark 1987, 1989), 204 (Finland 1987, 1989), 205 (Germany 1987), 206 (Germany 1989), 207 (Ireland 1987, 1989), 213 (Norway 1987), 214 (Norway 1989, Switzerland 1987, 1989), 216 (Sweden 1987, 1989); ILO, Yearbook of labour statistics. 1995. Geneva 1996, 164 (Austria 1987, 1989, Finland 1987, 1989), 165 (Germany 1987, 1989), 166 (Ireland 1987, 1989), 167 (Norway 1987, 1989), 168 (Switzerland 1987, 1989), 169 (Sweden 1987, 1989).

Table 11. Coverage of health insurance in Hungary and Western Europe, 1900-1990 (members as percentage of the labour force)

	1900	1910	1920	1930	1940	1950	1960	1970	1980	1990
Hungary "A"			25	27	27	46	63	79	83	
Hungary "B"						47	85	97	100	100
Austria	18	24	39	59		56	71	85	87	86
Germany/FRG	39	44	53	57	56	57	67	67	84	(100)
France	9	18	17	32	48	60	69	96		
Netherlands	-	-	-	(42)	(42)	54	60	74	85	(100)
Belgium	6	12	21	33	31	57	57	92		
Switzerland	-	-	43	69	86	89	(100)	(100)	(100)	99
United Kingdom	-	-	73	82	90	(100)	(100)	(100)	(100)	(100)
Ireland	-	-	-	34	44	53	58	67	78	89
Sweden	13	27	28	35	49	97	(100)	(100)	(100)	(100)
Denmark	27	54	97	(100)	(100)	(100)	(100	(100)	(100)	(100)
Finland	-	-	-	-	-	-	-	(100)	(100	(100)
Norway	-	-	55	56	86	(100)	(100)	(100)	(100)	(100)
Italy	(6)	(6)	(6)	7	47	44	76	92		

Legend: Hungary "A": persons eligible for cash sickness benefits as percentage of active earners; Hungary "B": insured persons as percentage of total population.

Notes: Numbers in parentheses refer to estimates partly based on legislative regulations and to coverage ratios exceeding 100 per cent of the labour force. For international comparisons the coverage is estimated at 100 per cent; national insurance scheme coverage is estimated at 100 per cent; Hungary "A" 1924-1980: own computations based on sources specified below; Ireland: cash benefit insurance figures (no medical scheme in effect); Netherlands: 1930-1940 only cash benefit scheme in effect; 1970 data refers to cash benefit scheme; Switzerland: pre-1945 data refer to persons insured for medical and/or cash benefits; post-1945 data refer to medical benefits insurance only; Hungary 1940: estimation for 1939 in present territory based on sources specified below; other dates: Hungary 1924, 1939; Austria 1989, Germany 1989, Netherlands 1989, Switzerland 1989, Ireland 1989, Sweden 1989,

Denmark 1989, Finland 1989, Norway 1989; data for Western Europe in 1980 are results of interpolation from data for 1975 and 1987.

Sources: ILO, International Survey of Social Services. Studies and Reports. Series M., No. 11. Geneva 1933, 363-370 (Hungary 1924, 1930; own computation); Statisztikai Negyedévi Közlemények, XLIII (1940), 204 (Hungary 1939; own computation); Statisztikai Évkönyv. 1990. Budapest 1991, 17 (Hungary 1950-1980, insured persons as percentage of total population); Egészségügyi helyzet. 1972. Budapest 1973, 90, 108, 114, 164, 167, 191 (Hungary 1950-1980, insured persons as percentage of total population); A társadalombiztosítás fejlődése számokban, 1950-1985. Budapest 1987, 52-55 (Hungary 1950-1980, persons eligible for cash sickness benefits); Time series of historical statistics, 1867-1992. Vol. I. Budapest 1993, 36 (Hungary, active earners; own computations); Statisztikai Évkönyv. 1990. Budapest 1991, 17 (Hungary 1990); Peter Flora ed., State, Economy, and Society in Western Europe, 1815-1975. Vol. I. Frankfurt/M. 1983, 460 (Western Europe 1900-1975); ILO, The cost of social security. Fourteenth international inquiry, 1987-1989. Geneva 1996, 201 (Austria 1987), 203 (Austria 1989, Denmark 1987, 1989), 204 (Finland 1987, 1989), 205 (Germany 1987), 206 (Ireland 1987, Germany 1989), 207 (Ireland 1989), 211 (Netherlands 1987), 212 (Netherlands 1989), 213 (Norway 1987), 214 (Switzerland 1987, 1989, Norway 1989), 216 (Sweden 1987, 1989); ILO, Yearbook of labour statistics. 1995. Geneva 1996, 164 (Austria 1987, 1989), 165 (Germany 1987, 1989), 166 (Ireland 1987, 1989), 167 (Netherlands 1987, 1989, Norway 1987, 1989), 168 (Switzerland 1987, 1989), 169 (Sweden 1987, 1989).

Table 12. Coverage of pension insurance in Hungary and Western Europe, 1900-1990 (members as percentage of the labour force)

	1900	1910	1920	1930	1940	1950	1960	1970	1980	1990
Hungary				16	30	47	85	97	100	100
Austria		2	(5)	43		51	75	78	82	85
Germany/FRG	53	53	57	69	72	70	82	81	91	(100)
France	(8)	13	14	(36)	48	69	92	93		
Netherlands			52	58	65	64	(100)	(100)	(100)	(100)
Belgium	9	29	(29)	51	(44)	57	89	100		
Switzerland						(100)	(100)	(100)	(100)	(100)
United Kingdom				82	90	94	86	83		
Ireland					44	55	64	71	86	(100)
Sweden			(100)	(100)	(100)	(100)	(100)	(100)	(100)	(100)
Denmark			-	95	(100)	(100)	(100)	(100)	(100)	(100)
Finland					-	(100)	(100)	(100)	(100)	(100)
Norway					-	(100)	(100)	(100)	(100)	(100)
Italy	0	(2)	(38)	38	38	(39)	89	99		

Notes: Numbers in parentheses refer to estimates partly based on legislative regulations and to coverage ratios exceeding 100 per cent of the labour force. For international comparisons the coverage is estimated at 100 per cent; national insurance scheme coverage is estimated at 100 per cent; Hungary 1950-1990: as percentage of total population; Hungary 1940: estimates for 1939 and present territory based on sources specified below; Denmark: 1930 invalidity insurance only; Ireland: up to 1960 survivors insurance only; United Kingdom: 1930-1940 medical benefit insurance data which better reflect the scope of active membership than official pension insurance data including lapsed insurances; data for Western Europe in 1980 are results of interpolation from data for 1975 and 1987; other dates: Hungary 1939; Austria 1925, 1989, Germany 1989, Switzerland 1989, Ireland 1989, Sweden 1989, Denmark 1989, Finland 1989, Norway 1989.

Sources: ILO, Compulsory Pension Insurance. Studies and Reports. Series M., No. 10. Geneva 1933, 106-107 (Hungary 1930); Magyar Statisztikai Évkönyv. 1940. Budapest 1941, 47, 56-57 (Hungary 1940); A társadalombiztosítás fejlődése számokban, 1950-1985. Budapest 1987, 59 (Hungary 1950-1980); Statisztikai Évkönyv. 1990. Budapest 1991, 17 (Hungary 1990); Time series of historical statistics, 1867-1992. Vol. I. Budapest 1993, 36 (Hungary; active earners; own computations); Peter Flora ed., State, Economy, and Society in Western Europe, 1815-1975. Vol. I. Frankfurt/M. 1983, 460 (Western Europe 1900-1975); ILO, The cost of social security. Fourteenth international inquiry, 1987-1989. Geneva 1996, 201 (Austria 1987), 202 (Austria 1989), 203 (Denmark 1987, 1989), 204 (Finland 1987, 1989), 205 (Germany 1987, 1989), 206 (Ireland 1987), 207 (Ireland 1989), 211 (Netherlands 1987), 212 (Netherlands 1989), 213 (Norway 1987, 1989), 215 (Switzerland 1987, 1989), 216 (Sweden 1987, 1989); ILO, Yearbook of labour statistics. 1995. Geneva 1996, 164 (Austria 1987, 1989), 165 (Germany 1987, 1989), 166 (Ireland 1987, 1989), 167 (Netherlands 1987, 1989, Norway 1987, 1989), 168 (Switzerland 1987, 1989).

Table 13. Work injury benefits in Hungary and Western Europe in 1930

	Temporary disability cash benefits	Permanent disability benefits	Partial disability benefits	In kind benefits
Hungary	60% of earnings for the first 10 weeks, thereafter 75%	66.6% of earnings; proportional part of 66.6% if incapacity above 10%; 100% if totally disabled	Proportionate to degree of incapacity	Free medical services and medicines
Germany	66.6% of earnings	66,6% of earnings	Proportionate to degree of incapacity	Free medical care including hospitalization
France	50% of earnings from the 5th day (but only 1/4-1/8 of earnings constitutes the base of the computation if yearly earnings above 8000 francs)	66.6% of earnings	Proportionate to degree of incapacity	Medical care and hospitalization
Netherlands	80%, for max. 43 days	70% of daily earnings	Proportionate to degree of incapacity	Medical care
Belgium	Half of the average daily wage, 66.6% from the 29th day (up to 20000 francs yearly earnings)	66.6% of average earnings; 100% if totally disabled		
Switzerland	80% of earnings from the 3rd day (up to daily maximum of 21 francs)	70% (up to a yearly maximum of 6000 francs); max. 100% if totally disabled	Pension proportionate to degree of incapacity	Medical care and medicines

	Temporary disability cash benefits	Permanent disability benefits	Partial disability benefits	In kind benefits
United Kingdom	50% (max. 30 s), if earnings above 50s; 50% plus the half of the earnings above 25s if earnings below 50s	50% (max. 30 s), if earnings above 50s; 50% plus the half of the earnings above 25s if earnings below 50s	50% (max. 30 s), if earnings above 50s; 50% plus the half of the earnings above 25s if earnings below 50s	None
Ireland	75% of weekly earnings, up to weekly maximum of 35s	75% of weekly earnings, up to weekly maximum of 35s	Half of the difference between earnings prior and after the injury (up to a weekly maximum of 20s)	None
Sweden	1-5 Kr depending on earnings, typically 60-70%	66.6% of yearly earnings (minimum 450 Kr, maximum 3000 Kr)	Partial benefits	Medical care and medicines
Denmark	66.6% of earnings after the 14th week (up to a daily maximum of 4.46 Kr and minimum of 1 Kr)	5-10 times of yearly earnings as a lump-sum payment (up to maximum yearly earnings of 2100 Kr, and minimum 1200 Kr)		Medical care and medicines
Finland	50% of earnings from the 3rd day (up to a maximum of 30 Marka and minimum 5 Marka) 66.6% if dependents	50% of earnings from the 3rd day (up to a maximum of 30 Marka and minimum of 5 Marka) 66.6% if dependents	Proportionate to degree of incapacity	Hospitalization, medicines etc.

	Temporary disability cash benefits	Permanent disability benefits	Partial disability benefits	In kind benefits
Italy	50% of earnings	Compensation equals 6 times the yearly base wage	Compensation equals 6 times the loss of earnings	None

Notes: United Kingdom: Great Britain and Northern Ireland; benefits for industrial employees; Sweden: level of benefits: own computation based on the source indicated below.

Source: ILO, International Survey of Social Services. Studies and Reports. Series M., No. 11. Geneva 1933, 364 (Hungary), 275 (Germany), 199-202 (France), 487-488 (Netherlands), 39-40 (Belgium), 611-612 (Switzerland), 317-318 (Great Britain and Northern Ireland), 393 (Ireland), 581-582 (Sweden), 156-157 (Denmark), 184 (Finland), 415-416 (Italy).

Table 14. Sickness cash benefits and qualifying conditions in Hungary and Western Europe in 1930

	Cash sickness benefits	Cash sickness benefits with allowance (for males)	Waiting period	Maximum period of payment
Hungary	60% of average earnings from the 4th day	60% of average earnings from the 4th day	None	52 weeks
Germany	50% of daily average earnings from the 4th day	Supplements up to 75% from a special fond		26 weeks (exceptionally 52 weeks)
France	50% from the 6th day		60 days	26 weeks
Netherlands	80%, up to daily maximum of 8 Fl. from the 3rd day			26 weeks
Belgium	50% if sickness is longer than 14 days			26 weeks
United Kingdom	Weekly 15 s (men) and 12 s (women) from the 4th day; Lowered: 9 and 7 s 6 d		26 weeks for lowered and 104 weeks for full benefits	26 weeks
Ireland	Weekly 15 s (men) and 12 s (women) from the 4th day; Lowered amount: 9 and 7 s 6 d		26 weeks for lowered and 104 weeks for full benefits	26 weeks

	Cash sickness benefits	Cash sickness benefits with allowance (for males)	Waiting period	Maximum period of payment
Sweden	Same amount for every member and members paying the same contributions; min. 90 öre			
Denmark	0.40-6 Kr from the 4th day, up to a maximum of 80% of daily earnings		6 weeks	26 weeks
Finland	Strongly different			2-6 months
Italy			18 weeks	90-180 days

Notes: Different date: Hungary: 1929; United Kingdom: Great Britain and Northern Ireland; benefits for industrial employees.

Sources: Béla Kovrig, Magyar társadalompolitika, 1920-1945. I. rész. New York 1954, 126 (Hungary); ILO, International Survey of Social Services. Studies and Reports. Series M., No. 11. Geneva 1933, 368 (Hungary), 278 (Germany), 205 (France), 493-494 (Netherlands), 42 (Belgium), 320-321 (Great Britain and Northern Ireland), 395 (Ireland), 585-586 (Sweden), 161 (Denmark), 185 (Finland), 419 (Italy).

Table 15. Old age pension benefits and qualifying conditions in Hungary and Western Europe in 1930 (major features)

	Cash benefits	Minimum age	Waiting period	Others
Hungary	Flat benefit of 120 P a year; plus a yearly 24% of the former total contributions for workers and 19% for white collar employees; 15% supplement for each child under 15	Age 65	400 weeks of contribution	
Germany	72 RM annually as a state pension; 168 RM paid by the insurance institute; 20% of the total contributions paid since 1924; and 4.30 RM per wage-classes for each insured week since the end of 1927	Age 65		120 RM bonus for each child above 15
France	40% of earnings and 10% supplement for 3 children	Age 60	30 years of contribution for full pension; otherwise eligible only for revenues from contributions paid	

	Cash benefits	Minimum age	Waiting period	Others
Netherlands	Yearly benefits: 260 times the average monthly contributions and 11.2% of total contributions paid	Age 65	None	
Belgium	Accumulated contributions and 50% state supplement (up to a maximum of 1200 francs a year)	Age 65 for men and 60 for women	None	
United Kingdom	10 s a week	Age 65	5 years of contribution immediately prior to age 65	
Ireland	0-10 s a week depending on earnings	Age 70		
Sweden	15-70% (males) and 12-56% (females) depending on the length of the insured period	Age 67	No waiting period, however, the length of the insured period determines the sum of the pension	
Denmark	Flat-rate between 402-678 Kr depending on type of residence	Age 65	Means-tested pension payable below 1000 Kr yearly income	

	Cash benefits	Minimum age	Waiting period	Others
Italy	5 times the average yearly contributions and 100 lire plus 30% of total contributions paid as a state supplement	Age 65	Minimum 240 biweekly contri-butions	

Notes: Other date: Hungary 1929; United Kingdom: Great Britain and Northern Ireland; benefits for industrial employees.

Sources: ILO, International Survey of Social Services. Studies and Reports. Series M., No. 11. Geneva 1933, 371 (Hungary), 280-281 (Germany), 206-207 (France), 494-496 (Netherlands), 44-46 (Belgium), 616-618 (Switzerland), 323-324 (Great Britain and Northern Ireland), 398 (Ireland), 587-588 (Sweden), 168-169 (Denmark), 431-432 (Italy).

Table 16. Work injury benefits and qualifying conditions in Hungary and Western Europe in 1981

	Temporal disability cash benefits	Permanent disability benefits	Partial disability benefits	Qualifying conditions	In kind benefits and other characteristics
Hungary	100% of average earnings.	65% of average earnings plus 1% of pension per year of insurance.	60 of earnings for over 67% incapacity; 8% of earnings for 16-24% loss of working capacity, increasing to 30% for 50-67% loss.	Incapacity for any paid work, or 67% of loss of working capacity. No minimum qualifying period.	Free medical services, medicines, and appliances.
Austria	Employer pays 100% of earnings for at least 8 weeks. Thereafter, sick funds pay 50% of covered earnings, plus up to 10% for wife and 5% per child to maximum 75%.	66% of average earnings, plus supplement of 20% of total disability pension if totally disabled. Child supplement 10% for each children. Constant-attendance supplement.	Percentage of full pension corresponding to loss of earning capacity. 14 payments a year.	No minimum qualifying period.	
Germany	100% of total earnings for first 6 weeks; thereafter, 80% for 78 weeks in 3 years.	67% of latest year's earnings, if totally disabled; supplement for severly disabled; child's supplement.	Percent of full pension corresponding to earning capacity loss if 20% or more.	No minimum qualifying period.	Free and comprehensive care, rehabilitation, and appliances.
France	50% of earnings during first 28 days; maximum 344 francs a day. Thereafter, 66%; maximum 458 francs a day.	100% of average earnings during last 12 months, if totally disabled; with minimum and maximum established by formula. Constant-attendance supplement.	Average earnings multiplied by ½ the degree of incapacity for the portion of disability between 10% and 50%, and by 1 ½ for the portion above 50%.	No minimum qualifying period.	All necessary medical care. No cost sharing by patient.

	Temporal disability cash benefits	Permanent disability benefits	Partial disability benefits	Qualifying conditions	In kind benefits and other characteristics
Netherlands	80% of earnings up to daily maximum earnings of 240 guilders.	80% of base amount of 70.29 guilders if 80% disabled. May be increased to 99.84 guilders for married pensioners if daily earned income less than 30% of base amount. Constant-attendance supplement.	20% to 65% of basis for 25% to 80% disability.	No minimum qualifying period. Loss over 80% of earning capacity, or 25% to 80% for partial pension.	Includes general and specialist care, hospitalisation etc.
Belgium	90% of average earnings during year preceding accident.	100% of earnings if totally disabled. Constant-attendance supplement.	Percent of full pension corresponding to degree of incapacity.	No minimum qualifying period.	Medical benefits.
Switzerland	80% of earnings. Maximum benefit 120 francs a day. Payable after 2-day waiting period.	70% of earnings if totally disabled. Maximum benefit 2730 francs a month. Constant-attendance supplement: 30% of earnings.	Percent of full pension corresponding to degree of incapacity.	No minimum qualifying period. Benefits payable for both occupational and non-occupational accidents.	Medical and other necessary care.
United Kingdom	Flat benefit of £23.40 a week, £ 12.75 for wife, £1.25 for each child. Earnings-related supplement. Maximum 85% of earnings.	Up to £44.30 a week if 100% disablement. Dependents' supplements, mobility allowance and constant attendance supplement.	From £8.90 a week for 20% to £39.90 for 90% disability. Special hardship supplement.	No minimum qualifying period.	Medical benefits provided under the National Health Service.

	Temporal disability cash benefits	Permanent disability benefits	Partial disability benefits	Qualifying conditions	In kind benefits and other characteristics
Ireland	£28.20 a week plus 40% to 20% (according to duration) of earnings between £14 and £140 a week. Dependents' supplements. Reduced rates for married women and youths. 0-14 days waiting period.	Same as temporary disability benefit. Unemployability supplement and constant-attendance supplement. Reduced rates for women and youths.	Percent of full pension proportionate to degree of disability for 20% to 99% incapacity.	No minimum qualifying period.	Medical and other necessary care and appliances.
Sweden	90% of income up to 7.5 times the base amount. (100% of income up to 7.5 times the base amount if incapacity lasts more than 90 days.)	If 100% disabled, 100% of income up to maximum 7.5 times the base amount.	If 1/15 or more disabled, proportionate to degree of disability.	No minimum qualifying period.	Patient pays 25 kr per visit. Free hospitalisation, free medicine for some chronic diseases, other medicine costs max. 40 Kr per purchase.
Denmark	90% of earnings, up to 236 kr a day, 6 days a week.	¾ of average earnings if totally disabled.	Percent of full pension proportionate to loss of earning capacity if 50% to 99% disabled. Lump sum (equal to commuted value of partial pension) if 5% to 49% disabled.	No minimum qualifying period.	Most medical services obtained under ordinary sickness insurance.

	Temporal disability cash benefits	Permanent disability benefits	Partial disability benefits	Qualifying conditions	In kind benefits and other characteristics
Finland	60% of earnings. Supplement for 1 or more dependents: 20% of earnings.	Basic pension equals to 30% of earnings, plus supplement up to 30% of earnings depending on degree of disability. Dependents' supplement: 30% of above for 1, 20% for each additional dependent. Constant-attendance supplement.	Proportional partial disability benefits for temporary incapacity of 20% or more.	No minimum qualifying period.	Medical and other necessary care and appliances.
Norway	100% of covered earnings. Maximum 521 kr a day. Self-employed: 65% of assessed covered earnings after 14 days waiting.	100% of base amount if totally disabled.	Percent of full pension proportionate to degree of disability. (Lump-sum payment if disability less than 30%.) Supplements for spouse and children. Constant-attendance supplement.	No minimum qualifying period.	Comprehensive care; no sharing of costs by patient.
Italy	60% of earnings for first 90 days of disability; 75% thereafter.	100% of earnings in the prior year if totally disabled. Constant-attendance supplement. Dependents' supplements: 5% of pension for wife and each child.	If 65-99% disabled, pension proportionate to degree of incapacity. If 11-64% disabled, pension equals 50% to 98% of the degree of incapacity.	No minimum qualifying period.	Medical and other necessary care.

Notes: Major features; benefits for workers.

Source: U.S. Department of Health and Human Services ed., Social Security Throughout the World. 1981. Washington D.C. 1982, 108-109 (Hungary), 90-91, 12-13 (Austria), (Germany), 82-83 (France), 176-177 (Netherlands), 20-21 (Belgium), 236-237 (Switzerland), 260-261 (United Kingdom), 120-121 (Ireland), 234-235 (Sweden), 64-65 (Denmark), 80-81 (Finland), 186-187 (Norway), 124-125 (Italy).

Table 17. Health insurance cash and medical benefits and qualifying conditions in Hungary and Western Europe in 1981

	Cash sickness benefits	Qualifying period/ conditions (waiting period) for cash benefits. Duration of payments	Medical benefits	Qualifying conditions for medical benefits. Duration of benefits	Medical benefits for dependents
Hungary	65% of earnings, or 75 if 2 years of continuous employment. Max. benefit 400 forints a day.	Currently in insured employment. Payable from 1st day of incapacity for up to 1 year.	Medical services provided through public health services. Includes comprehensive care. Patients pay 15% of cost of medicines and appliances. Life-saving medicines and those for maternity and infant care are free of charge.	No special qualifying conditions. Duration: No limit.	Same as for insured.
Austria	Employer pays 100% of earnings for first 4-10 weeks for wage earners and 6-12 weeks for salaried employees, according to workers' length of service in establishment. Thereafter, sick funds pay 50% of covered earnings, plus up to 10% for wife and 5% per child to maximum 75%.	Currently in covered employment (funds may require 6 months of contribution in last year for optional benefits only.)	Includes general and specialist care, hospitalisation etc. Patients pay 15 schilling per prescription up to 20% of dental care cost; some cost sharing for appliances. (Exceptions for patients of limited means.)	See cash benefits. Duration: No limit.	Same as for insured persons, but with 10% cost sharing (except for maternity) during first 4 weeks of hospitalisation.

	Cash sickness benefits	Qualifying period/ conditions (waiting period) for cash benefits. Duration of payments	Medical benefits	Qualifying conditions for medical benefits. Duration of benefits	Medical benefits for dependents
Germany	Employer pays 100% of total earnings for first 6 weeks. Thereafter, sickness funds pay 80% of covered earnings for up to 78 weeks in 3 years.	Membership in sickness fund. No minimum employment period.	Includes comprehensive medical and dental care, hospitalisation, prescribed medicines etc. Patients pay DM 1 per prescription.	No minimum employment period. Duration: No limit.	Same as for insured.
France	50% of covered earnings, rising 66.6% after 30 days if 3 or more children. Benefits reduced during hospitalisation if less than 2 dependent children or relatives.	200 hours of employment in last 3 months, or 6 months at minimum wage. For extended cash benefits, entry into insurance 12 months before incapacity and 800 hours of employment. Payable after 3-day waiting period for up to 1 months. Extended up to 3 years if chronic illness. Max. 96 francs a day or 127 francs if 3 or more children.	Cash refunds of part of medical expenses. Includes general and specialist care, hospitalisation etc. Insured normally pays for services, and is reimbursed by local sickness fund for 75% of amounts provided for such services in negotiated and approved fee schedules.	600 hours of paid employment in last 6 months, or 6 months at minimum wage; 200 hours in last quarter, or 120 hours in last month. (No minimum qualifying period during first 3 months after entry into insurance.) Duration: No limit.	Same as for insured.

	Cash sickness benefits	Qualifying period/ conditions (waiting period) for cash benefits. Duration of payments	Medical benefits	Qualifying conditions for medical benefits. Duration of benefits	Medical benefits for dependents
Netherlands	80% of earnings up to daily maximum earnings of 240 guilders.	Fully incapable of doing one's own work. Payable after 2-day waiting period for up to 52 weeks.	Includes general and specialist care, hospitalisation etc. Patients share cost of maternity and long-term hospitalisation. (No cost sharing if income below specified limit.)	Membership in approved sickness fund. No minimum contribution period for compulsory insured. Max. duration: No limit.	Same as for insured person.
Belgium	60% of earnings; max. 1352 francs a day. Employer pays 100% of earnings for up to 30 days.	6 months of insurance, including 120 days of actual or credited work and insurance during last quarter. Duration: 1 year.	Cash refunds of part or all medical expenses. Includes general and specialist care, hospitalisation etc. Insured normally pays for health care, and is then reimbursed by fund up to 75% of cost of doctor's fees and 50-100% of medicines. The insured pays 125 francs a day for hospitalisation. Pensioners, widows, orphans are reimbursed 100% for most medical benefits.	See cash benefits. Duration: No limit.	Same as for insured person.

	Cash sickness benefits	Qualifying period/ conditions (waiting period) for cash benefits. Duration of payments	Medical benefits	Qualifying conditions for medical benefits. Duration of benefits	Medical benefits for dependents
Switzerland	Federal minimum applicable to all funds, 2 francs a day. Higher benefits according to fund and rate for which person is insured.	Funds may require 3 months of membership. Payable after waiting period of not over 3 days for at least 720 in 900 consecutive days.	Includes general and specialist care, hospitalisation etc. Patients pay up to 10%, on the average, of medical and pharmaceutical expenses, plus certain fixed fees for first treatment in adult illness.	See cash benefits. Duration: No limit is permitted except at least 720 in 900 days for hospitalisation.	Receive same benefits in own right if member of fund. Otherwise, no benefit even if family head insured.
United Kingdom	Flat benefit of £20.65 a week, £12.75 for wife or dependent husband, 1.25 for each child. Earnings-related supplement up to £14.00 a week. Maximum 85% of earnings.	26 weeks of contributions; plus 50 weeks paid or credited in last year (reduced benefits if 26 to 49 weeks). Payable after 3-day waiting period for up to 6 months.	Includes GP care, specialist services, hospitalisation etc. Patients pay full cost up to £5 for routine dental treatment, 0.20 for each prescription, 30 for dentures. Children, new mothers and certain low-income persons are exempt from fees.	See cash benefits. Duration: No limit.	Same as for family head.

	Cash sickness benefits	Qualifying period/ conditions (waiting period) for cash benefits. Duration of payments	Medical benefits	Qualifying conditions for medical benefits. Duration of benefits	Medical benefits for dependents
Ireland	£20.45 a week, plus £13.25 for adult dependent; £5.95 each for 1st and 2nd child; £4.90 for each other child; plus 40% or 20% of earnings between £14 and £140 a week.	26 weeks of paid contributions and 48 weeks paid or credited in last year. Payable after 3-day waiting period for up to 52 weeks; duration unlimited after 156 weeks of paid contributions until age 66.	Includes general and specialist care, hospitalisation etc. Patients pay hospital consultant's fees if annual income above £7000.	Available to any person whose income is below £7000 a year, those medically needy and small farmers.	Same as for insured.
Sweden	90% of income up to 7.5 times the base amount. Max. daily benefit 298 Kr; min. 15 Kr. Benefits taxed for contribution purposes.	No minimum qualifying period. Payable from 2nd day of incapacity for duration of illness, 7 days a week.	Doctor's consultation, patient pays 25 Kr per visit. Free hospitalisation, free medicine for some chronic diseases, other medicine costs max. 40 Kr per purchase. Pensioners limited to 365 days of free hospital care, thereafter 30 Kr per day.	No minimum qualifying period.	Same as for family head.

	Cash sickness benefits	Qualifying period/ conditions (waiting period) for cash benefits. Duration of payments	Medical benefits	Qualifying conditions for medical benefits. Duration of benefits	Medical benefits for dependents
Denmark	90% of earnings, up to 236 kr a day, 6 days a week.	Income from employment or self-employment. Others may insure voluntarily. No time limit.	Free service benefits (financed through general revenue funds) include general and specialist care, hospitalisation, 50% to 75% of cost of certain medicines etc.	Resident of metropolitan Denmark. If moving from another country, 6 weeks' qualifying period. Duration: No limit.	Same as for family head.
Finland	0.15% of annual income below 25000 marks a day; min. and max.: 20 and 38.25 marks a day. Supplements: 15% for wife, 10% for each child under age 16; maximum supplement 50%.	Employment during last 3 months, unless involuntarily unemployed. Payable after a 7-day waiting period for up to 300 days.	Cash refunds of part of medical expenses. Includes 60% of doctor's fees, 50% of cost of medicines over 11 marks etc. Hospitalisation available free or for small fee.	Residence in country.	Same as for family head.
Norway	100% of covered earnings, max. 521 kr a day, 6 days a week. Self-employed 65% of assessed covered earnings.	14 days of insurance. Payable from 1st day of incapacity, up to 312 days, for self-employed after 14 days waiting period.	Cash refunds of part or all of medical expenses. Includes 51% to 100% of cost of doctors' fees, free care in public hospitals etc.	Currently insured. Duration: No limit.	Insured in their own right (since based on residency).

	Cash sickness benefits	Qualifying period/ conditions (waiting period) for cash benefits. Duration of payments	Medical benefits	Qualifying conditions for medical benefits. Duration of benefits	Medical benefits for dependents
Italy	50% of earnings for 1-20 days; 66.6% thereafter. Salaried employees not entitled to cash benefits.	Currently insured. No minimum qualifying period for wage earners. Payable after 3-day waiting period for up to 180 days.	Includes general and specialist care, hospitalisation etc. Patients pay 200-600 lire for nonessential prescribed medicines.	Currently insured. No minimum qualifying period for wage earners. No qualifying period for hospitalisation. Duration: No limit.	Same as for insured.

Notes: Major features; benefits for workers.

Source: U.S. Department of Health and Human Services ed., Social Security Throughout the World. 1981. Washington D.C. 1982, 108-109 (Hungary), 12-13 (Austria), 90-91 (Germany), 82-83 (France), 176-177 (Netherlands), 20-21 (Belgium), 236-237 (Switzerland), 260-261 (United Kingdom), 120-121 (Ireland), 234-235 (Sweden), 64-65 (Denmark), 80-81 (Finland), 186-187 (Norway), 124-125 (Italy).

Table 18. Old-age pension benefits and qualifying conditions in Hungary and Western Europe in 1981

	Benefits	Qualifying conditions (waiting period)	Other characteristics
Hungary	33% of average earnings during best 3 of 5 years, rising in steps to 75% for 42 years of coverage. Increment of pension for manual workers; deferral past retirement age (7% of pension for each year up to maximum of 95% of earnings). Spouse's supplement: If pension below 1820 forints, 680 forints a month; if above, amount necessary to raise pension to 2320 forints a month.	Age 60 (men) or 55 (women); reduced for unhealthy work. 10 years of employment; 20 years for those retiring after 1990.	Automatic annual adjustment: 2%, minimum 70 forints.
Austria	30% of average earnings in last 5 years, or, if higher, the 60 months before age 45 (recorded earnings revalued for national average earnings changes); plus 0.6% of earnings for each of first 10 insurance years; 0.9% for 11-20, 1.2% for 21-30, and 1.5% for 31-45 insurance years. Up to 10% added if pension plus supplements below 50% of earnings; max. pension 79.5% of covered earnings. Increment for deferred pension: 2% a year (women' age 61-64); 3% a year (men' age 66-70);	Age 65 (men) or 60 (women). 180 months of contribution, including 12 months in last 3 years. Payable at age 60 (men) or 55 (women) after year of sickness or unemployment, or 35 years of contribution with 24 months in last 3 years.	14 payments a year. Automatic annual adjustment of pensions for changes in national-average covered earnings.

	Benefits	Qualifying conditions (waiting period)	Other characteristics
Austria (cont.)	5% a year thereafter. Child supplement: 5% of earnings for each child under 18. Income-tested allowance.		
Ger-many	1.5% of worker's as-sessed wages times years of insurance (including credited periods of incapacity, unemploy-ment, schooling after age 16). Deferred pension increment: 0.6% per month worked between age 65 and 67.	Age 63 with 35 years of insurance, or 65 with 15 years; payable at age 60 if unemployed 1 year in last 18 months, or woman with 10 years of insurance in last 20. 180 months of contribution.	'Assessed wages' repre-sent ratio of worker's earnings to national average over period of coverage, multiplied by current 'general compu-tation base'. Latter is changed annually and corresponds to average of national wage levels in 3 prior calendar years. 1981 computation base: DM 22787.
France	25% of average earnings in 10 highest years after 1947, or 50% if entitled to hypothetical credits. Past earnings revalued for wage changes. Increment of 1.25% for each quarter pension deferred beyond age 60 (30% at age 61, 50% at age 65 etc.). Reduced pension: 1/150 of full pension times quarters of insurance. Minimum: 8500 francs a year if 60 quarters; oth-erwise, proportionately reduced.	Age 60 and 37.5 years (150 quarters) of coverage; otherwise, proportionately reduced. Credited at age 60 as if age 65 to: manual worker with long service, invalidity etc.	Spouse's supplement, child's supplement, old-age allowance. Automatic semi-annual adjustment of pensions for changes in national average wages.

	Benefits	Qualifying conditions (waiting period)	Other characteristics
Netherlands	Full pension 1098 guilders a month. Supplement for wife of any age: 479 guilders a month. Pension reduced by 2% for each unexcused year of non-contribution.	Age 65. Contributions paid each year from age 15 through 64, for full pension; otherwise reduced pension (no decrements for pre-1957 period if resident citizen with 6 years of residence after age 59).	Automatic adjustment of all pensions twice a year for changes in net minimum wages.
Belgium	Full pension 60% of average lifetime earnings, or 75% for married couple; in computing pension, past earnings are revalued for wage and price changes. Reduced pension if full qualifying period not met: Percent of full pension corresponding to portion of period completed. Early retirement: Unemployment benefit plus 1000 francs a month. Minimum pensions: 189648 francs a year (236988 francs if married couple).	Age 65 (men) or 60 (women); payable up to 5 years earlier, with 5% reduction per year. For full pension, actual or credited employment totalling 45 years for men, 40 for women (credited if work in all years since 1946); otherwise, proportionately reduced pension. Early retirement benefit paid at age 60 (men) or 55 (women) if unemployed for more than 1 year.	Automatic periodic adjustment of pensions for price changes. Annual lump sum for wage changes and other economic factors. Means-tested allowance. Vacation allowance.
Switzerland	Monthly pension: 805 of minimum monthly pension plus 1.67% of average annual revalued earnings. Minimum and maximum pension, 550 and 1100 francs a month. Couple's pension, 150% of single pension if wife age 62 or more than 50% disabled.	Age 65 (men) or 62 (women). For full pension, contributions in all years since 1948 (or age 21); for partial pension, at least 1 year of contribution.	Pensions reviewed every two years for increases in price and wage indexes.

	Benefits	Qualifying conditions (waiting period)	Other characteristics
Swit-zerland (cont.)	Partial pension: Percent of full pension related to number of years since 1948 (or age 20) in which contributions were paid. Dependents' supplements: Wife, 30% of pension if age 48-61. Each child under age 18 (25 if student), 40% of pension. Constant-attendance supplement: 80% minimum pension. Means-tested allowance payable to aged citizens ineligible for benefits or with benefits below specified limits.		
United King-dom	Basic component £27.15 a week, plus earnings-related component of 1.25% of covered earnings per year. Dependent's supplements: £16.30 a week for dependent wife, £7.50 for each child. Increment for deferred retirement: 1/7% of pension for each week worker delays retirement between age 65-70 (men) or 60-65 (women). Old-persons' pension. Age addition if age 80 or over.	Age 65 (men) or age 60 (women). 50 weeks of paid contributions before. 50-52 weeks of paid contributions before 1978; plus 'reckonable years' equal to approximately 9/10ths of the years in working life. Pensions reduced proportionately with shorter coverage.	Pension adjusted annually according to price changes.

	Benefits	Qualifying conditions (waiting period)	Other characteristics
Ireland	Flat-rate pension of £24.50 a week, increased by £1.75 a week if age 80 or over. Dependents' supplement: £15.65 a week for adult dependent under age 66; £6.40 each for 1st and 2nd child under age 18 (21 if student); £5.30 for each other eligible child. Non-contributory means-tested allowance for old age pensioner, blind person: Up to £21 a week payable at age 66 to persons whose other means are below £1196 a year. Living-alone allowance.	Age 66 and initial coverage before age 56. 156 weeks of paid contributions, and annual average of 48 weeks paid or credited (reduced pension if 24-47 weeks).	
Sweden	Universal old-age pension: 95% of current base amount, or 155% for aged couple (1274 kr or 2079 kr a month). Increment of 0.6% of pension per month of deferral until age 70. Supplements: 41% of base amount if ineligible for earnings-related pension; 25% of base amount per child under age 16; housing-supplement. Earnings-related pension: 60% of the difference between average annual covered earnings and the base amount, based on coverage since 1960.	Age 65. Universal pension, no contribution or income test. Earnings-related pension, 3 years' coverage. Retirement unnecessary for either pension. Partial pension (age 60-64) reduced work schedule, employed at least 5 to 12 months before entitlement, and 10 years' earnings-related coverage after age 45.	Automatic adjustment for price changes.

	Benefits	Qualifying conditions (waiting period)	Other characteristics
Sweden (cont.)	Increment of 0.6% of pension per month of deferral until age 70. Partial pension: 65 of income loss connected with changeover to part-time work.		
Denmark	Universal old-age pension: 2098 kr a month (single) or 3854 kr (aged couple); increased 5% for each 6 months deferment until age 70. Supplements (income-tested): 387 kr a month (single) or 832 kr (aged couple); spouse under age 62, 178 kr; wife age 62-66 1080 kr a month. Supplements for children. Voluntary early retirement. Employment-related old-age pension: 100 kr times years of contribution (if covered in 1965, calculated on more favourable terms). Max.: 4000 kr a year after 40 years, or 35 years if covered in 1965. 5% increment per half-year deferral of pension until age 70.	Universal pension, age 67 (men, married women), 62 (single women), or 55 (adverse social or employment-related circumstances); full pension, 40 years' residence, or 10 years if 5 of these immediately prior to age 67; citizenship. Employment-related pension: age 67; 3 years' contribution. Retirement unnecessary for either pension. Voluntary early retirement: Resident aged 60 (including self-employed) and member of unemployment fund for 5 years during last 10 years.	Automatic adjustment of pensions each 6 months for price changes.
Finland	Universal old-age pension: 215 marks a month, or 430 marks for aged couple. Increment of 12.5% of pension for each year deferred after 65; maximum 62.5%.	Universal pension, age 65 and 5 years of residence. Means-tested allowance, age 65. Employment-related pension, age 65 and retirement from covered	Automatic adjustment of pensions and supplements for changes in cost-of-living index.

	Benefits	Qualifying conditions (waiting period)	Other characteristics
Finland (cont.)	Small supplement for each child. Means-tested allowance: Up to 971 marks a month. Supplements to allowance: 30% for wife age 60-64 or invalid. Old-age, attendance supplement. Employment-related pension: Full pension, 1/8% of average monthly earnings times months of coverage as if worked until age 65. Partial pension, ½ of full pension.	employment. 40 years' coverage for full pension. All pensions, early retirement if age 60 and unemployment at least 200 days during last 60 weeks.	
Norway	Universal old-age pension: Up to 100% of base amount if single, 150% for aged couple. Supplements: 50% of pension for spouse not drawing old-age pension; 25% of base amount for each child under age 18; up to 44% of base amount if ineligible for earnings-related pension. Deferred pension, ¾% increase per month of deferral until age 70. Earnings-related old-age pension: 45% of the difference between average covered earnings and the base amount, based on coverage since 1967 (full pension, 20 years' coverage until 1987, thereafter increasing year by year to 40).	Both pensions, age 67; income limit (pension plus wages) 80% of former earnings; no limit from age 70. Universal pension, 3 years coverage ages 16-66 (full pension 40 years coverage, reduced for shorter coverage). Earnings-related pension, 3 years earnings above base amount.	Automatic adjustment of pensions for changes in cost-of-living index and income levels.

	Benefits	Qualifying conditions (waiting period)	Other characteristics
Nor-way (cont.)	For shorter coverage, pension reduced proportionally. Deferred pension, see universal pension above.		
Italy	2% of highest 3 of last 10 years times number of years of contribution, up to maximum of 80% for those with 40 years of contribution. Minimum pension: 188 250 lire a month (200 450 lire with 15 or more years of contribution). Lower for self-employed. Dependents' supplement. Means-tested old-age benefit: Up to 119850 lire a month payable at age 65, if resident citizen.	Age 60 (men) or 55 (women), and 15 years of coverage. Pre-retirement pension at 57 and 52 respectively, if unemployed due to economic crisis or industrial reorganization. Also payable at any age after 35 years of contribution. Earnings reduce benefits above the minimum pension level. Maximum monthly pension for working pensioners: 142950 lire.	Automatic adjustment of pensions every 4 months for changes in wages and cost of living. 13th monthly pension.

Notes: Major features; benefits for workers.

Source: U.S. Department of Health and Human Services ed., Social Security Throughout the World. 1981. Washington D.C. 1982, 108-109 (Hungary), 12-13 (Austria), 90-91 (Germany), 82-83 (France), 176-177 (Netherlands), 20-21 (Belgium), 236-237 (Switzerland), 260-261 (United Kingdom), 120-121 (Ireland), 234-235 (Sweden), 64-65 (Denmark), 80-81 (Finland), 186-187 (Norway), 124-125 (Italy).

Appendix

Appendix. Indicators of welfare development in Hungary and Western Europe, 1900-1990

Year	Hungarian data (1)	West. Eu. mean (2)	West. Eu. standard deviation (3)	West. Eu. coeff. of variation	Standardized Hungarian data = (1–2)/3
		Social insurance expenditures (as % of GDP)			
1930	(1.60)	2.53	1.67	.66	(-.56)
1940	(2.70)	4.30	.	.	.
1950	3.20	4.99	1.62	.32	-1.11
1960	5.00	7.23	1.47	.20	-1.51
1970	7.50	11.12	1.86	.17	-1.94
1980	11.50	15.45	3.59	.23	-1.10
1990	14.50	16.86	5.10	.30	-.46
		Social expenditures of central government (as % of GNP)			
1890	.	.67	.30	.44	.
1900	.	.79	.38	.48	.
1910	.	.99	.46	.47	.
1920	.	1.18	.68	.58	.
1930	.64	2.16	1.42	.66	-1.07

		Social security expenditures (as % of GDP)			
1950	3.80	9.38	2.88	.31	-1.94
1960	5.80	11.43	2.38	.21	-2.36
1970	8.90	15.77	2.96	.19	-2.32
1980	14.20	22.82	5.12	.22	-1.68
1990	18.40	24.03	5.77	.24	-.98
		Social expenditures (as % of GDP)			
1950	.	12.31	3.57	.29	.
1960	11.30	15.62	3.50	.22	-1.24
1970	13.90	21.44	4.33	.20	-1.74
1980	19.60	29.99	5.84	.19	-1.78
1990	27.80	30.23	5.19	.15	-1.32
		Distribution of social security expenditures and family allow. in 1960 (%)			
Health care	33.1	15.39	9.61	.62	1.84
Pensions	38.7	49.98	11.31	.23	-1.00
Unempl.	-	4.32	4.09	.95	-
Family allow.	12.20	17.28	10.66	.62	-.48
Others	16.00	13.02	5.31	.41	.56
		Distribution of social security expenditures and family allow. in 1980 (%)			
Health care	17.50	30.32	7.52	.25	-1.70
Pensions	55.10	45.99	9.94	.22	.92
Unempl.	-	6.45	5.56	.86	-
Family allow.	13.30	8.04	4.47	.56	1.18
Others	14.10	9.19	3.61	.39	1.36

Distribution of social security revenues in 1960 (%)

Employees	13.10	20.78	10.12	.49	-.76
Employers	49.20	34.73	17.80	.51	.81
Special taxes	-	.36	.86	2.37	-
From government	37.10	39.71	21.97	.55	-.12
Capital rev.	.10	2.95	3.00	1.01	-.95
Others	.40	1.46	2.11	1.45	-.50

Distribution of social security revenues in 1980 (%)

Employees	14.60	19.15	12.76	.67	-.36
Employers	41.10	36.69	13.69	.37	.32
Special taxes	-	.22	.54	2.52	-
From government	43.60	40.0	19.87	.50	.18
Capital rev.	-	3.15	2.94	.94	-
Others	.60	.78	.93	1.18	-.20

Coverage of employment injury insurance (as % of economically active population)

1900	.	16.17	20.39	1.26	.
1910	.	30.67	22.72	.74	.
1920	.	39.85	22.77	.57	.
1930	39.00	50.46	14.45	.29	-.79
1940	35.00	52.92	17.18	.32	-1.04
1950	47.00	60.77	16.33	.27	-.84
1960	85.00	71.54	14.79	.21	.91
1970	97.00	78.15	12.52	.16	1.51
1980	100.00	85.13	13.24	.16	1.12
1990	100.00	88.88	17.85	.20	.62

Coverage of health insurance (members as % of the labour force)

1900	.	9.83	12.56	1.28	.
1910	.	15.42	18.61	1.21	.
1920	(25.00)	33.23	30.46	.92	(-.27)
1930	(27.00)	46.62	28.00	.60	(-.70)
1940	(27.00)	56.58	28.89	.51	(-1.02)
1950	47.00	66.69	29.44	.44	-.67
1960	85.00	73.69	28.41	.39	.40
1970	97.00	90.23	12.85	.14	.53
1980	100.00	93.40	8.81	.09	.75
1990	100.00	97.40	5.27	.05	.49

Coverage of sickness cash benefits (insured persons as % of the labour force)

1900	.	9.83	12.56	1.28	.
1910	.	15.42	18.61	1.21	.
1920	25.00	33.23	30.46	.92	-.27
1930	27.00	46.62	28.00	.60	-.70
1940	27.00	56.58	28.89	.51	-1.02
1950	46.00	66.69	29.44	.44	-.70
1960	63.00	73.69	28.41	.39	-.38
1970	79.00	90.23	12.85	.14	-.87
1980	83.00	93.40	8.81	.09	-1.18
1990	(100.00)	97.40	5.27	.05	(.49)

Coverage of pension insurance (members as % of the labour force)

1900	.	5.83	15.21	2.61	.
1910	.	8.25	16.54	2.01	.
1920	.	22.69	31.31	1.38	.
1930	16.00	44.00	36.40	.83	-.77
1940	30.00	66.83	32.48	.49	-1.13
1950	47.00	76.85	22.77	.30	-1.31
1960	85.00	90.54	11.49	.13	-.48
1970	97.00	92.69	10.53	.11	.41
1980	100.00	95.90	6.94	.07	.59
1990	100.00	98.50	4.74	.05	.32

Notes: Brackets refer to serious limitations in the comparability of data.

Sources: For Hungarian data, see Tables 1-12; other data are own calculations based on Tables 1-12.

BIBLIOGRAPHY

A lakosság jövedelme és fogyasztása, 1960-1980. Budapest 1984.

A magyar állam zárszámadása az 1930-31. évről. Budapest 1932.

A magyar társadalombiztosítás húsz éve, 1945-1964. Budapest 1967.

A magyar társadalombiztosítás ötven éve, 1892-1942. Budapest 1943.

A munkásbetegsegélyezési törvény módosítása. I. kötet. Hazai anyag. Budapest 1905.

A társadalombiztosítás fejlődése számokban, 1950-1985. Budapest 1987.

A Világbank szociálpolitikai jelentése Magyarországról, in: Szociálpolitikai Értesítő, 1992. 2. szám.

Ádám, György, Az orvosi hálapénz Magyarországon. Budapest 1986.

Adema, Willem, Uncovering Real Social Spending. The OECD Observer, No. 211, April/May 1998, 20-23.

Alber, Jens, Government Responses to the Challenge of Unemployment: The Development of Unemployment Insurance in Western Europe, in: Peter Flora and Arnold J. Heidenheimer eds., The Development of Welfare States in Europe and America. New Brunswick 1981, 151-183.

— Vom Armenhaus zum Wohlfahrtsstaat. Analysen zur Entwicklung der Sozialversicherung in Westeuropa. Frankfurt/M. and New York 1987.

— Germany, in: Peter Flora ed., Growth to Limits. The Western European Welfare States Since World War II. Vol. 2. Berlin and New York 1987, 1-154.

Alestalo, Matti and Uusitalo, Hannu, Finland, in: Flora ed., Growth to Limits. Vol. 1. 197-292.

Ambrosius, Gerold and Hubbard, William H., A Social and Economic History of Twentieth Century Europe. Cambridge/Mass. 1989.

Andorka, Rudolf, The Use of Time Series in International Comparison, in: Else Oyen ed., Comparative Methodology. London 1990, 203-223.

— and Kolosi, Tamás and Vukovich, György eds., Társadalmi riport. 1992. Budapest 1992.

— and Tóth, István György, A szociális kiadások és a szociálpolitika Magyarországon, in: Andorka Rudolf and Kolosi Tamás and Vukovich György eds., Társadalmi riport. 1992. Budapest 1992, 396-507.

— and Kondratas, Anna and Tóth, István György, A jóléti rendszer átalakulása Magyarországon: felépítése, kezdeti reformjai és javaslatok. A Magyar-Nemzetközi Kék Szalag Bizottság 3. sz. Gazdaságpolitikai tanulmánya. Budapest 1994.

— et al. ed., A Society Transformed: Hungary in Time-Space Perspective. Budapest 1999.

Andreff, Wladimir, Nominal and Real Convergence, in: Jozef M. van Brabant ed., Remaking Europe. The European Union and the Transition Economies. Lanham 1999, 111-138.

Armour, Philip K. and Coughlin, Richard M., Social Control and Social Security: Theory and Research on Capitalist and Communist Nations, in: Social Science Quarterly, 66 (1985) 3, 770-788.

Attir, Mustafa O. et al. ed., Directons of Change. Boulder/Co. 1981.

Augusztinovics, Mária ed., Körkép reform után. Budapest 2000.

Az Országos Társadalombiztosító Intézet jelentése az 1940. évi működéséről. Budapest 1941.

Bak, Hans and van Holthoon, Frits and Krabbendan, Hans eds., Social and Secure? Politics and Culture of the Welfare State. Amsterdam 1996.

Baldwin, Peter, The Politics of Social Solidarity and the Bourgeois Basis of the European Welfare State, 1875-1975. Cambridge 1990.

— Can We Define a European Welfare State Model?, in: B. Greve ed., Comparative Welfare Systems: the Scandinavian Model in a Period of Change. London 1996, 29-44.

Barát, Mária ed., A magyar gazdaság vargabetűje. Budapest 1994.

Barr, Nicholas ed., Munkaerőpiac és szociálpolitika Közép- és Kelet-Európában. Budapest 1995.

Barro, Robert J. and Sala-i-Martin, Xavier, Economic Growth. New York 1995.

Berghman, Jos and Peeters, Jan and Vranken, Jan, Belgium, in: Flora ed., Growth to Limits. Vol. 3.

Beruházási Évkönyv. 1980. Budapest 1981.

Béry, László and Kun, Andor, Magyarország évkönyve. 1934. Budapest s. a.

Bikkal, Dénes, Betegségi biztosítás Magyarországon. Budapest 1932.

— Társadalombiztosítás Magyarországon, in: Közgazdasági Szemle, LVIII (1934) 6-8, 341-389.

Borchert, Jens, Ausgetretene Pfade? Zur Statik und Dynamik wohlfahrtsstaatlicher Regime, in: Stephan Lessenich and Ilona Ostner (Hrsg.), Welten des Wohlfahrtskapitalismus. Der Sozialstaat in vergleichender Perspektive. Frankfurt/M. and New York 1998, 137-176.

Borgetta, Edgar F. and Borgetta, Marie L. eds., Encyclopaedia of Sociology. Vol. 1. New York 1992.

Botos, József, A magyar társadalombiztosítás kialakulása és fejlődése. Budapest 1998.

Castles, Francis G., Whatever Happened to the Communist Welfare State?, in: Studies in Comparative Communism, XIX (1986) 3-4, 213-226.

— ed., Families of Nations. Patterns of Public Policy in Western Democracies. Aldershot 1993.

— and Mitchell, Deborah, Worlds of Welfare and Families of Nations, in: Francis G. Castles ed., Families of Nations. Patterns of Public Policy in Western Democracies. Aldershot 1993, 93-128.

Clasen, Jochen ed., Social Insurance in Europe. Bristol 1997.

— ed., Comparative Social Policy: Concepts, Theories and Methods. Oxford 1999.

— Introduction, in: Clasen, Jochen ed., Comparative Social Policy: Concepts, Theories and Methods. Oxford 1999, 1-12.

Clement, Wallace and Mahon, Rianne eds., Swedish Social Democracy: A Model in Transition. Toronto 1994.

Cochran, Allan and Clarke, John, Comparing Welfare Sates: Britain in International Context. London 1993.

Collier, David and Messick, Richard, Prerequisites versus Diffusion: Testing Alternative Explanations of Social Security Adoption, in: American Political Science Review, 69 (1975), 1299-1315.

Comission of the European Communities, Comparative Tables of the Social Security Schemes in the Member States of the European Communities. Luxembourg 1989.

Comission of the European Communities, Social Protection in Europe, 1993. Luxembourg 1994.

Conrad, Christoph, The Emergence of Modern Retirement: Germany in an International Comparison (1850-1960), in: Population. An English Selection, 3 (1991), 171-200.

— Mixed Incomes for the Elderly Poor in Germany, 1880-1930, in: Michael B. Katz and Christoph Sachsse eds., The Mixed Economy of Social Welfare. Baden-Baden 1996, 340-367.

Coughlin, Richard M. and Armour, Philip K., Sectoral Differentiation in Social Security Spending in the OECD Nations, in: Comparative Social Research, 6 (1983), 175-199.

Cox, Robert H., The Development of the Dutch Welfare State. Pittsburgh 1993.

Crouch, Colin, Social Change in Western Europe. Oxford 1999.

Csaba, Iván and Tóth, István György eds., A jóléti állam politikai gazdaságtana. Budapest 1999.

— and Tóth, István György, A jóléti állam politikai gazdaságtana. Budapest, 1999, in: Csaba, Iván and Tóth, István György eds., A jóléti állam politikai gazdaságtana. 7-41.

Csöppüs, István, Komáromi norma – egy szociálpolitikai kísérlet, in: Századok, 126 (1992) 2, 259-283.

Cutright, Philips, Political Structure, Economic Development, and National Social Security Programs, in: American Journal of Sociology, 70 (1965), 537-550.

Darányi Ignác emlékkonferencia. Budapest 2000.

Deacon, Bob, Social Policy and Socialism. London 1983.

De Swaan, Abram, Der sorgende Staat. Wohlfahrt, Gesundheit und Bildung in Europa und den USA der Neuzeit. Frankfurt/M. 1993.

Dixon, John and Macarov, David eds., Social Welfare in Socialist Countries. London and New York 1992.

Dréhr, Emerich von, Die soziale Arbeit in Ungarn. Budapest 1930.

Eckstein, Alexander, National Income and Capital Formation in Hungary, 1900-1950, in: Simon Kuznets ed., Income and Wealth. Series V. London 1955, 152-223.

Egészségügyi helyzet. 1972. Budapest 1973.

Eisenstadt, S. N. and Ahimeir, Ora eds., The Welfare State and its Aftermath. London and Sydney 1985.

Erikson, Robert and Goldthorpe, John H. and Portocarero, Lucienne, Intergenerational Class Mobility and the Convergence Thesis: England, France, and Sweden, in: British Journal of Sociology, 34 (1983), 303-343.

Esping-Andersen, Gosta, The Three Worlds of Welfare Capitalism. Cambridge 1990.

— Welfare States and the Economy, in: Neil J. Smelser ed., Handbook of Economic Sociology. Princeton/NJ 1994, 711-732.

— Social Foundations of Postindustrial Economies. Oxford 1999.

Esztergár, Lajos, A szociálpolitika tételes jogi alapja. Pécs 1936.

Evers, Adalbert, Shifts in the Welfare Mix – Introducing a New Approach for the Study of Transformations in Welfare and Social Policy, in: A. Evers and H. Wintersberger eds., Shifts in the Welfare Mix. Frankfurt/M. 1990, 7-30.

— and Wintersberger, H. eds., Shifts in the Welfare Mix. Frankfurt/M. 1990.

Ferge, Zsuzsa, A Society in the Making: Hungarian Social and Societal Policy, 1945-1975. New York 1979.

— Társadalompolitikai tanulmányok. Budapest 1980.

— Fejezetek a magyarországi szegénypolitika történetéből. Budapest 1986.

— The Changing Hungarian Social Policy, in: Else Oyen ed., Comparing Welfare States and their Futures. Aldershot 1986.

— A szociálpolitika hazai fejlődése, in: Ferge Zsuzsa and Várnai Györgyi eds., Szociálpolitika ma és holnap. Budapest 1987, 40-61.

— and Kolberg, Jon Eivind eds., Social Policy in a Changing Europe. Frankfurt/M. and Boulder/Co. 1992.

— Social Policy Regimes and Social Structure, in: Zsuzsa Ferge and J. E. Kolberg eds., Social Policy in a Changing Europe. Frankfurt/M. and Boulder/Co. 1992, 201-222.

Ferrera, Mauricio, Italy, in: Peter Flora ed., Growth to Limits. Vol. 2. Berlin 1986, 385-482.

Fischer, Wolfram (Hrsg.), Handbuch der europäischen Wirtschafts- und Sozialgeschichte. Bd. 6. Stuttgart 1987.

Flora Peter, Solution or Source of Crises? The Welfare State in Historical Perspective, in: W. J. Mommsen ed., The Emergence of the Welfare State in Britain and Germany, 1850-1950. London 1981, 343-389.

— and Alber, Jens, Modernization, Democratization, and the Development of Welfare States in Western Europe, in: Flora and Heidenheimer eds., The Development of Welfare States in Europe and America. New Brunswick and London 1981, 37-80.

— and Heidenheimer, Arnold J. eds., The Development of Welfare States in Europe and America. New Brunswick and London 1981.

— and Heidenheimer, Arnold J., The Historical Core and Changing Boundaries of the Welfare State, in: Flora and Heidenheimer eds., The Development of Welfare States in Europe and America. 17-34.

— ed., State, Economy, and Society in Western Europe, 1815-1975. Vol. I. Frankfurt/ M. 1983.

— On the History and Current Problems of the Welfare State, in: S. N. Eisenstadt and Ora Ahimier eds., The Welfare State and its Aftermath. London and Sydney 1985, 11-30.

— ed., Growth to Limits. The Western European Welfare States Since World War II. Vol. 1. Berlin 1986; Vol. 2. Berlin 1986; Vol. 3. Berlin 1988; Vol. 4. Berlin 1987.

Fraternité Rt., Jelentés a társadalombiztosítás reformjáról. Budapest 1991.

Fretwell, David and Jackman, Richard, Munkaerőpiacok: munkanélküliség, in: Nicholas Barr ed., Munkaerőpiac és szociálpolitika Közép- és Kelet-Európában. Budapest 1995, 194-228.

Furniss, Norman and Tilton, Timothy, The Case for the Welfare State. From Social Security to Social Equality. Bloomington-London, 1979.

Gács, Endre, Szociális kiadásaink nemzetközi összehasonlításban, in: Statisztikai Szemle, 63 (1985) 12, 1226-1236.

Gál, László et al., Szociálpolitikánk két évtizede. Budapest 1969.

Gauthier, Anne Héléne, The State and the Family. Oxford 1996.

Gordon, Margaret S., Social Security Policies in Industrial Countries. Cambridge 1988.

Gough, Ian, Welfare Regimes: On Adapting the Framework to Developing Countries. University of Bath, Institute for International Policy Analysis. Working Paper. 2000.

Greve, Bent, The Historical Dictionary of the Welfare State. Lanham, Md. and London 1998.

Griffin, Larry J., Comparative-historical Analysis, in: Edgar F. Borgetta and Marie L. Borgetta eds., Encyclopedia of Sociology. Vol. 1. New York 1992, 263-271.

Gross, Peter and Puttner, Helmut, Switzerland, in: Flora ed., Growth to Limits. Vol. 3.

Gyáni, Gábor, A szociálpolitika múltja Magyarországon. Budapest 1994.

— Könyörületesség, fegyelmezés, avagy a szociális gondoskodás genealógiája, in: Történelmi Szemle, XLI (1999) 1-2, 57-84.

— A szociálpolitika első lépései hazánkban: Darányi törvényei, in: Darányi Ignác emlékkonferencia. Budapest 2000, 94-110.

Hage, Jerald and Hannemann, Robert and Gargan, Edward T., State Responsiveness and State Activism. London 1989.

Hagfors, Robert, The Convergence of Financing Structure, 1980-1995, in: Juho Saari and Kari Välimäki eds., Financing Social Protection in Europe. Helsinki 1999.

Hámori, Péter, A magyarországi agrár-szociálpolitika kezdetei, in: Századok, 137 (2003) 1, 3-42.

Haney, Lynne, Familial Welfare: Building the Hungarian Welfare Society, 1948-1968, in: Social Politics, 7 (2000) 1, 101-122.

Hansen, Hans, Elements of Social Security. Copenhagen 1998.

Hauser, Richard, Soziale Sicherung in westeuropäischen Staaten, in: Stefan Hradil and Stefan Immerfall (Hrsg.), Die westeuropäischen Gesellschaften im Vergleich. Opladen 1997, 521-545.

Heclo, Hugh, Modern Social Politics in Britain and Sweden. From Relief to Income Maintenance. New Haven and London 1974.

— Toward a New Welfare State?, in: Flora and Heidenheimer eds., The Development of Welfare States. 383-406.

Hegyesi, Gabor and Gondos, Anna and Orsos, Eva, Hungary, in: John Dixon and David Macarov eds., Social Welfare in Socialist Countries. London and New York 1992, 98-130.

Heidenheimer, Arnold J. and Heclo, Hugh and Adams, Carolyn Teich, Comparative Public Policy. The Politics of Social Choice in America, Europe, and Japan. New York 1990.

Heller, Farkas, Magyarország socialpolitikája. Budapest 1923.

Higgins, Joan, States of Welfare. Comparative Analysis of Social Policy. Oxford 1981.

Hill, Michael, Social Policy: A Comparative Analysis. London 1996.

Hilscher, Rezső, Bevezetés a szociálpolitikába. Budapest 1928.

Hockerts, Hans Günter, Die Entwicklung vom Zweiten Weltkrieg bis zur Gegenwart, in: Peter A. Köhler and Hans F. Zacher (Hrsg.), Beiträge zur Geschichte und aktuellen Situation der Sozialversicherung. Berlin 1983.

Hofmeister, Herbert, Landesbericht Österreich, in: Köhler and Zacher (Hrsg.), Ein Jahrhundert Sozialversicherung. 445-730.

Hollós, István, A közszolgálati alkalmazottak nyugdíjkérdése és a megoldási lehetőségek. Budapest 1940.

Horowitz, Irving Louis ed., Equity, Income, and Policy. Comparative Studies in Three Worlds Development. New York and London 1977.

Hradil, Stefan and Immerfall, Stefan (Hrsg.), Die westeuropäischen Gesellschaften im Vergleich. Opladen 1997.

Huszár Tibor, Gondolatok a munkaerkölcsről. Budapest 1982.

ILO, Compulsory Pension Insurance. Studies and Reports. Series M., No. 10. Geneva 1933.

ILO, Compulsory Sickness Insurance. Studies and Reports. Series M., No. 6. Geneva 1927.

ILO, Financing social security: The options. An international analysis. Geneva 1984.

ILO, International Survey of Social Services. Studies and Reports, Series M., No. 11. Geneva 1933.

ILO, The cost of social security. Eleventh international inquiry, 1978-1980. Geneva 1985.

ILO, The cost of social security. Fourteenth international inquiry, 1987-1989. Geneva 1996.

ILO, World Labour Report 2000. Income Security and Social Protection in a Changing World. Geneva 2000.

ILO, Yearbook of labour statistics. 1995. Geneva 1996.

Inkeles, Alex, Convergence and Divergence in Industrial Societies, in: Mustafa O. Attir et al. ed., Directions of Change. Boulder/Co. 1981, 3-38.

— and Sasaki, Masamichi eds., Comparing Nations and Cultures. Englewood Cliffs, 1996.

International Bank for Reconstruction and Development, Hungary: Reform of social policy and expenditures. Washington DC 1992.

Janoski, Thomas and Hicks, Alexander M. eds., The Comparative Political Economy of the Welfare State. Cambridge 1994.

Johansen, Lars Norby, Denmark, in: Flora ed., Growth to Limits. Vol. 1. 293-381.

Johnson, Paul, Welfare States, in: Max-Stephan Schulze ed., Western Europe. Economic and Social Change Since 1945. London/NewYork 1999, 122-139.

Jones, Catherine, Patterns of Social Policy. An Introduction to Comparative Analysis. London 1985.

Kaelble, Hartmut, Auf dem Weg zu einer europäischen Gesellschaft. München 1987.

— A Social History of Western Europe, 1880-1980. Dublin 1990.

— Der Wandel der Erwerbstruktur im 19. und 20. Jahrhundert, in: Struktur und Dimension. Festschrift für K. H. Kaufhold. Stuttgart 1997, 73-93.

— Europäische Besonderheiten des Massenkonsums, 1950-1990, in: Hannes Siegrist, Hartmut Kaelble, Jürgen Kocka (Hrsg.), Europäische Konsumgeschichte. Frankfurt/M. 1997, 169-203.

— Europäische Vielfalt und der Weg zu einer europäischen Gesellschaft, in: Stefan Hradil and Stefan Immerfall (Hrsg.), Die westeuropäischen Gesellschaften im Vergleich. Opladen 1997, 27-68.

— Der historische Vergleich. Frankfurt/M. 1999.

— Wie kam es zum Europäischen Sozialmodell?, in: Jahrbuch für Europa- und Nordamerika-Studien, 4 (2000), 39-53.

Kangas, Olli, The Politics of Social Rights. Studies on the Dimensions of Sickness Insurance in OECD Countries. Stockholm 1991.

Katz, Michael B. and Sachsse, Christoph eds., The Mixed Economy of Social Welfare. Baden-Baden 1996.

Kaufmann, Franz-Xaver, The Blurring of the Distinction 'State Versus Society' in the Idea and Practice of the Welfare State, in: Franz-Xaver Kaufmann et. al. ed., Guidance, Control, and Evaluation in the Public Sector. Berlin and New York 1986.

— and Leisering, Lutz, Demographic Challanges in the Welfare State, in: Else Oyen ed., Comparing Welfare States and their Futures. Aldershot 1986, 96-113.

— et. al. ed., Guidance, Control, and Evaluation in the Public Sector. Berlin/New York 1986.

Kerr, Clark et al., Industrialism and Industrial Man. Cambridge/Mass. 1960.

Kocka, Jürgen, Asymmetrical Historical Comparison: The Case of the German Sonderweg, in: History and Theory, 38 (1999), 40-50.

Kohl, Jürgen, Staatsausgaben in Westeuropa. Analysen zur langfristigen Entwicklung der öffentlichen Finanzen. Frankfurt/M. 1985.

Komlossy, Andrea and Parnreiter, Christof and Stacher, Irene and Zimmermann, Susan (Hrsg.), Ungeregelt und unterbezahlt. Der informelle Sektor in der Weltwirtschaft. Frankfurt/M. and Wien 1997.

Korpi, Walter, Social Policy and Distributional Conflict in the Capitalist Democracies, in: West European Politics, 3 (1980) 3, 296-316.

— The Democratic Class Struggle. London 1983.

— Power, Politics, and State Autonomy in the Development of Social Citizenship: Social Rights during Sickness in Eighteen OECD Countries since 1930, in: American Sociological Review, 54 (1989) 3, 309-328.

Kosonen, Pekka, European Integration: A Welfare State Perspective. Helsinki 1994.

— European Welfare State Models: Converging Trends, in: International Journal of Sociology, 4 (1995), 81-110.

Kovrig, Béla, A társadalombiztosítási választások eredményei, in: Társadalombiztosítási Közlöny, 1929. május-június.

— A társadalombiztosítási önkormányzati választások eredményéről, in: Munkaügyi Szemle, 1935. 5. szám. 1-22.

— and Nádujfalvy, V. József, Társadalombiztosítási kézikönyv. Budapest 1938.

— Magyar társadalompolitika. II. kötet. Társadalompolitikai feladatok. Kolozsvár 1944.

— A munka védelme a dunai államokban. Kolozsvár 1944.

— Magyar társadalompolitika. 1920-1945. I. rész. New York 1954.

Köhler, Peter A. and Zacher, Hans F., (Hrsg), Ein Jahrhundert Sozialversicherung in der Bundesrepublik Deutschland, Frankreich, Grossbritannien, Österreich und der Schweiz. Berlin 1981.

— and Zacher, Hans F. (Hrsg.), Beiträge zur Geschichte und aktuellen Situation der Sozialversicherung. Berlin 1983.

Kövér, György and Gyáni, Gábor, Magyarország társadalomtörténete a reformkortól a második világháborúig. Budapest 1998.

Kuhnle, Stein, Norway, in: Flora ed., Growth to Limits. Vol. 1. 117-196.

— The Growth of Social Insurance Programs in Scandinavia: Outside Influences and Internal Forces, in: Flora and Heidenheimer eds., The Development of Welfare States. 125-150.

Kuznets, Simon ed., Income and Wealth. Series V. London 1955.

Laczkó, István, A magyar munkás- és balesetbiztosítás története. Budapest 1968.

Ladik, Gusztáv, Jóléti intézményeink. Budapest 1940.

Langlois, Simon et al., Convergence or Divergence? Comparing Recent Social Trends in Industrial Societies. Frankfurt/M. and London 1994.

Leibfried, Stephan, Towards a European Welfare State? On Integrating Poverty Regimes into the European Community, in: Zsuzsa Ferge and Jon Eivind Kolberg eds., Social Policy in a Changing Europe. Frankfurt/M. and Boulder/Co. 1992, 245-279.

Lessenich, Stephan and Ostner, Ilona (Hrsg.), Welten des Wohlfahrtskapitalismus. Der Sozialstaat in vergleichender Perspektive. Frankfurt/M. and New York 1998.

Lindert, Peter H., The Rise of Social Spending, 1880-1930. Agricultural History Center, University of California, Davis. Working Paper, No. 68. 1992.

— The Rise of Social Spending, 1880-1930, in: Explorations in Economic History, 31 (1994), 1-37.

— What Limits Social Spending?, in: Explorations in Economic History, 33 (1996), 1-34.

Lőrincz, Ernő, A munkaviszonyok szabályozása Magyarországon a kapitalizmus kezdeteitől az első világháború végéig, 1840-1918. Budapest 1974.

Maguire, Maria, Ireland, in: Flora ed., Growth to Limits. Vol. 2. 241-384.

Magyar Statisztikai Évkönyv. 1930. Budapest 1931.

Magyar Statisztikai Évkönyv. 1940. Budapest 1941.

Magyar Statisztikai Évkönyv. 1970. Budapest 1971.

Magyar Statisztikai Évkönyv. 1980. Budapest 1981.

Magyar Statisztikai Negyedévi Közlemények, XLIII (1940)

Magyarország nemzeti számlái. Főbb mutatók. 1991. Budapest 1993.

Maltby, Tony, Social insurance in Hungary: the individualisation of the social?, in: Jochen Clasen ed., Social Insurance in Europe. Bristol 1997, 205-222.

Marshall, Thomas H., Citizenship and Social Class. Cambridge 1950.

Maurer, Alfred, Landesbericht Schweiz, in: Köhler and Zacher (Hrsg.), Ein Jahrhundert Sozialversicherung. 731-833.

Midgley, James, Social Welfare in Global Context. London 1997.

Minkoff, Jack and Turgeon, Lynn, Income Maintanance in the Soviet Union in Eastern and Western Perspective, in: Irving Louis Horowitz ed., Equity, Income, and Policy. Comparative Studies in Three Worlds Development. New York and London 1977, 176-211.

Mommsen, W. J. ed., The Emergence of the Welfare State in Britain and Germany, 1850-1950. London 1981.

Munkásbiztosítás a Magyar Szent Korona országaiban. Budapest 1911.

Népesség- és társadalomstatisztikai zsebkönyv. 1985. Budapest 1986.

Népgazdasági mérlegek, 1949-1987. Budapest 1989.

Niemelä, Heikki and Salminen, Kari and Vanamo, Jussi, Converging Social Security Models? The Making of Social Security in Denmark, France and the Netherlands. Helsinki 1996.

Nordic Social-Statistical Committee, Social Security in the Nordic Countries. Scope, expenditure and financing, 1990. Statistical Reports of the Nordic Countries, 59. 1990.

OECD, National Accounts. Main Aggregates, 1960-1997. Vol. I. Paris 1999.

OECD, Net Public Social Expenditure. OECD Working Papers. Vol. V. Occasional Papers, No. 19. Paris 1997.

OECD, Social Expenditure Statistics of OECD Member Countries. Labour Market and Social Policy Occasional Papers. No. 17. Paris 1996.

OECD, Social Expenditure, 1960-1990. Problems of growth and control. Paris 1985.

OECD, The Future of Social Protection. Paris 1988.

Ogus, Anthony I., Landesbericht Großbritannien, in: Köhler and Zacher (Hrsg.), Ein Jahrhundert Sozialversicherung. 269-443.

Olson, Sven, Sweden, in: Flora ed., Growth to Limits. Vol. 1. 1-116.

Országos Társadalombiztosító Intézet, A magyar társadalombiztosítás tíz éve, 1919-1929. Budapest é.n.

Oyen, Else ed., Comparing Welfare States and their Futures. Aldershot 1986.

— ed., Comparative Methodology. London 1990.

Palme, Joakim, Pension Rights in Welfare Capitalism. Stockholm 1990.

Pampel, Fred C. and Williamson, John B., Jóléti kiadások a fejlett demokráciákban, 1950-1980, in: Csaba and Tóth eds., A jóléti állam politikai gazdaságtana. 42-68.

Perry, Richard, United Kingdom, in: Flora ed., Growth to Limits. Vol. 2. 155-240.

Petrák, Katalin, A szervezett munkásság küzdelme a korszerű társadalombiztosításért. Budapest 1978.

Pierson, Christopher, Beyond the Welfare State? The New Political Economy of Welfare. Cambridge 1991.

Pryor, Frederick, Public Expenditure in Capitalist and Communist Nations. Homewood/ Ill. 1968.

Rimlinger, Gaston, Welfare Policy and Industrialization in Europe, America and Russia. New York 1971.

Ritter, Gerhard A., Social Welfare in Germany and Britain. Origins and Development. Leamington Spa/New York 1986.

— Der Sozialstaat. München 1989.

Roenbroek, Joop and Berben, Theo, Netherlands, in: Flora ed., Growth to Limits. Vol. 3.

Rosenthal, Uriel, Welfare State or State of Welfare? Repression and Welfare in Modern State, in: Richard F. Tomasson ed., The Welfare State, 1883-1983. Greenwich, Connecticut and London 1983, 279-297.

Saari, Juho and Välimäki, Kari eds., Financing Social Protection in Europe. Helsinki 1999.

Saint-Jours, Yves, Landesbericht Frankreich, in: Köhler and Zacher (Hrsg.), Ein Jahrhundert Sozialversicherung. 181-268.

Sala-i-Martin, Xavier, The Classical Approach to Convergence Analysis, in: Economic Journal, 106 (1996), 1019-1036.

Schmidt, Manfred G., Sozialpolitik. Opladen 1988.

— Wohlfahrtsstaatliche Regime: Politische Grundlagen und politisch-ökonomisches Leistungsvermögen, in: Lessenich and Ostner (Hrsg.), Welten des Wohlfahrtskapitalismus. 179-200.

Schneider, Saundra K., The Sequential Development of Social Programs in Eighteen Welfare States, in: Comparative Social Research, 5 (1982), 195-219.

Schulze, Max-Stephan ed., Western Europe: Economic and Social Change Since 1945. London/NewYork 1999.

Shalev, Michael, The Social Democratic Model and Beyond, in: Comparative Social Research, 6 (1983), 315-351.

Sik, Endre, New Trends in the Hungarian Welfare System, in: A. Evers and H. Wintersberger eds., Shifts in the Welfare Mix. Frankfurt/M. 1990, 281-296.

— and Svetlik, Ivan, Similarities and Differences, in: A. Evers and H. Winterberger eds., Shifts in the Welfare Mix. Frankfurt/M. 1990, 273-279.

Skocpol, Theda and Somers, Margaret, The uses of comparative history, in: Comparative Studies in Society and History, 22 (1980), 174-197.

Sorokin, Pitirim A., Mutual Convergence of the United States and the U.S.S.R. to the Mixed Sociocultural Type, in: International Journal of Comparative Sociology, 1 (1960), 143-176.

Statistisches Bundesamt (Hrsg.), Bevölkerung und Wirtschaft, 1872-1972. Stuttgart 1972.

Statisztikai Évkönyv. 1940. Budapest 1941.

Statisztikai Évkönyv. 1970. Budapest 1971.

Statisztikai Évkönyv. 1990. Budapest 1991.

Statisztikai Havi Közlemények, (1925).

Statisztikai Negyedévi Közlemények, XLIII (1940).

Szikra, Dorottya, Modernizáció és társadalombiztosítás a 20. század elején, in: Augusztinovics, Mária ed., Körkép reform után. Budapest 2000, 11-27.

Társadalmi riport. 1992. Budapest 1992.

Társadalombiztosítási évkönyv. I. évf. Budapest 1930, and other volumes.

Therborn, Göran, Classes and States: Welfare State Developments, 1881-1981, in: Wallace Clement and Rianne Mahon eds., Swedish Social Democracy: A Model in Transition. Toronto 1994, 13-43.

— Europan Modernity and Beyond. The Trajectory of European Societies, 1945-2000. London 1995.

Tilly, Charles, Big structures, large processes, huge comparisons. New York 1984.

Time series of historical statistics, 1867-1992. Vol. I. Budapest 1993.

Tinbergen, J., Do Communist and Free Economies Show a Converging Pattern?, in: Soviet Studies, 12 (1961), 333-341.

Titmuss, Richard M., Essays on 'The Welfare State'. London 1958.

— Social Policy. London 1974.

Tomasson, Richard F. ed., The Welfare State, 1883-1983. Greenwich, Connecticut and London 1983.

Tomka, Béla, Családfejlődés a 20. századi Magyarországon és Nyugat-Európában: konvergencia vagy divergencia? Budapest 2000.

— Társadalmi integráció a 20. századi Európában: Magyarország esete, in: Századvég, 17 (2000), 3-40.

— Jóléti rendszerek a 20. századi Magyarországon: Nemzetközi összehasonlítás, in: Történelmi Szemle, 43 (2001) 3-4, 209-236.

— Social Integration in 20th Century Europe: Evidences from Hungarian Family Development, in: Journal of Social History, 35 (2001) 2, 327-348.

— Demographic Diversity and Convergence in Europe, 1918-1990: The Hungarian Case, in: Demographic Research, 6 (2002) 2, 17-48.

— A jóléti intézmények fejlődésének meghatározói a 20. századi Európában – hosszú távú összehasonlítások néhány tanulsága, in: Valóság, 45 (2002) 6, 55-68.

— A jóléti kiadások alakulása Magyarországon nemzetközi összehasonlításban, 1918-1990, in: Statisztikai Szemle, 81 (2003) 1, 52-69.

— Social security in Hungary in a long-run and comparative perspective: expenditures, social rights, and organization, 1918-1990. Arbeitspapiere des Osteuropa-Instituts der Freien Universität Berlin. Arbeitsbereich Politik und Gesellschaft. Nr. 43. 2002. 45 pp.

— Western European Welfare States in the 20th Century: Convergences and Divergences in a Long-Run Perspective, in: International Journal of Social Welfare, 12 (2003) 4, 249-260.

Tóth, István György, A jóléti rendszer az átmenet időszakában, in: Közgazdasági Szemle, XLI (1994) 3, 313-340.

— Welfare Programmes and the Alleviation of Poverty, in: Rudolf Andorka et al. ed., A Society Transformed: Hungary in Time-Space Perspective. Budapest 1999, 128-146.

U.S. Department of Health and Human Services ed., Social Security Throughout the World. 1981. Washington D.C. 1982.

UNESCO, Statistical Yearbook. 1993. Paris 1993.

United Nations, Statistical Yearbook. 1961. New York 1961.

Valuch, Tibor, Magyarország társadalomtörténete a XX. század második felében. Budapest 2001.

Van Brabant, Jozef M. ed., Remaking Europe. The European Union and the Transition Economies. Lanham 1999.

Van den Braembussche, A. A., Historical Explanation and Comparative Method: Towards a Theory of the History of Society, in: History and Theory, 28 (1989), 1-24.

Van der Veen, Romke J., Social Solidarity: The Development of the Welfare State in the Netherlands and the United States, in: Hans Bak and Frits van Holthoon and Hans Krabbendan eds., Social and Secure? Politics and Culture of the Welfare State. Amsterdam 1996.

Van Kersbergen, Kees, Social Capitalism: A Study of Christian Democracy and the Welfare State. London 1995.

Vígh, Győző, Az öregségi, rokkantsági, özvegységi és árvasági biztosítás szolgáltatásainak megindulása. Budapest 1933.

Weigel, Wolfgang and Amann, Anton, Austria, in: Flora ed., Growth to Limits. Vol. 3.

Wilensky, Harold L., Leftism, Catholicism, and Democratic Corporatism: The Role of Political Parties in Recent Welfare State Development; in: Flora and Heidenheimer eds., The Development of Welfare States. 345-382.

— and Lebeaux, Charles, Industrial Society and Social Welfare. New York 1965.

— The Welfare State and Equality: Structural and Ideological Roots of Public Expenditures. Berkeley 1975.

— et. al., Comparative Social Policy: Theory, Methods, Findings. Berkeley/Calif. 1985.

Williamson, John B. and Fleming, Jeanne J., Convergence Theory and the Social Welfare Sector: A Cross-National Analysis, in: Alex Inkeles and Masamichi Sasaki, eds., Comparing Nations and Cultures. Englewood Cliffs 1996, 348-355. (Orig.: International Journal of Comparative Sociology, 18 (1977) 3-4, 242-253.)

Zimmermann, Susan, Prächtige Armut. Fürsorge, Kinderschutz und Sozialreform in Budapest. Das "sozialpolitische Laboratorium" der Donaumonarchie im Vergleich zu Wien, 1873-1914. Sigmaringen 1997.

— and Melinz, Gerhard, A szegényügy "szerves" fejlődése vagy radikális reform? Kommunális közjótékonyság Budapesten és Bécsben (1873-1914), in: Aetas, 8, (1994) 3, 37-70.

— Geschützte und ungeschützte Arbeitsverhältnisse von der Hochindustrialisierung bis zur Weltwirtschaftskrise. Österreich und Ungarn im Vergleich, in: Andrea Komlossy and Christof Parnreiter and Irene Stacher and Susan Zimmermann (Hrsg.), Ungeregelt und unterbezahlt. Der informelle Sektor in der Weltwirtschaft. Frankfurt/M. and Wien 1997, 87-115.

Zöllner, Detlev, Landesbericht Deutschland, in: Köhler and Zacher (Hrsg.), Ein Jahrhundert Sozialversicherung. 45-179.

www.ingramcontent.com/pod-product-compliance
Lightning Source LLC
LaVergne TN
LVHW081337011026
849161LV00013BB/2940